Boys Do Cry

Schools are undergoing a mental health crisis and adult statistics surrounding male suicide paint a bleak picture of the future for boys in our schools. From bullying and sexism to traditional 'ideals' of masculinity, outdated expectations of what it is to be male are causing boys to suffer. Research also shows that this is having a negative impact on girls in our schools. Clearly, the issue of boys' mental wellbeing has never been so important. *Boys Do Cry* examines key research on factors impacting boys' mental health and arms teachers with a range of practical strategies to start enacting positive change.

Combining the latest research, personal anecdote, expert advice, and a uniquely engaging writing style, **Matt Pinkett** provides focused, evidence-based guidance on what those working in schools can do to improve and maintain the mental wellbeing of boys. The chapters follow an easy-to-navigate three-part structure, detailing personal stories, key research, and practical solutions to the problems raised. With sensitivity, Pinkett deals with a diverse range of topics relating to boys' mental health including:

- Anger
- Self-harm and suicide
- LGBTQ+ masculinity
- Body image
- Friendships
- Pornography

This is an essential read for teachers and school leaders who want to ensure they are improving the mental health of boys in their schools, challenging toxic behaviours, and equipping the current generation of boys to become happy, healthy, emotionally articulate men.

Matt Pinkett is an English teacher in Surrey with a personal and professional interest in gender and masculinity in schools. He is co-author of the bestselling *Boys Don't Try?* Matt has also blogged, written for several publications, and delivers regular CPD sessions on the topic of teaching and masculinity.

'Matt Pinkett tackles some deeply uncomfortable issues relating to boys' mental health. It's searingly honest, written from the heart and with a whopping intent to open up some of this tricky terrain. It is one thing to name that terrain, it is quite another to expand on it in a way that really makes you think, and then quitter another to provide some sensitive yet punchy potential solutions. It's a cliché to say that certain books should be read by everyone working in schools. In the case of *Boys Do Cry*, it's absolutely true.'

Mary Myatt

'For people who teach, this book reminds us why we do it. For people who don't, it will give you a chance to look into boys' lives and experiences and consider how we need to talk, support, and provide role models to give boys the happy and healthy adulthoods they deserve.'

Dr Poppy Gibson

Boys Do Cry

Improving Boys' Mental Health and Wellbeing in Schools

Matt Pinkett

Designed cover image: Sarah Hoyle

First published 2023
by Routledge
4 Park Square, Milton Park, Abingdon, Oxon OX14 4RN

and by Routledge
605 Third Avenue, New York, NY 10158

Routledge is an imprint of the Taylor & Francis Group, an informa business

© 2023 Matt Pinkett

The right of Matt Pinkett to be identified as author of this work has been asserted in accordance with sections 77 and 78 of the Copyright, Designs and Patents Act 1988.

All rights reserved. No part of this book may be reprinted or reproduced or utilised in any form or by any electronic, mechanical, or other means, now known or hereafter invented, including photocopying and recording, or in any information storage or retrieval system, without permission in writing from the publishers.

Trademark notice: Product or corporate names may be trademarks or registered trademarks, and are used only for identification and explanation without intent to infringe.

British Library Cataloguing-in-Publication Data
A catalogue record for this book is available from the British Library

Library of Congress Cataloging-in-Publication Data
Names: Pinkett, Matt, author.
Title: Boys do cry : improving boys' mental health and wellbeing in schools / Matt Pinkett.
Description: Abingdon, Oxon ; New York, NY : Routledge, 2023. | Includes bibliographical references and index.
Identifiers: LCCN 2022048854 (print) | LCCN 2022048855 (ebook) | ISBN 9781032168685 (hardback) | ISBN 9781032168692 (paperback) | ISBN 9781003250722 (ebook)
Subjects: LCSH: Boys--Education. | Teenage boys--Education. | Boys--Mental health. | Teenage boys--Mental health. | Sex differences in education. | School mental health services.
Classification: LCC LC1390 .P559 2023 (print) | LCC LC1390 (ebook) | DDC 371.8211--dc23/eng/20221220
LC record available at https://lccn.loc.gov/2022048854
LC ebook record available at https://lccn.loc.gov/2022048855

ISBN: 978-1-032-16868-5 (hbk)
ISBN: 978-1-032-16869-2 (pbk)
ISBN: 978-1-003-25072-2 (ebk)

DOI: 10.4324/9781003250722

Typeset in Melior
by SPi Technologies India Pvt Ltd (Straive)

Printed in Great Britain
by Bell & Bain Ltd, Glasgow

For Robin Wye,
You did more for people than you ever knew.
I love you, and I miss you, and I will always talk to you.
'Matt-man'.

Contents

	Acknowledgements	viii
	Introduction	1
1	Anger	6
2	Exclusions	26
3	Suicide and self-harm	47
4	Talk	72
5	Friendships	95
6	LGBTQ+ masculinity in schools	112
7	Sport and physical activity	136
8	Body image and eating disorders	165
9	Pornography	183
10	The final, final word	217
	Index	218

Acknowledgements

Thanks to Megan James, Priya Pillay, Steve Daniels, Emmanuel Awoyelu, Chelsea McDonagh, Carol Carter, Charlotte Woolley, Bennie Kara, Clare Milford-Haven, Dennis Ougrin, The Samaritans, Joseph Ford, Andrea Vaughan, Richard Clutterbuck, Phil Denton, Nic Ponsford at the Global Equality Collective, Paul Beeson, Chris Wright, Lee Sullivan, Lee Andersen, Darryn Knight, Thomas Green, David Fawcett, Mary Myatt, Poppy Gibson, James Downs, Tommy Hatto, Charlotte Markey, Rachel Barber-Mack, Beyond Equality, Jo Morgan, Daniel Gunn, Andrew Daville, Rebecca Bownas, Justin Hancock, and all the other academics, experts, and teachers whose effort, patience, and time helped to create this book.

Thanks to all the students who turned up to my lessons because the law required them to do so.

Thanks to all the teachers and schools who bought *Boys Don't Try?* Your stories, tweets, and comments about how the book persuaded you to do things even a little differently are inspiring.

Thanks to Alex Foster, Gemma Astley and Matt Stone, Brendan Bartram, Thomas Cope, Tom Mackenzie-Chalmers, Louise Belshaw, Becky, and Laura Evans and Faheem Khan for their contributions to Chapter Six. I love what you've written and your adherence to deadlines puts me to shame!

I want to thank all the friends who see me for who I really am. I love you.

Thanks to all the reprobates from The Jolly Farmer. Because of you I'm never lonely.

Ben Sink. Somehow, you're always there for me. Let's not ever change that.

I want to thank Dad, Mum, Pat, and Nick for always coming through for me. I hope that with this book, you feel like I've come through for you.

Donna – I never take you for granted. I love you. Thank you for being in my life.

Lily, my sweet, sweet girl, who only sees the good in me. I love you and I adore you, but can you please stop adding the 'Poo Bum Poo Bum' song to my Spotify playlist?

Finally, to Roz Burrows, Queen of the Footnotes, proof-reader and line editor extraordinaire. Without your attention to detail, intelligence, and compassion, this book wouldn't have happened. Thanks for the laughs, and, on the hottest day since recorded history began, introducing me to the word 'mafting[1]'.

Note

1 Look it up.

Introduction

Girls cry too, of course.

And given what we know about girls' mental health, it's hardly surprising; more than two thirds of anti-depressants prescribed to teenagers are for girls. Although eating disorders for girls *and* boys are on the rise, more than 90% of those who receive treatment in hospital for eating disorders are girls. The number of girls cutting themselves has risen four-fold in the past decade and girls are five times more likely than boys to harm themselves by self-poisoning through drugs or alcohol.[1]

Why write a book on boys' mental health?

If this is the case, one might reasonably question my decision to write a book about the mental health and wellbeing of those who identify as boys. There are several reasons. Firstly, it was regularly suggested to me, based on the success of *Boys Don't Try?*[2] (*BDT?*), that I write a follow-up about girls. A *Girls Do Try*, if you like. I considered it, but not for long. I'm of the opinion that the success of *BDT?* lies in the fact that my co-author, Mark Roberts, and I were once boys ourselves. *BDT?* is peppered with anecdotes from our own experiences of growing up that helped the research to come alive. Never having been a girl myself, the idea of writing a book about the female experience felt awkward, disingenuous, and potentially insulting. Besides, why try and light a fire on the blazing landscape of the written female experience when people like Laura Bates, Charlotte Woolley, and Caitlin Moran are already doing it so well?

This will be uncomfortable for some to read, but I also feel – and I'm sorry if I'm giving men too much credit here – that a lot of the mental health struggles that young girls deal with stem from the pressures of living up to expectations, *as dictated by men*, of what it means to be a female; the pressures to look, act, even think in ways that the patriarchy decrees to be 'appropriately' female or feminine. I fervently believe that we can teach boys that there is value in being kind, considerate, vulnerable, and emotionally open; we can make boys feel that school is a place of happiness and security; we can show boys that there are right and wrong

DOI: 10.4324/9781003250722-1

ways to deal with the confusion and chaos that teenage life provides. Perhaps this will benefit those girls and women who suffer as a consequence of the anger, emotional mutism, and insecurity of men who are not given adequate mental health guidance, advice, or intervention.

A compelling study[3] in Australia, looking at the mental health of 1,943 adolescents over a 16-year period, found that mental health disorders in adolescence 'often precede mental disorders in young adults'. And yet, the study also found that early mental health intervention in adolescence could prevent 'much morbidity[4]' in adulthood. Despite the grim statistics surrounding girls' mental health, teenage boys are still twice as likely as girls to die by suicide. And, when the boys we teach become men, they are three times more likely than women to die by suicide. It is my belief that if we want to stop men dying in the future, we must address the issue of boys' mental health *now*.

If, as I have suggested, author experience is integral to creation of a book, what then do I – an English teacher and father to a young daughter – know about male mental health? I know that I'm depressed. I know that I hate my body. I know that addiction, anxiety, and self-loathing are as much a part of me as anything else. I know that the complex interrelation between my poor mental health and my masculinity means that when I've been fragile, I've often sought to repair myself through self-destructive habits and behaviours. I've often hurt, taken advantage of, or exploited others. So, on a personal level, whilst this book stems from a genuine desire to improve the present and future lives of young people and those that love them, there's a selfish aspect too: I want to attempt to make some amends for the bad I've done. I want to do *some* good.

Stories, research, and solutions

As with *BDT?*, each chapter of *Boys Do Cry*, with the exception of the LGBTQ+ chapter, follows a three-part structure. The opening of each chapter begins with a story. Although the format of each story differs, one thing remains constant: lived human experience. These are stories that shine a light on the personal. They're not about data sets, methodologies, or statistical significance. They're about feeling. You'll hear stories from – and about – people who have suffered, and people who have triumphed. You'll hear from people who are still suffering and who are yet to triumph. But you will hear *people*.

Each chapter of the book relies on extensive research. I have engaged with as much of the research as I could in creating this book. I've read countless journals, reports, and articles in an attempt to more fully understand those topics I have chosen to write about. I have also interviewed academics and experts in the field to get a more comprehensive grasp on topics as diverse as anger, male friendships, and body dysmorphia. The fruit of this quite joyous labour can be found in the 'Research' section of each chapter.

The final part of each chapter looks at 'Solutions.' Of course, the subject of mental health in schools necessitates that there are times when only those primarily working in a pastoral capacity within a school can facilitate change, improvement, and support where mental health is concerned. But my guiding question when looking for answers to the problems raised in each chapter was always: *what can classroom teachers do to help with this issue?* And when I say classroom teachers, I don't mean just personal, social, health, and economic (*PSHE)* education teachers. Whether I was writing about talk, pornography, friendships, body image, anger, or sport and exercise, I always asked myself, 'What could a geography teacher, or a business studies teacher, or a maths teacher do to help with this issue?' As a result, I hope that the advice contained herein helps everyone, regardless of their role within a school, to make things a little better.

A summary of the book's content

In Chapter One, you'll read about anger. I'll ask you to reframe your thinking about overt displays of aggression and, instead, see angry boys as victims of an emotion that's as natural as love, joy, hate, or jealousy. You'll learn strategies for dealing with anger in the classroom and learn to recognise and differentiate between the feeling of anger, and the expression of anger.

Exclusion rates for boys are disproportionately high, in comparison to girls. If you are a Black-African/Caribbean boy, or a Gypsy, Roma, or Traveller boy, those rates are even higher. Through positioning a lens on these two ethnic minority groups, Chapter Two looks at how schools can make these boys feel more included and valued members of the school community. It forms part of the broader picture on our attempts to reduce school exclusions and the damaging impact they have on young people's mental wellbeing.

Whilst, as Chapter Three acknowledges, there are significant gender differences in how self-harm and suicide behaviours present, there are things schools and teachers can do to protect all children against the dangers of self-harm and suicide, regardless of gender. The chapter ends with practical instruction on how all teachers can discuss suicide responsibly in the classroom.

The answer, the narrative goes, to improving male mental health is for men to talk more. Chapter Four interrogates the myth of male emotional mutism and looks at what is preventing men from engaging in the talk that's meant to save them. The chapter helps teachers to prepare boys to communicate effectively. And, as you'll find, effective communication isn't just about talk. It's about listening too.

Chapter Five shines a light on boys' friendships. Whilst to many, boys' friendships seem built on a foundation of banter bordering on abuse, often befuddlingly so, the reality is that boys' friendships are complex and nuanced. Practical advice is given to help facilitate emotional connection between boys and help build friendships that are supportive.

Mental health statistics for LGBTQ+ pupils are distressing. A Stonewall report from 2017,[5] looking into the school experience of LGBTQ+ students, found that 92% of trans pupils have considered taking their own life. For non-trans pupils who are gay, lesbian, or bisexual, this figure remains worryingly high at 70%. Chapter Six, comprised of a collection of essays by LGBTQ+ educators, explores the complex relationship between LGBTQ+ identity and masculinity.

Physical activity is inextricably linked to improved mental wellbeing. However, in many schools, toxic changing room cultures, and an unnecessary emphasis on sporting acumen, mean that many boys are not getting the regular exercise they need to be mentally well. Chapter Seven, on sport and physical activity, provides advice on how all teachers – and not just the ones that wear shorts in winter – can raise the physical activity levels of boys in schools.

Eating and body image disorders are increasing for boys. Chapter Eight explores anorexia and bulimia, but also the recent increase in cases of 'Bigorexia' and steroid abuse. It provides advice as to how teachers can prepare boys for a world that is repeatedly telling them that the toned, muscular bodies of men in the media are the masculine physical ideal to which they should aspire.

The final chapter of the book explores the topic of pornography, but also those sexist behaviours and attitudes often closely linked to accessing and watching porn from a young – and therefore inappropriate – age. Some readers may be shocked, or even offended by the content, but it would be irresponsible of me to avoid it given the extent of the problem engendered by a lack of pornography education.

The aim of the book

It is my hope that this book empowers those working in education, parents, and those whose work brings them into regular contact with young people. More importantly, it is my hope that this book empowers young people who are struggling or suffering. That it helps our boys to understand and engage in protective behaviours that enable them to be, whenever possible, happy.

I hope it helps to make boys – and the men they will one day become – realise that to feel angry, scared, weak, lonely, anxious, terrified is not failure, but human.

An important note

Whilst I have carried out hundreds of hours of research in my endeavour to produce a book that is insightful as well as useful, it is my responsibility to iterate that I am not a qualified mental health professional. As I emphasise throughout the book, the help of trained professionals, where available, should always be sought where there are serious concerns about a person's mental or physical wellbeing.

Notes

1 Bokzam, B. (2017, September 23). Mental health data shows stark difference between girls and boys. *The Guardian*. https://www.theguardian.com/society/2017/sep/23/mental-health-data-shows-stark-difference-between-girls-and-boys (Accessed: 27th July 2022).
2 Pinkett, M., & Roberts, M. (2019). *Boys Don't Try? Rethinking Masculinity in Schools* (1st ed.). UK: Routledge.
3 Patton, G. C., Coffey, C., Romaniuk, H., Mackinnon, A., Carlin, J. B., Degenhardt, L., Olsson, C. A., & Moran, P. (2014). The prognosis of common mental disorders in adolescents: A 14-year prospective cohort study. *Lancet, 383*(9926), 1404–1411.
4 'Morbidity' is a medical term referring to the condition of *suffering from* a disease or condition, for example depression.
5 Stonewall. (2017). *The School Report: The experience of lesbian, gay, bi and trans young people in Britain's schools in 2017*.Stonewall. Available at: https://www.stonewall.org.uk/system/files/the_school_report_2017.pdf (Accessed: 27th July 2022).

References

Bokzam, B. (2017, September 23). Mental health data shows stark difference between girls and boys. Available at: *The Guardian*. https://www.theguardian.com/society/2017/sep/23/mental-health-data-shows-stark-difference-between-girls-and-boys (Accessed: 27th July 2022).
Patton, G. C., Coffey, C., Romaniuk, H., Mackinnon, A., Carlin, J. B., Degenhardt, L., Olsson, C. A., & Moran, P. (2014). The prognosis of common mental disorders in adolescents: A 14-year prospective cohort study. *Lancet, 383*(9926), 1404–1411.
Pinkett, M., & Roberts, M. (2019). *Boys Don't Try? Rethinking Masculinity in Schools* (1st ed.). UK: Routledge.
Stonewall. (2017). *The School Report: The experience of lesbian, gay, bi and trans young people in Britain's* schools in 2017. Stonewall. Available at: https://www.stonewall.org.uk/system/files/the_school_report_2017.pdf (Accessed: 27th July 2022).

1 Anger

The story

Three students: a thought experiment

I want to tell you about three students.

These fictional students are in Year 10. All three attend the same large, mixed comprehensive school in Surrey. These students have impeccable academic records and excel in all subjects. Although these students have excellent results, near-flawless behaviour records, and a zestful enthusiasm for extension tasks, homework, and extra-curricular activities, each of these students also has significant personal problems that they are dealing with.

Jamar has a history of anxiety and depression. There are times when he wants to crawl up into a ball on the floor and wail with despair. Jamar has two therapy sessions a week to help him with these problems.

Joel suffers from Obsessive-Compulsive Disorder (OCD). His compulsions aren't completely debilitating but they are there, every day. Joel's parents have recently employed the services of a behavioural therapist to help him manage his OCD.

Jack has a problem with anger. Sometimes, he is overcome with an irrepressible rage at things others might consider trivial. Although his peers and teachers would never know it, there are times when Jack wants to punch walls and shout and swear at the top of his voice. Jack's parents have recently enrolled their son onto an anger management programme to help him control his anger.

I'd now like you to think about a child you care about very much. It may be your own son or daughter, a niece or nephew, perhaps someone you teach. Imagine that this child goes to the large, mixed comprehensive in Surrey where Jamar, Joel, and Jack study. Now answer this question:

> Of the three students I've told you about, which student would you least like to be best friends with your child?

Now, read everything you've just read to somebody close to you and ask them the same question. What answer did they give? Was it the same as yours?

More often than not, Jack is the student whom people would least want as friend for their own child. Perhaps this is understandable. After all, countless philosophers, spiritual leaders, and rock stars tell us that anger is a weakness.[1] We are led to believe that anger is a destructive and dangerous emotion; we believe that angry people are likely to inflict harm upon us and the people we – and they care – about.

The research

Why anger?

Anger is one of the last taboos in education. We only have to look at how teachers deal with their own anger to see that this is true. As teachers, we have no problem telling our colleagues – and sometimes even our superiors – that we feel stressed, anxious, or overworked. But conversations about anger, if they happen at all, are typically limited to whispered confessions to our closest friends or disguised as jokes in drinking establishments at the end of the school week. In those unfortunate times when a colleague's anger becomes apparent – perhaps they shout at a class, slam a door in frustration, or allow a swear word to erupt from their mouth – it is often professional condemnation that these colleagues receive, with little professional support offered to help them manage the anger that could not only frighten children, but ultimately destroy their own career. As far as students' emotions are concerned, when it comes to anger, we tend to focus on the aggressive behaviour that angry students demonstrate, rather than the underlying anger that prompts the aggressive acts in the first place.

In my thought experiment above, people's tendency to name Jack as the child they are wary of shows us that, in 21st century Britain, despite how far we've come as a society when it comes to discussing and talking about our emotions, anger is something shameful; something to be regarded with fear, scorn, and disdain. We do not attempt to understand anger adequately because it scares us. It is this fact, along with the fact that as adults, males are more likely to commit physically aggressive, violent, and sexually violent acts where anger often plays a part, which has made anger the subject of the first chapter of the book which you now hold in your hands.

Anger: it's not all bad

Although anger can certainly be a destructive force, it's not all bad.

Research has shown that despite its poor reputation, anger has several benefits. People are more likely to confer social status, in the form of higher-status job roles and higher salaries, upon those who display anger or aggression, rather than sadness, in organisational settings[2] such as the office or boardroom.[3] Also, angry people are more likely to take risks, which could be beneficial in situations where a tendency to *avoid* risk could prove detrimental to outcomes.[4] Situations like having to decide on whether to invest in an innovative new product like the iPad, Kindle, or even – that nemesis of classroom teachers everywhere – the fidget spinner, for example. Furthermore, where a lack of confidence in oneself is a barrier to progress, 'anger increases perceived control and certainty' whereas 'fear decreases such perceptions.'[5] Finally, and rather counter-intuitively, anger has also been shown to induce positive opinions of the self in a similar way to happiness.[6]

The fact that anger is a perfectly normal human emotion means that viewing it through a wholly negative lens, in the way we typically do, could have quite catastrophic implications for our mental health. Anger is as natural as happiness, sadness, love, guilt, and regret. It is hard to imagine a human being alive – let alone a teacher – who has not felt anger in some capacity.[7]

What is anger?

The human brain is constantly assessing the environment for potential threats. When something occurs in our environment that goes beyond what we expect, a region of the brain – a region called the amygdala – kicks into action. The amygdala initiates the fight, flight, or freeze response. If 'fight' looks like the best option, the adrenal glands are pumped with stress hormones (adrenaline, cortisol, testosterone), which prepare us for a right proper dust-up. Luckily, we tend not to give in to our desire to smash in the face of the Geography teacher who smugly tells us in the staffroom, 'Well, he behaves for *me*,' because another part of our brain – the prefrontal cortex, which helps us to make reasonable decisions – keeps us in check and tells us that actually, a staffroom isn't an appropriate place to rid a Geographer of his teeth.[8]

For the non-scientists reading this, possibly glazing over as you read phrases like, 'adrenal glands' and words like 'amygdala,' the hormonal and physiological responses to anger are crucially important to understand. Teachers who recognise that anger is a physiological response to the body being flooded with hormones are better able to see that the angry child in front of them is the victim of a debilitating physiological process, rather than a calculating and scheming perpetrator of violence and destruction, hell-bent on destroying everything that crosses his or her path. If we can recognise this, we're in a good position to offer the best kind of help – help free from judgement and misconceptions.

> **Physical effects of anger**
>
> Anger has a range of physical effects. It can be useful for angry people to recognise the physical impact of anger on their own bodies as these symptoms may serve as triggers for anger-reduction techniques. Mental health charity *Mind* describes the following physical signs of anger:
> - A churning feeling in your stomach
> - Tightness in your chest
> - An increased and rapid heartbeat
> - Legs go weak
> - Tense muscles
> - You feel hot
> - You have an urge to go to the toilet
> - Sweating, especially your palms
> - A pounding head
> - Shaking or trembling
> - Dizziness
>
> *Taken from https://www.mind.org.uk/media-a/2962/anger-2018.pdf*

Why do we get angry?

I've already mentioned that anger is the product of a hormonal response to something we perceive to be a threat. But what is it that human beings define as threatening? There has been much research into the causes of anger and the explanations provided are varied. However, the causes of anger noted by Ekman and Friesen[9] are useful in the sense that anybody who has experienced anger can likely relate to either one of the five antecedents of anger that Ekman and Friesen identify. These are:

1. Frustration

2. Physical threat

3. Insult

4. Witnessing someone else being violated

5. Being on the receiving end of someone else's anger

Certainly, in a school context, a student could experience up to four of these antecedents in a single lesson (assuming that incidences of physical threats in the classroom environment are rare in most classrooms). For example, Ed may feel frustration at the fact he needs to learn what an isosceles triangle is when he believes, without a thread of doubt, that the job he has lined up as a plumber's apprentice will not require any knowledge of trigonometry whatsoever. So, when the teacher asks Ed why he 'looks so grumpy,' he may feel a little insulted. Of course, Ed's burgeoning anger could be quelled by the late arrival into the classroom of his best friend, Martin. Unfortunately, however, the teacher decides to reprimand Martin for having his coat on, something that makes Ed furious as it's clear to him – and presumably everyone in the world that isn't a teacher – that it's positively arctic in the classroom because, once again, the adults in the school have decided that central heating is unnecessary. Naturally, Ed's anger incites him to intervene on Martin's behalf, causing the teacher to round on him. And that's when a table gets thrown and a fist finds a wall.

Dr Jennifer Lerner, an expert in anger at Harvard University, believes that anger is different from guilt, fear, or anxiety in that it is dependent on the blaming of a *person* (as opposed to external forces or the self) for the occurrence of a negative event (likely to be one of the five antecedents of anger identified by Ekman and Friesen):

> Specifically, anger has been associated with a sense that the self (or someone the self cares about) has been offended or injured with a sense of certainty or confidence about the angering event and what caused it.

She goes on to explain that anger is often triggered by:

> ...the belief that another person (as opposed to the situation or the self) was responsible for the event and with the notion that one can still influence the situation or cope with it.[10]

According to Lerner and her team, when negative events occur, we experience differing emotions depending on *who* or *what* we perceive to be responsible for the negative event's occurrence. The table below helps to explain:

Who we blame (for a negative event occurring)	What we feel	Example
Ourselves	Guilt or shame	*Nicholas couldn't be bothered to do his homework. His teacher is really nice. She even smiled at him once. Because of this, he feels guilty about receiving a detention.*
External forces	Sad	*The wind blew Patrick's homework out of his hand, straight into a large body of water from which it could not be recovered. Genuinely. Because of this, he feels sad about receiving a detention.*
A person (or people)	Anger	*Jordan feels that his teacher didn't explain the homework clearly enough and that is why he didn't hand it in on time. Because of this, he loathes his teacher and wants to shout in his face. Loudly.*

However anger is caused, it is fair to say that schools are high-pressure environments. They are hives of power, buzzing with imbalanced relationships where the opportunity for frustration and the stings of insults, threat, and blame are rife. Because of this, it's important teachers understand anger, and the way it impacts them, more fully.

Anger and gender

There are marked differences in the way that anger manifests itself in boys and girls, and men and women. The damaging impact of poor anger management in boys doesn't present itself most severely until adulthood, where incidences of male violence[11] and suicide[12] increase dramatically. As such, it is important to consider now, before we look at child and adolescent anger, how anger might affect our boys as they reach adulthood. It is only with this long-term picture in mind that we can rationalise and justify the need to make changes in the way we handle anger in school in the here and now, whilst these 'future adults' are still children.

Adult gender differences in the expression and experience of anger

Largely, the research shows that there are no significant differences in the manner and frequency with which adult men and women *experience* anger: as *Guardian* science correspondent Hannah Devlin says in her article, *Science of Anger*, 'Research has consistently found that women experience anger as frequently and as intensely as men.'[13] A study from 2000, by researchers at Southwest Missouri State University, found that 'in day-to-day interactions, women appear to take advantage of their anger just as frequently as men.'[14] The only difference the study found was that whilst women tend to regard anger as counterproductive, men 'seem to embrace their anger' and in fact feel less effective when they are asked to suppress it. Presumably, this is because positive or normalised depictions of male anger, force, and aggression in society and the media make it more acceptable for them to do so.

In terms of how men and women *express* (rather than experience) their anger, again, there is little difference between men and women in terms of the frequency with which they express anger. The only differences noted are in the manner of how that anger is expressed. In 1996, Jerry Deffenbacher and his team published research[15] which found that whereas women tend to cry more often when they are angry, men are more likely to express their anger physically, by hitting objects or people, or through name-calling.

The problems with adult male anger

The way that adult males express their anger has significant ramifications for society and our boys. Although figures from various studies show that women are between 1.2 and 3 times more likely than men to attempt suicide,[16] men are more likely to succeed in their suicide attempts because they 'are more prone to aggressive, antisocial and externalising behaviours,' meaning they are more 'likely to make more impulsive, lethal, active and determined suicide attempts,'[17] like using guns or jumping from a height in order to kill themselves.

74% of violent crimes committed in the UK are committed by males[18] whilst, shockingly, according to figures from the Office for National Statistics, 98% of perpetrators of rape or assault by penetration were male.[19] It is more than reasonable to assume that underpinning the violent acts that inform these appalling statistics is, far too frequently, anger. Anger is the catalyst for explicit and violent rage as well as underlying and simmering bitterness and resentment, both of which have devastating consequences for the victims and the perpetrators of these crimes.

Research also suggests that anger in adult life can have a severe physical impact on our bodies. As Smith and Furlong note, 'It is becoming increasingly clear... that high levels of anger are causally related to a wide range of physical ailments including hypertension, coronary heart disease, gastrointestinal distress, and even cancer.'[20] Many of these diseases – such as heart disease[21] and hypertension[22] – are much more likely to affect men.

Child and adolescent gender differences in the expression and experience of anger

The reality of these potentially disastrous consequences of adult male anger means that we need to attend to the anger of boys during their time at school. Before we look at ways of dealing with this, it's important to have a better understanding of the way that child and adolescent boys experience and express their anger.

As with adults, there is little to no evidence to suggest there is a difference in the frequency or intensity with which boys and girls *experience* anger. However, studies by Macklin and Jacoby,[23] and Crick[24] suggest that boys are more likely to *express* their anger physically. A more recent study by Cox, Hulgus, and Stabb[25] has shown that boys are more likely to express their anger outwardly.

In 2003, Peter Boman conducted a study[26] looking at adolescent anger in the context of the school setting. It provides some interesting reading for teachers. Boman found significant differences in the way that boys and girls experienced anger: girls were far more likely to be open about their feelings and talk to someone when feeling angry. Interestingly, they were also more likely to use positive calming techniques such as reading or writing. Girls were also more likely to cry or have a stomach-ache when angry. Boys, on the other hand, were far more likely to be destructive as a means of coping with their anger. They would break things and would voice a determination to get back at the teacher who had made them angry. When looking for a reason for these differences in coping with anger and anger-expression, Boman noted that 'The relationship between positive coping and lower levels of hostility towards school was particularly strong.'[27] In other words, improving boys' attitudes to school could have a significant impact on reducing the likelihood of them expressing their anger in destructive and threatening ways.[28]

Why do boys express their anger the way they do?

Boys are more likely to express anger outwardly and in a destructive or physically aggressive manner, but what causes this? Various studies point the finger at parents as the cause of the differences in the way that children express anger. A study[29] from 2005, which observed mothers and fathers as they watched their children play a game, showed that fathers are far more likely to respond to their sons when they display anger than when they display sadness. This could suggest that boys realise from an early age that if they want attention from an adult, anger is an effective way to get it. This theory is backed up by a 1985 study[30] conducted by Beverly Fagot et al., which looked at the behaviour of toddlers at infant play groups. Even though there was no difference in the play and social behaviours that boys and girls exhibited at this stage of their development, adults in this setting were far more likely to respond to boys' assertive behaviours – which included hitting and trying to grab toys from other children – than they were girls' assertive behaviours. Furthermore, adults were far more likely to respond to boys' 'intense' attempts at communication and more likely to respond to girls' 'less intense' attempts. When the researchers returned 11 months later, they noticed that now, boys and girls *did* differ significantly in one type of behaviour: the boys were more assertive than the girls.

The solutions

A. Teach students about anger

Whilst most classroom teachers will find it difficult to teach students about anger in any detail (although I think there is plenty of potential in English and Humanities subject classrooms), a school with a strong pastoral team and a robust PSHE or RSE[31] curriculum should be teaching students about anger. Ideally, this would be a proactive – rather than reactive – strategy which is delivered regularly and with solid understanding from those leading the sessions and buy-in from all staff. In addition, there will always be those students who would benefit from either small group work or even 1:1 sessions after they've displayed anger negatively.

Teach students what anger is

It's important that students – particularly students who are displaying anger – know what anger is: a physiological, hormonal response to a threat. They need to know that this threat may be physical, but it may also be a threat to one's principles, belief system, loved ones, or public persona. Students should also be taught that anger is not inherently bad and is actually an ingrained evolutionary tool to help us deal with the threats that life presents. Students should never be made to feel guilty for *feeling* angry.

Teach students the difference between anger and aggression

That's not to say that students shouldn't feel guilty for letting their anger cause them to be destructive. This is why it's important that students need to know the difference between the *experience* or *feeling* of anger and the *expression* of anger. It's okay to feel a burning injustice at the state of the world. It's not okay to frighten and intimidate people, or damage property, because of this. Furthermore, students who are taught to recognise the difference between the feeling and expression of anger find it easier to accept that the two don't have to come as a pair. These students have acquired, and can use, the meta-language to articulate calming thoughts, such as *I am **feeling** angry now. This is okay. I must do whatever it takes to ensure that I do not **express** this anger in a destructive way.*

Teach students to recognise the physical signifiers of anger

Students who can recognise the physical symptoms (see *Physical effects of anger*, above) of their impending anger will be able to implement their own anger management plan into effect, faster and more effectively. Anger will affect different students in different ways, but as with anything, when students are more knowledgeable about the intricacies of something – be it the Irish Potato Famine, musical time signatures, or the experience and appropriate expression of anger – they are better able to use that information effectively when the situation requires it.

B. Help angry students to manage their anger

Anger management techniques

On a general level, all students can be taught some basic anger management techniques. Bill Rogers, world-renowned expert in behaviour management and childhood anger, says that the following can help in what he calls 'initial calming.'

- Consciously untensing face, shoulder, and neck muscles
- Counting backwards
- *Calm* breathing (rather than *deep* breathing): a calm breath in for a count of two, hold for a count of three, and then breathe out for a count of two[32]

Rogers recommends that these skills are practised 1:1 in specialised behaviour support sessions. Given the universal nature of anger (it's not just the kids who punch and scream that suffer as a result of *feeling* angry), I see no reason why time in the tutor or PSHE programme cannot be dedicated to this vital and useful skill. In fact, I think teachers could benefit from learning these techniques too!

Articulating anger

Often, when anger escalates, it is miscommunication somewhere along the line that causes it to do so. A frustrated tut or silent eyeroll from a student is perceived by the teacher to be a downright belligerent attack on the lesson they've spent hours planning, whilst a polite 'Pick up your pen and start writing please,' from the teacher is perceived by a student to be an unnecessarily public, vicious insult directed solely towards him and everything he holds dear. Communication, as the saying goes, is key (or not, if you're the person to whom this important information wasn't communicated). Rogers advocates teaching students to use simple, 'I am' or 'I can' statements to help them articulate and manage their anger. Phrases such as, 'I *am* angry with this task because…' or 'I *can* calm myself when I'm feeling annoyed' really help children to process their anger. A child who is taught to articulate their anger is less likely to sit in silence as it boils over.

Anger management plans

Some students, normally those who find anger management difficult, will need this information visually – a one-page, step-by-step plan, accompanied by drawings. Examples of such plans can be found here:

https://dmbcwebstolive01.blob.core.windows.net/media/Default/ChildrenYoungPeopleFamilies/01%20Anger%20and%20aggression%20at%20school%202020.pdf

The case study below provides a real-life look at the efficacy of student anger management programmes in action within a SEND[33] setting:

> **Case study: Calm Plans**
>
> As we are a specialist school serving primary - and secondary-age children with Autism, many of our students arrive at various stages in their school career and bring with them a differing array of experiences of learning environments and behaviour management from their previous schools. This can mean they experience elevated levels of anxiety in school and trouble regulating their emotions, making accessing learning very difficult. Our students' autism means they may not always be able to identify or understand the physiological signs associated with emotions, leading to outbursts of aggression. This is the reason we use individualised 'Calm Plans' to support our students.
>
> The aim of a Calm Plan is to give our students independence over how they regulate their emotions at school. Calm Plans are developed by the students during a 1:1 SALT[34] session, so that they have ownership over the plan and can help learn about and inform on the strategies that work for them. The plans incorporate strategies from various therapeutic inputs lacking in most mainstream schools but can also rely on,

or be centred around, the students' own interests and self-soothing techniques. For example, reading or throwing a ball. Initially, plans are very visual for our students as we know this benefits those with an Autism diagnosis. However, as time goes on and these strategies become more embedded, the students no longer use the visuals, and it just becomes part of their day-to-day life. It is our hope that these strategies move with them throughout life, and not just in school.

We have many examples of Calm Plan success stories: Keith came to us when he was in Year 2. He arrived from mainstream and had been taught in isolation frequently, due to his aggressive behaviour. He came to us with a complete distrust for school and very low self-esteem. At first, he described himself as 'always angry,' and said that he didn't know how to help himself or change that feeling. Our staff worked closely alongside him and his family to create structure in his day-to-day life and create a Calm Plan that made sense to him. For him, art, Lego, and music were things he could identify as being calming, so these were incorporated into his Calm Plan. This was shared with home, so that they could replicate it for use in his home environment and shared with all staff who work with Keith. Staff then knew that if Keith was showing any signs of emotional dysregulation, or importantly, if Keith could *identify* any signs of emotional dysregulation, he could take time out of the classroom and use any of his identified strategies – doodle on a piece of paper, play with some Lego – to calm him. Over time, Keith's plan was adapted as he matured, so that the strategies grew with him and could be applied to any environment. Keith himself has identified that these strategies help him understand himself and give him the tools he needs when he is dysregulated. Once these strategies were embedded, Keith could also identify how his behaviour impacted those around him and vice versa, which made him even more responsive to using the strategies. We don't only see a happier, calmer, and more engaged Keith in school, but we also see data (both academic and behavioural) that reflect the progress he has made since these strategies were introduced.

Calm Plans are not a 'one size fits all' and certainly will not solve problems overnight; they need careful thought and effort in their design and implementation, but for lots of students, Calm Plans are a very effective, very worthwhile use of the resources available to us, whatever setting we're in.

This case study was written by Megan James and Priya Pillay, during their time at Heathermount School.

Case study commentary

It's great to see the impact that Heathermount's Calm Plans have had on students like Keith. Being a specialist school means that Heathermount has resources available to them that many mainstream schools do not. However, it's also important to note that whilst many mainstream schools don't have specialist school resources available to them, they do have SEND students, many of whom would be better off in a specialist setting.

Eight years into my career I took a job as an Assistant Head at a specialist school for Autistic pupils. Now I'm back in mainstream, I fully realise the extent to which many

> mainstream schools neglect the needs of SEND pupils, not because of a lack of good intentions or care, but because of a lack of understanding, a lack of funding, and a lack of adequate support and consistency. I wince with shame when I think of how, early on in my career, I regarded the emotional meltdowns of Autistic children as wilful naughtiness. And it wasn't just me. If only I knew then what I know now.
>
> I think mainstream schools could learn a lot from Heathermount's use of Calm Plans, in order to help students, regardless of their background, neurodivergent and neurotypical alike, who may struggle to regulate their behaviour.

Destigmatise anger

The effective use and implementation of anger management techniques for pupils to deploy themselves relies on a whole-school commitment to destigmatising anger. It's all well and good a student counting backwards from ten as they clench and unclench their fists under the desk in an effort to calm themselves, but if a teacher feels that managing anger isn't a suitable reason for a student to take a quick break from his History essay, anger management is not going to work. Equally, it's great if a student can say to a teacher, 'I am angry because I don't understand the task.' However, if the teacher then turns round and reproaches them for that fact, anger management is not going to work.

Teachers need to accept and be on board with the fact that students get angry and that things they may consider trivial could cause students to feel annoyed, angry, or absolutely apoplectic. If we as teachers accept this, then – just like when we spot a child sobbing in class, or when a child tells us they have a debilitating headache or an uncontrollable urge to urinate – when a child tells us that they are angry and explains why, we can give them the time and support needed to lessen the impact anger is having on their ability to take part in the lesson. Which leads us onto the rather thorny issue of time-outs…

C. Use time-outs effectively

Anger is rarely conducive to learning.

The use of the 'time-out' – a period of time where a child in a heightened emotional state is withdrawn from a potentially aggravating environment or situation in order to calm down – is something often offered to students who are visibly upset, or students who are very disruptive, but it could also help students who are in the early stages of anger, so as to avoid a catastrophe later on.

The TIME time-out saga

The phrase 'time-out' evokes images of mischievous scamps wearing untucked shirts and tiny caps waiting nervously outside the headteacher's office as they look sheepishly at their feet; of exiled middle fingers being shown to the backs of unknowing teachers through the glass windows of classroom doors; of students dreading the moment the teacher steps outside of the classroom into the corridor to quietly ask them in a strange, soft voice, 'Is everything okay at home?'

And yet, the once-innocent process of classroom banishment became the source of considerable controversy in 2014 when *TIME* magazine published an article ominously titled *'Time-outs' Are Hurting Your Child*.[35] The authors of the article, Daniel Siegel and Tina Bryson, experts in child development, stated that the 'primary experience a time-out offers a child is isolation.'[36] They argued that, 'even when presented in a patient and loving manner, time-outs teach [children] that when they make a mistake, or when they are having a hard time, they will be forced to be by themselves.'[37] Siegel and Bryson contended that when a student is struggling, the thing they need most is connection, and not isolation. Perhaps the most shocking thing from the article – and the thing that got parents and teachers across the pond quaking in their time-out-giving boots – was the assertion that the experience offered by being in isolation from others 'looks very similar to the experience of physical pain in terms of brain activity.' Whilst this article was aimed at parents, it sparked widespread fervent debate and discussion (albeit *internet*-based widespread fervent debate and discussion) amongst teachers, who seemed to be in either one of two camps: those who believed that whacking kids into corridors was simply good behaviour management or those who believed that whacking kids into corridors was tantamount to just whacking kids, full stop.

The *TIME* time-out controversy took another exciting turn when a month later, in October 2014, Siegel posted a blog post[38] in which he accused *TIME* of misrepresenting his and Bryson's beliefs about time-outs. In the blog post, Siegel clarified that it wasn't time-outs that he was critical of, but *bad* time-outs. A *bad* time-out is any time-out that doesn't follow the tenets of a *good* time-out as laid out by Siegel in his blog post. A *good* time-out is:

- Short
- Infrequent (that is, unusual in the sense that it's not something given regularly)
- Explained (the reason for the time-out is explained by the giver of the time-out and understood by the recipient)
- Followed up by positive feedback
- Followed up by human connection

Let me tell you about a 'hypothetical' *bad* time-out, that no doubt reflects the reality of my use of time-outs in the long-distant past:

> Scott is really annoyed with me for telling him to remove the coat – the coat his dying grandfather bought him – indoors and so Scott starts to disrupt the lesson by tapping his pen incessantly. Naturally, I think I'm above the school's

very effective behaviour system and so I ignore it and bark at Scott to be quiet. Scott likes the fact that he's getting to me and realises that, for some reason, I'm not giving him the formal warning as outlined by the school's behaviour policy that he's familiar with in other lessons. Understandably believing he's getting away with it, Scott continues to tap his pen loudly. Of course, I eventually get frustrated and yell at him to, 'Get out!' Seething, Scott stands up, tells me to, 'F*@k off!' and leaves the classroom. As I've still got 29 other kids to teach, I don't go and speak to Scott. Nor do I direct the Teaching Assistant (TA), sitting there doing nothing as I bang on about independent clauses and comma splicing, to go and speak to him. Eventually, after about ten minutes, I ask another student to fetch him in. Scott's not there. He doesn't come back. The lesson carries on.

And now, let me tell you how the new, enlightened me would handle the same situation, keeping in mind the facets of *good* time-outs:

Scott is really annoyed with me for telling him to remove the coat – the coat his dying grandfather bought him – indoors and so Scott starts to disrupt the lesson by tapping his pen incessantly. Sensing that Scott is annoyed, I approach him and quietly ask him if he'd like three minutes outside. Perhaps he tells me, very directly, 'I am angry,' or perhaps he can't articulate his anger, but I am familiar with the signs of anger so notice it myself. Rather than be affronted, I explain to Scott that I feel he should leave the classroom and stand outside for a few minutes. I tell him I recognise that he's angry and his behaviour right now is disruptive to others and could be the precursor for a worse situation if he continues. Scott begrudgingly leaves. After one minute, I ask the TA to watch the class as I go out and check on Scott. I offer sympathy and tell him I'll speak to his tutor about getting someone he can talk to about what he's going through. I then tell him I'll give him another minute to calm down. As he re-enters the classroom, coat now in hand, I whisper, 'Well done, Scott. Good lad,' as he sits down. Scott learns something. The lesson ends.

Okay, so in reality of course the coat wouldn't have come off, but the point is that Scott remained in lesson and at no point did anyone a) tell someone to 'F*@k off' or b) *actually* f*@k off.

I realise that, to some, such an approach will seem like pandering. I get it, I really do. For a large part of my career, I wouldn't dare to let a student leave my lesson, simply because to let them leave would be to go against my principles: *Lessons are for learning. I am a good teacher. Students don't leave **my** lessons. They **will** remain here and learn.* However, I realise now, as a (slightly more) mature adult, that in situations where I can feel my own blood boiling, I need to remove myself from that situation in order to calm down and refocus my thoughts. Why would I not afford the students I teach the same opportunity? The fact is, for many of us, we experience huge difficulty separating our 'teacher' self from our 'real' self, which is what can make approaches like this appear unacceptable or somewhat like pandering.

By 'reframing' both the behaviour and our response to it, our self-concept and dignity can remain intact. The frame is now a slightly different shape or possibly, just possibly, a tad more flexible. This can help to remove a lot of the cognitive dissonance that we experience when we see this type of response as 'losing' or 'backing down' or even as being inconsistent with the school's policy. In that case, the policy has to be much clearer, or the amount of flexibility we have must be clarified by the Senior Leadership Team (SLT).

D. Hold students (and teachers) accountable for their behaviour

Steve Daniels is the founder of Strengthening Minds, a company which works with schools up and down the country to help students manage their emotions. I interviewed Daniels, and he explained that whilst it's important to help students identify their emotions and manage them, it's also important to hold students accountable for their behaviour when it becomes destructive:

> We can give students all the tools they need to recognise their anger and to manage it optimally. But ultimately, when students find themselves in a difficult situation or an altercation with a teacher, I have to ask them: *How did you enter the classroom? Did you say hello to the teacher? Were you polite?* Because, sometimes, managing anger isn't always about being responsive. Sometimes it takes a proactive approach and being polite can go a long way.

Interestingly, Daniels took it upon himself to remind me (and rightly so) that teachers must ensure that their own anger and irritations (it can be a slightly frustrating job, after all) never impede their own ability to be polite and courteous at all times:

> When teachers or schools teach kids about anger, it's great because it reminds them to practise what they preach. When I worked in schools, I remember, on INSET[39] days, there was always a big emphasis on expecting manners and respect from students, but there can be some adults in schools not modelling these manners and this respect. Teaching is a hard job, and I take my hat off to all teachers, but teachers must always remember that if they're not polite and courteous to students, they could potentially invite a situation into their classroom that they do not want, which may involve making a student angry and then potentially destructive.

At the time of speaking to Daniels, for me this was a timely reminder. Only a few days prior to speaking to him a student came to see me at breaktime as they wanted to move seats in class. I'd had a terrible morning and was still reeling from the disruptive behaviour of the student's class the previous day. As the student spoke to me, I didn't even turn to look them in the eye and simply grunted my response to their plea, as I continued to stare at the computer screen in front of me. I'm very glad an angry parent (who was able to use their anger far more effectively than I had that day) called me that afternoon to tell me very firmly and clearly what a fool I'd been.

Daniels went on to tell me that it's imperative that teachers sanction destructive behaviours in accordance with the school behaviour policy:

> Knowing about your own anger and how it manifests itself is not about finding an excuse to misbehave. It's about making sure you don't allow your anger to become destructive and the moment it does, you have to accept responsibility.

This is good advice. I was acutely aware, as I penned this chapter, how many of the solutions offered may be seen by some to 'excuse or pander to anger.' That was not my intention. If I have excused or pandered to anything, it is the *experience* of anger. I have excused and will continue trying to excuse the fact that someone might *feel* angry. Anger is a normal, human emotion after all. It's important that I try and empathise with others. However, what I will not excuse or pander to is anger expressed in a manner that is intimidating or destructive. Daniels' advice is a good reminder to us all to that effect.

The final word

Perhaps we'll never know who really said it, but someone, somewhere, once said, 'Anger is a weakness.' They were right – it can be. However, the aphorism doesn't really capture the true essence of anger. Nor does it do justice to the people who experience it. It's important, therefore, that teachers and students learn to differentiate between the *feeling* of anger and the *expression* of it. This subtle distinction between feeling and expression will also enable us to consider how we might express our own anger constructively rather than let it cause us to harm ourselves and those around us.

We can then start to think about how feeling anger – and thereby knowing anger – can be a strength; an opportunity to know yourself and to manage yourself in such a way that the feeling of anger doesn't leave you feeling like a failure.

Notes

1 A quick Google search reveals that the Dalai Lama, philosopher Alain De Botton, and the lead singer of The Strokes, Julian Casablancas, have all stated, one way or another, that anger is synonymous with weakness.
2 Tiedens, L. (2001). Anger and advancement versus sadness and subjugation: The effect of negative emotion expressions on social status conferral. *Journal Of Personality And Social Psychology*, *80*(1), 86–94.
3 Or the staffroom, perhaps?

4 Loewenstein, G., & Lerner, J. S. (2003). The role of affect in decision making. In R. Davidson, K. Scherer, & H. Goldsmith (Eds.), *Handbook of affective science* (pp. 619–642). London: Oxford University Press.
5 Litvak, P., Lerner, J. S., Tiedens, L. Z., & Shonk, K. (2010). Fuel in the fire: How anger impacts judgment and decision making. In M. Potegal, G. Stemmler, & C. Spielberger (Ed.), *International Handbook of Anger* (pp. 287–311). New York, Springer.
6 Lerner, J., & Keltner, D. (2001). Fear, anger, and risk. *Journal Of Personality And Social Psychology, 81*(1), 146–159.
7 If you are a teacher who has not yet experienced anger, I urge you to take an IT lesson in which 30 pupils have forgotten the login details given to them only the previous lesson.
8 The preferable and more traditional place, of course, would be behind the bike sheds.
9 Ekman, P., Friesen, W. V. (1975). *Unmasking the Face.* Englewood Cliffs, NJ: Prentice-Hall.
10 Litvak et al. (2010).
11 Office for National Statistics. (2019). The nature of violent crime in England and Wales. Available at: https://www.ons.gov.uk/peoplepopulationandcommunity/crimeandjustice/articles/thenatureofviolentcrimeinenglandandwales/yearendingmarch2018#what-do-we-know-about-perpetrators-of-violent-crimes (Accessed: 29th April 2021).
12 Office for National Statistics. (2020). Suicides in England and Wales: 2019 registrations. Available at: https://www.ons.gov.uk/peoplepopulationandcommunity/birthsdeathsandmarriages/deaths/bulletins/suicidesintheunitedkingdom/2019registrations#suicide-patterns-by-age (Accessed: 29th April 2021).
13 Devlin, H. (2019). Science of anger: How gender, age and personality shape this emotion. *Guardian Online.* Available at: https://www.theguardian.com/lifeandstyle/2019/may/12/science-of-anger-gender-age-personality (Accessed: 5th September 2021).
14 Science Daily. (2000). Comparison Of Anger Expression In Men And Women Reveals Surprising Differences. Available at: www.sciencedaily.com/releases/2000/01/000131075609.htm (Accessed: 29th April 2021).
15 Deffenbacher, J. L., Oetting, E. R., Lynch, R. S., Morris, C. A. (1996). The expression of anger and its consequences. *Behaviour Research and Therapy, 34*, 575–590.
16 Vijayakumar L, (2015). Suicide in Women. *Indian Journal of Psychiatry. 57*(6).
17 Tsirigotis, K., Wojciech, G., Tsirigotis, M. (2011). Gender differences in methods of suicide attempts. *Medical Science Monitor, 17*(8) 65–70).
18 Office for National Statistics (2019).
19 Office for National Statistics. (2020b). Nature of sexual assault by rape or penetration, England and Wales: Year ending March 2020. Available at: https://www.ons.gov.uk/peoplepopulationandcommunity/crimeandjustice/articles/natureofsexualassaultbyrapeorpenetrationenglandandwales/yearendingmarch2020#perpetrator-characteristics (Accessed: 5th September 2021).
20 Smith, D. C., Furlong, M., Bates, M., Laughlin, J. D. (1998). Development of the Multidimensional School Anger Inventory for males. *Psychology in the Schools, 35*(1), 1–15.
21 Cardiovascular Risk In Men – Why Is Heart Disease A Male Problem. (2020). Available at: https://www.newvictoria.co.uk/about-us/news-and-articles/cardiovascular-risk-in-men-why-is-heart-disease-a-male-problem#:~:text=Overall%2C%20men%20are%20more%20likely,(CVD)%20numbers%20in%20men. (Accessed: 5th June 2022).
22 Choi, H., Kim, H., & Kang, D. (2017). Sex differences in hypertension prevalence and control: Analysis of the 2010–2014 Korea National Health and Nutrition Examination Survey. *PLOS ONE, 12*(5), 4.
23 Maccoby, E. E., & Jacklin, C. N. (1980). Sex differences in aggression: A rejoinder and reprise. *Child* Development, 51, 964–980.

24 Crick, N. R. (1997). Engagement in gender normative versus nonnormative forms of aggression: Links to social-psychological adjustment. *Developmental Psychology*, *33*(4), 610–617.
25 Cox, D. L., Stabb, S. D., & Hulgus, J. F. (2000). Anger and depression in girls and boys: A study of gender differences. *Psychology of Women Quarterly*, 24, 110–112.
26 Boman, P. (2003). Gender differences in school anger. *International Education Journal*, *4*(2).
27 Ibid.
28 *Boys Don't Try?* offers many solutions as to how schools can improve boys' relationship with teachers and schools. Chapter Two, on Exclusions, also looks at how schools can help to make students feel more included.
29 Chaplin, T. M., Cole, P. M., Zahn-Waxler, C. (2005). Parental socialization of emotion expression: Gender differences and relations to child adjustment, *Emotion, 5*(1), 80–88.
30 Fagot, B. I., Hagan, R., Driver leinbach, M., Kronsberg, S. (1985). Differential reactions to assertive and communicative acts of toddler boys and girls. *Child Development, 56*, 1499–1505.
31 Relationships and Sex Education. Up to 2017 this was referred to as SRE – Sex and Relationships Education – but was changed to emphasise the importance of relationships *before* sex. A new and compulsory RSE curriculum, introduced in England in 2020, means that schools have a duty to deliver age-appropriate education about relationships and sex to students. Parents do not have the right to withdraw their child from Relationships education, but may do so from Sex education.
32 Rogers, B. (2017). Anger and Aggression at School. Available at: https://dmbcwebstolive01.blob.core.windows.net/media/Default/ChildrenYoungPeopleFamilies/01%20Anger%20and%20aggression%20at%20school%202020.pdf (Accessed: 28th October 2021).
33 Special Educational Needs and Disabilities.
34 Speech and Language Therapy.
35 Siegel, D. J. & Bryson, T. P. (2014). 'Time-outs' are hurting your child. *TIME Online*. Available at: https://time.com/3404701/discipline-time-out-is-not-good/ (Accessed: 12th October 2021).
36 Ibid.
37 Ibid.
38 Siegel, D. J. (2014). You said WHAT about time-outs?! *Dr Dan Siegel*. Available at: https://drdansiegel.com/you-said-what-about-time-outs (Accessed: 13th October 2021).
39 **IN-SE**rvice **T**raining days. In English schools, five of the 195 days of directed time that a teacher works are dedicated to these development days.

References

Boman, P. (2003). Gender differences in school anger. *International Education Journal*, *4*(2).
Cardiovascular Risk In Men – Why Is Heart Disease A Male Problem. (2020). Available at: https://www.newvictoria.co.uk/about-us/news-and-articles/cardiovascular-risk-in-men-why-is-heart-disease-a-male-problem#:~:text=Overall%2C%20men%20are%20more%20likely,(CVD)%20numbers%20in%20men (Accessed: 5th June 2022).
Chaplin, T. M., Cole, P. M., Zahn-Waxler, C. (2005). Parental socialization of emotion expression: Gender differences and relations to child adjustment. *Emotion*, *5*(1), 80–88.
Choi, H., Kim, H., & Kang, D. (2017). Sex differences in hypertension prevalence and control: Analysis of the 2010–2014 Korea National Health and Nutrition Examination Survey. *PLOS ONE*, *12*(5), 4.

Cox, D. L., Stabb, S. D., & Hulgus, J. F. (2000). Anger and depression in girls and boys: A study of gender differences. *Psychology of Women Quarterly*, 24, 110–112.

Crick, N. R. (1997). Engagement in gender normative versus nonnormative forms of aggression: Links to social-psychological adjustment. *Developmental Psychology*, 33(4), 610–617.

Deffenbacher, J. L., Oetting, E. R., Lynch, R. S., Morris, C. A. (1996). The expression of anger and its consequences. *Behaviour Research and Therapy*, 34, 575–590.

Devlin, H. (2019). Science of anger: how gender, age and personality shape this emotion. *Guardian Online*. Available at: https://www.theguardian.com/lifeandstyle/2019/may/12/science-of-anger-gender-age-personality (Accessed: 5th September 2021).

Ekman, P., Friesen, W. V. (1975). *Unmasking the Face*. Englewood Cliffs, NJ: Prentice-Hall.

Fagot, B. I., Hagan, R., Driver Leinbach, M., Kronsberg, S. (1985). Differential reactions to assertive and communicative acts of toddler boys and girls. *Child Development*, 56, 1499–1505.

Lerner, J., & Keltner, D. (2001). Fear, anger, and risk. *Journal Of Personality And Social Psychology*, 81(1), 146–159.

Litvak, P., Lerner, J. S., Tiedens, L. Z., & Shonk, K. (2010). Fuel in the fire: How anger impacts judgment and decision making. In M. Potegal, G. Stemmler, & C. Spielberger (Ed.), *International Handbook of Anger* (pp. 287–311). New York, Springer.

Loewenstein, G., & Lerner, J. S. (2003). The role of affect in decision making. In R. Davidson, K. Scherer, & H. Goldsmith (Eds.), *Handbook of affective science* (pp. 619–642). London: Oxford University Press.

Maccoby, E. E., & Jacklin, C. N. (1980). Sex differences in aggression: A rejoinder and reprise. *Child Development*, 51, 964–980.

Office for National Statistics. (2019). The nature of violent crime in England and Wales. Available at: https://www.ons.gov.uk/peoplepopulationandcommunity/crimeandjustice/articles/thenatureofviolentcrimeinenglandandwales/yearendingmarch2018#what-do-we-know-about-perpetrators-of-violent-crimes (Accessed: 29th April 2021).

Office for National Statistics (2020a). Suicides in England and Wales: 2019 registrations. Available at: https://www.ons.gov.uk/peoplepopulationandcommunity/birthsdeathsandmarriages/deaths/bulletins/suicidesintheunitedkingdom/2019registrations#suicide-patterns-by-age (Accessed: 29th April 2021).

Office for National Statistics (2020b). Nature of sexual assault by rape or penetration, England and Wales: Year ending March 2020. Available at: https://www.ons.gov.uk/peoplepopulationandcommunity/crimeandjustice/articles/natureofsexualassaultbyrapeorpenetrationenglandandwales/yearendingmarch2020#perpetrator-characteristics (Accessed: 5th September 2021).

Rogers, B. (2017). Anger and Aggression at School. Available at: https://dmbcwebstolive01.blob.core.windows.net/media/Default/ChildrenYoungPeopleFamilies/01%20Anger%20and%20aggression%20at%20school%202020.pdf (Accessed: 28th October 2021).

ScienceDaily. (2000). Comparison Of Anger Expression In Men And Women Reveals Surprising Differences. Available at: www.sciencedaily.com/releases/2000/01/000131075609.htm (Accessed: 29th April 2021).

Siegel, D. J. (2014). You said WHAT about time-outs?! *Dr Dan Siegel*. Available at: https://drdansiegel.com/you-said-what-about-time-outs (Accessed: 13th October 2021).

Siegel, D. J., & Bryson, T. P. (2014). 'Time-outs' are hurting your child. *TIME Online*. Available at: https://time.com/3404701/discipline-time-out-is-not-good (Accessed: 12th October 2021).

Smith, D. C., Furlong, M., Bates, M., Laughlin, J. D. (1998). Development of the Multidimensional School Anger Inventory for males. *Psychology in the Schools*, *35*(1), 1–15.

Tiedens, L. (2001). Anger and advancement versus sadness and subjugation: The effect of negative emotion expressions on social status conferral. *Journal Of Personality And Social Psychology*, *80*(1), 86–94.

Tsirigotis, K., Wojciech, G., & Tsirigotis, M. (2011). Gender differences in methods of suicide attempts. *Medical Science Monitor*, *17*(8) 65–70).

Vijayakumar L. (2015). Suicide in Women. *Indian Journal of Psychiatry. 57*(6).

2 Exclusions

The story

Originally, this chapter began as an attempt to bring wider attention to the injustices faced by Black-African/Caribbean boys in schools. Injustices which go some way to explaining why Black-African/Caribbean boys are three times more likely to be excluded from school than White boys.

The research phase of any writing project is exciting, because if research is done properly, it can take your writing project in an entirely new direction. Uncharted territory. As I pored over the depressing statistics around exclusion and Black-African/Caribbean boys, something nagged at me. How could I write about Black-African/Caribbean boys and the disproportionate risk of exclusion they face, whilst ignoring the fact that another group of students – Gypsy, Roma, and Irish Traveller (GRT) boys – are up to *five* times more likely to be excluded from school than White boys?

Surely, I surmised, I could just write a chapter about both Black-African/Caribbean *and* GRT boys. But then, how could I do that in a way that is coherent and cohesive without conflating two very different groups of people, each with their own traditions, culture, and belief systems?

I did what I could.

I read lots and I spoke to people within the Black-African/Caribbean and GRT communities. The revelation was that although Black-African/Caribbean and GRT boys come from very different backgrounds, the reasons for their high exclusion rates are very similar: both groups of boys are *excluded* because in many schools they simply don't feel *included*.

What do school exclusions have to do with boys' mental wellbeing? Recent research from Exeter University proposes that exclusion from school increases the likelihood that a child will experience a mental health disorder in the next three years after initial exclusion. In other words, exclusion and mental health are inextricably linked. And, as you read on, you'll see that the way to tackle exclusion is inclusion. Inclusion means making students feel valued. Boys who feel as though they are valued members of their school community are not only less likely to be excluded from school, but they are more likely to be happy, too.

As you read the 'Solutions' section to this chapter, I'd ask you to recognise that any students, regardless of gender or ethnicity, who are persistently excluded from school can benefit from the solutions on offer. And yet, I urge you, as you read, not to forget the reality that Black-African/Caribbean and GRT boys are facing obstacles that others simply aren't.

The research

'Those' boys

According to the most recent data, if you are a boy, you are three times more likely to be permanently excluded from school than your female classmates.[1] Things are even worse for you if you happen to be a Black-Caribbean boy; this same data shows that Black-Caribbean boys are two times more likely than White British boys to be excluded, although in some areas – such as Cambridgeshire in England – their risk of exclusion is seven times higher than that of White British boys. If these figures are shocking, then consider statistics for boys of Gypsy, Roma, or Irish Traveller descent, whose likelihood of staying in school is even more precarious: GRT children are six times more likely to be excluded from school than their White classmates, but in some areas – such as Sheffield in South Yorkshire, which has the second-highest number of Roma children in the country – the exclusion rate is *nine* times higher than it is for White students.

> **Some notes on terminology**
>
> **Black-African/Caribbean boys**
>
> Emmanuel Awoyelu is a teacher and director of The Reach Out Project, a charity that aims to tackle youth violence and educational disengagement through mentoring programmes. In an interview with Awoyelu about the Black experience of school he was keen to point out that:
>
> > Although high exclusion rate statistics are specifically for Black boys of Caribbean heritage, the experience of informal exclusion through micro-aggressions and formal exclusions is something experienced by the Black diaspora. As an African born to Nigerian parents, I experienced school exclusions in both primary and secondary school. The experience was very similar to my Black peers who were

> from both the Caribbean and Africa. I'm African, but my experience is the Black experience.
>
> Whilst I fully acknowledge that the cultural beliefs, practices, and experiences of these two groups will vary significantly in many ways, I am also of the opinion that both Caribbean and African Black students fall victim to the same racial prejudices and injustices in the education system. Therefore, in this chapter, instead of referring specifically to 'Black-Caribbean boys,' I will use Awoyelu's preferred term, 'Black-African/Caribbean boys,' apart from when discussing exclusion rates of Black-Caribbean boys specifically, which are higher than for Black-African boys.
>
> Where quoted literature and contributors have used the term, 'Black' I have kept this.
>
> **GRT**
>
> As The Traveller Movement explains, 'Gypsies, Roma and Travellers are often categorised together under the "Roma" definition in Europe and under the acronym "GRT" in Britain[2]. However, although the umbrella term GRT is used, people should remember that Gypsies, Roma and Travellers each have their own distinct customs, languages and beliefs. It is particularly important that schools acknowledge this.
>
> 'However, the groups do share a number of common characteristics. For example: [a shared emphasis on] the importance of family and/or community networks; the nomadic way of life, a tendency toward self-employment, experience of disadvantage and having the poorest health outcomes in the United Kingdom.'[3]

Faced with these statistics, some people might assume that boys, particularly Black-Caribbean and GRT boys, are just *naturally* badly behaved. Of course, such assumptions are totally fallacious. As we discussed in *BDT?*, the notions that boys are 'naturally' more violent or aggressive – and therefore more likely to enact behaviours that lead to exclusion – are flimsy at best. We know that essentialist[4] beliefs about male behaviours (such as the belief that greater levels of testosterone lead males to be more violent) are deeply flawed and neglect the idea that gender is a social construct, rather than a biological one.[5] In fact, while men are the more violent sex, they are so because society has made it so and not because of predetermined characteristics in their biology. Therefore, if boys are more likely to commit violent acts which lead to higher exclusion rates in school, there are environmental factors that play a part. Environments can, nevertheless, demonstrably change and adapt to provide better, more suitable, outcomes.

If we go beyond 'boys' generally and focus in on the boys from Black-Caribbean and GRT backgrounds who are far more likely to be excluded than boys of other ethnicities, are we then to say that these boys are just *naturally* more badly behaved? Of course not. Such beliefs belong to eugenicist racists and not to anybody worthy of any role in the education system.

But let's play devil's advocate. Let's pretend that boys *are* naturally naughtier than girls. Let's even go as far to say that Black-African/Caribbean boys and GRT boys *are* naturally *even naughtier* than other boys. If this were the case, are we, as teachers and school leaders, to just accept this? Do we carry on with our lives accepting that every year nearly 80% of exclusions will be issued to boys? Do we blithely accept the fact that GRT children will always be, on average, five times more likely to be excluded than their White peers? Or do we do our jobs as we should be doing them? Do we adapt our practice and our language and our viewpoint to ensure that these so-called 'naturally' naughtier boys are given the same chances as everybody else in school?

I know which I choose.

An alternative explanation

Let's consider a more plausible explanation for the disproportionate statistics around the exclusion of Black-Caribbean and GRT pupils. Let's consider the wealth of evidence that suggests teachers stereotype Black-African/Caribbean students as ill-disciplined and wayward. Let's consider the experiences of those children who feel sidelined in school because the curriculum doesn't reflect their experience or heritage or provide any meaningful narrative about success and achievement in their communities. Let's consider the lack of diversity in staff ethnicity. And let's consider the way families from these backgrounds are often fundamentally misunderstood, ignored, and stigmatised by schools.

Teachers' racial bias

Both GRT and Black-African/Caribbean boys are the subject of teacher bias that can negatively impact their outcomes in school. Way back in 2003 the Department for Education and Skills (DfES) acknowledged that when it comes to GRT children:

> Low expectations which may be based on misplaced ideas that the pupils will not be staying long in the school or unchallenged stereotypes can lead them to not being encouraged to reach their potential.[6]

Comments made by teachers, outlined in a report into teachers' attitudes towards GRT children in UK schools, certainly seem to confirm that some teachers have a disturbingly negative attitude towards GRT children:

> …some of the Traveller kids…think they can do what they want…

> Their behaviour – both verbally and physically – is uncontrollable. They have no respect for authority or for teachers.

> I don't see why education should be different for them…They stand out because they *want to* stand out.[7]

One teacher, Rachael,[8] told me of her disgust at the racism of teachers she experienced at her school:

> My grandad was Scottish Traveller, and my father was brought up in that culture. Sadly, our family stopped practising the Traveller lifestyle in my generation. Unfortunately, what I have noticed since becoming a teacher is the way Traveller communities are still spoken about pejoratively. I have heard teachers referring to students as 'pikey' and speaking about them in a negative manner. When I've called staff out on these terms, explaining that they're offensive, the majority of teachers have just laughed it off. They don't seem to grasp that what they're doing is racist...
>
> I spoke with one Irish Traveller boy in my class who says that teachers and students still use 'banter' to get away with saying things to him that they simply wouldn't say to other minority ethnic students.

Decades of not recognising GRT children as belonging to distinct ethnic groups – they weren't included in UK school census data until 2003 – combined with the transient nature of many GRT children's lives, means statistical data on the stigma faced by these children is scant, although there are many small-scale studies which highlight attitudes similar to those outlined above. For Black-African/Caribbean children there is, conversely, an embarrassing wealth of evidence into the way teachers stereotype against them.

Disciplining Black boys

A study published by Stanford University in 2015[9] investigated teachers' reactions to misbehaviour by White[10] and Black children. In the study, teachers were asked to read an account of two incidences of misbehaviour by an imaginary pupil. After reading the account, teachers were then asked to comment on how severely they thought the student should be disciplined and asked to rate how likely it was that the student was a 'troublemaker.' The imaginary student was given either a 'stereotypically Black or White name' to see if the presumed race of the student impacted the teacher judgements. Sadly, it did. The study found that when a White student and a Black student commit two behaviour 'infractions,' teachers 'felt significantly more troubled by the second infraction than the first infraction when the student was Black.' Furthermore, when both a Black-African/Caribbean and a White child commit a second behaviour infraction, teachers think that the Black-African/Caribbean student should be disciplined more severely after the second infraction than a White student should. The study also found that, 'the more likely teachers were to *think* a student was Black-African/Caribbean (on the basis of the student's name), the more likely they were to label the student a troublemaker.' When it comes to exclusions, it's important to mention that the study also found that teachers were more likely to, 'imagine themselves suspending the Black-African/Caribbean student in the future compared with the White student.' In other words, teachers judge Black-African/Caribbean students' misbehaviours more harshly than those of White students.

Racial prejudice: start 'em young

This unfairly punitive stance in how teachers perceive Black-African/Caribbean boys' behaviour begins early. A Yale University study called *Do early educators' implicit biases regarding sex and race relate to behaviour expectations and recommendations of preschool expulsions and suspensions*[11]? is far more interesting than its title. In this study, 132 teachers were asked to watch a six-minute video clip of four preschool children – a Black-African/Caribbean boy, a White boy, a Black-African/Caribbean girl, and a White girl – seated around a classroom table. Participants were told that at some point in the video they might witness some challenging behaviour. Their job was to simply press the *Enter* key on a keypad every time they saw a behaviour that they felt could become a potential challenge. Then, once the video had finished, participants were asked to select which child they felt required most of their attention during the activity. Like all great studies, the participants were being lied to. The videos contained no challenging behaviours. Instead, the direction of the participants' gaze was being tracked by sophisticated eye-monitoring technology.

The study found that despite none of the children exhibiting any potentially challenging behaviours, teachers spent far longer gazing at the Black-African/Caribbean boy than all other children, even when all other factors were controlled for. Furthermore, at the end of the activity, when the teacher participants were asked to say which child required most of their attention, 42% said the Black-African/Caribbean boy compared to 34% for the White boy, 13% for the White girl, and 10% for the Black-African/Caribbean girl. The study concluded that:

> Regardless of the nature of the underlying biases, the tendency to observe more closely classroom behaviours based on the sex and race of the child may contribute to greater levels of identification of challenging behaviours with Black pre-schoolers.

The study goes on to assert that for Black boys in particular, this 'contributes to the documented sex and race disparities in preschool expulsions and suspensions.'[12]

No such thing as Black boys

The tendency for teachers to assume that Black-African/Caribbean boys are more likely to cause trouble and to punish them more severely when this belief is vindicated stems from a wider societal problem that deprives many Black-African/Caribbean boys of the right to childhood. A US study[13] asked participants to judge how 'innocent' they perceived children of different ages and racial backgrounds were, based on appearance. Up until the age of nine, children were judged to be 'innocent' regardless of race. However, after nine years old, Black-African/Caribbean children were judged to be 'significantly less innocent than White children.' In fact, participants tended to think Black-African/Caribbean boys' innocence rating was equal to that of White boys four years older than them. In other words, Black-African/Caribbean boys aged 10–13 were judged as equally innocent (or not innocent as the case may be) as White boys aged 14–17, whilst Black-African/Caribbean boys aged 14–17 were judged as equally innocent as White boys aged 18–21.

The same study asked participants to judge the age of Black-African/Caribbean, White, or Latino criminals. Black-African/Caribbean criminals were judged, on average, to be 4.53 years older than they actually were. This means that Black-African/Caribbean boys could be 'misperceived as legal adults at roughly the age of 13 and a half.' This 'adulting' of young Black-African/Caribbean boys happens in UK schools too. I spoke to Stacey Rye,[14] a teacher at a school in Birmingham with a high proportion of Black-African/Caribbean students. The picture she paints is unsettling:

> I once had to deal with an incident where a young, White, female newly qualified teacher (NQT) accused a 13-year-old Black student of sexual harassment – she said she didn't feel comfortable around him. When I investigated, it turned out there were three boys involved – the other two were White. Witnesses and the teacher admitted that the two White boys had also said things about her appearance and had been very inappropriate, but it was only the Black student who she said made her feel uncomfortable. All boys were the same age.

There is no excuse for the appalling harassment this female NQT received. However, what this incident shows is that White boys are not held to the same level of accountability as Black-African/Caribbean boys. Rye believes that often, the misbehaviour of Black-African/Caribbean boys is facilitated by a lack of understanding from White people in authority:

> It is the teachers who are often in the wrong. They are seeing Black-African/Caribbean students as something to fix, something to normalise. The reality is, it is the teachers who need to change their own understanding of what is and is not appropriate. They are barraging these children with their own micro-aggressions and worse, they are not recognising when their own prejudice is the instigator of serious incidents, for which Black-African/Caribbean students are then punished. It's a cycle which just adds to their pain and lack of engagement with White authority.

Interestingly, a similar phenomenon of 'premature aging' can happen to boys from GRT backgrounds too: Martin Myers' study[15] into Gypsy and Traveller parents' perceptions of education described this phenomenon as 'early onset adulthood.' This refers to the process by which, in many GRT communities, teenagers are 'deemed by their families and communities to have reached the status of adulthood shortly after making the transition to secondary school.' A teacher in the study explained how this can negatively impact teacher–student relationships because there are many teachers who struggle to manage GRT children 'because they are not "fawning and deferential enough" towards them.' The study goes on to say that:

> It's particularly difficult for GRT boys who are seen as men and breadwinners in their communities to have to come to school where not only are they treated like children, but they don't get to earn money either.[16]

What's more, many GRT children benefit from being widely travelled and are often exposed to cultural experiences during childhood in a way that many children are not. Many work from a young age. Because of this, many GRT students are used to talking with adults as equals. Where schools don't allow for this, there comes added conflict.

Who are schools for?

Children need to feel like they belong in a school. Children who feel alienated from a school's community, practices, curriculum, and teachers are unlikely to thrive. It's not surprising that students who feel informally excluded from schools will look for ways to make the arrangement a little more formal. For many Black-African/Caribbean and GRT children, school is a place where they are made to feel marginalised. This process of ostracism manifests itself in many ways: explicit and implicit racist abuse; curricula that refuse to acknowledge the lived experience and histories of ethnic minorities; an unwillingness to engage with the language, dialect, and customs of those who aren't White. Sometimes, the stigmatisation of ethnic minorities is even built into the very policies of the school. For example, as recently as 2020, schools have upheld rules about physical appearance that actively disadvantage Black-African/Caribbean children with afro hair.[17] Often, styles more suited to afro hair are banned, with one school objecting to haircuts that 'block the views of others.'

Daniel is one of many such children who was unfairly victimised at his predominantly White secondary school because of the way his afro hair contravened school policy:

> There was a rule that haircuts were not allowed to be below a number two grade[18] – we were told this was because they wanted our hair to look 'smart.' At this time I had a 'hi-top fade'.[19] When cutting my hair, I always made sure to tell my barber to double and triple check that he cut the sides of my hair no shorter than a number two grade. My dad made sure of this too. Yet, I still found myself regularly in isolation[20] because my hair was deemed to be 'too short' by teachers. At the time, I wasn't equipped with the vocabulary or knowledge to stand up for myself. The fact was my hair was 'afro-y' and that of other students wasn't. I started to assume

it was my fault that I kept ending up in detentions. I changed barbers three times! Of course, whenever I tried to defend myself, I was labelled a troublemaker.

The experience taught me that what made me different was punishable and that my academic survival meant that I had to be complicit.

Daniel's story is interesting because of the way it chimes with so much of the research we've discussed so far which suggests that adults play a role in the mistreatment of ethnic minority pupils in schools.

Of course, other students play a role too: a recent survey[21] showed that over a quarter (26%) of GRT boys have been bullied by other pupils.

The solutions

Clearly, there is work to be done. Work to be done in educating teachers and pupils about their own bias. Work to be done in dismantling teacher stereotyping and in making schools feel inclusive places where all can learn and thrive.

A. Tackle teacher bias

In Chapter Two of *BDT?* we wrote in some detail about how teachers can protect against their own, sometimes unconscious bias. Too often in schools, when we try to find solutions for problems we look outwards when in fact we'd be better off looking inwards. School leaders need to encourage staff to confront their bias via the use of question-directed discussions and attitude audit forms. Emmanuel Awoyelu also believes in an inward-centred approach:

> Good leaders should provide their staff with training on unconscious bias, helping them to learn how their prejudice and stereotyping of other groups informs how they treat or mistreat students and staff members in school. Schools should draw upon the experiences of staff members and families to help this process where appropriate so assumptions are not made that could be more damaging.

B. Be mindful of policing language

As well as trying to police Black-African/Caribbean hair, schools are policing Black-African/Caribbean language too. A recent report by linguist Ian Cushing[22] found many instances of schools banning words such as 'peng,' 'fam,' and 'bare,' all of which have their etymological roots in Black-African/Caribbean culture. GRT children suffer too, when using the language of their heritage. I spoke to Chelsea McDonagh, an Irish Traveller, who until recently worked for a well-known Traveller charity, who told me how she was reprimanded for how she pronounced words in her Irish Traveller accent when she started at a new school:

> I used it in class and my teacher told me, 'What you're saying is wrong.' She said that to me in front of the whole class. She kept getting me to repeat a different pronunciation. That was a defining moment for me.

As teachers, we should be celebrating the diverse richness of students' speech and recognise that often, when we're telling students to always speak using the language of middle-class White people – Standard English – we're asking them to abandon an aspect of their identity and heritage.

Appreciating the richness of student dialect isn't about abandoning Standard English. We can't do that – we have to teach it because it's in the Teachers' Standards. But we'd be wrong to assume that in order to write in Standard English, we need to speak in Standard English. Think about the dialect and slang words you use in your everyday interactions with friends and loved ones. Do these words slip into your transactional or formal writing? I find that teaching students explicitly, about the benefits of code switching – a recognised linguistic term that describes the ability to switch between more familiar, informal and dialectical forms of spoken English and more formal, Standard English when required for examinations or the workplace – helps students to recognise the power of language and use it more discerningly.

C. Audit your provision

Rudine Sims Bishop, Professor Emerita of Education at Ohio State University, is an expert on children's literature. In her seminal article, 'Mirrors, Windows and Sliding Glass Doors'[23] Bishop explains that children's books are like windows: they offer views into other worlds, cultures, and experiences. But books can also be mirrors: they can tell stories that reflect our own experience, culture, and heritage. In this sense, books provide self-affirmation; they make us see that we are an important – but tiny – piece in a world that exists beyond the scope of our own experience. The problem, as Bishop explains, is that for non-White children, there are too many windows and not enough mirrors. In other words, there just aren't enough books featuring BAME[24] characters, cultures, and experiences. This is borne out by the statistics. The *Reflecting Realities* report by the Centre for Literacy in Primary Education (CLPE)[25] found that:

- Of the 5,875 UK children's books published in 2020, only 15% featured BAME characters[26]
- Only 8% of these books had a BAME main character, despite the fact that 34% of children in UK primary schools in 2020 came from a BAME background

While many commend J. K. Rowling's *Harry Potter* series for promoting inclusivity and tolerance, as well as challenging themes such as racial purity and oppression, it is important to remember that this is within the context of a world populated by mythical figures: wizards, giants, and elves. Educator Darren Chetty highlights this problem eloquently in his discussion of the *Harry Potter* stories where he argues that:

> ...at Hogwarts, there are very few people of colour and no clear explanation of why that might be. So a story that has so much to say about racism on an allegorical level at the same time depicts people of colour as marginal without exploring their marginalisation.[27]

As Emmanuel Awoyelu explained to me, diversifying the books and texts we provide isn't just beneficial for students of ethnic minority backgrounds: 'We have to adopt the idea that if it's okay to show children of colour books related to the White experience, it's also okay for White children to hear stories about other people who exist in society.'

Sims Bishop provides a useful manifesto for consideration when thinking about the whitewashing of children's literature.

> When children can't find themselves reflected in the books they read...they learn a powerful lesson about how they are devalued in the society of which they are a part. Our classrooms need to be places where all children...can find their mirrors.[28]

With this manifesto in mind, schools need to ask: *What can we do to ensure that the literature we provide better reflects – like a mirror – the UK population,* **as well as** *our school population?*

Carol Carter, Library Co-ordinator at Headlands Primary School in Northampton, has done just this and created an audit form that schools can use to assess the diversity of the reading texts they are providing. I include it on the next page.

You can sign up to receive a comprehensive – and free – list of reading books that feature BAME characters and settings by typing this link into your web browser:

http://www.towerhamlets-sls.org.uk/perspectives

A list of books featuring GRT characters can be accessed with this URL:

http://www.newsfromnowhere.org.uk/books/DisplayBooklist.php?BookListID=1451

Diverse texts appraisal form

Use this form to analyse where gaps in your text offerings exist. In a small classroom bookshelf, it will not be possible to achieve perfect diversity, but you can decide which gaps are most important to fill. Use the blank rows to add other options specific to your setting, as identified by the first question.

What specific realities do I need to reflect in my setting (classroom/school/library)? e.g., *deafness, grief/loss, traveller families.*			
How well-represented is each of the following:			
Representation	**0** No texts Available	**1** 1–2 texts available	**2** Small range of texts	**3** Large range of texts
BAME				
Disability				
LGBTQ+				
Wider Horizons/Life Experiences				
Accessibility:	0	1	2	3
Varied reading age				
Dyslexia-friendly				
Text type:	0	1	2	3
Novels				
Short stories				
Graphic novels				
Poetry				
Newspapers				
Magazines/comics				
Genre:	0	1	2	3
Humorous				
Contemporary/realism				
Historical				
Fantasy/sci-fi/horror				
Mystery/thriller				
Factual				
Authorship:	0	1	2	3
BAME				
Gender balance				

Of course, it is not just books that should be mirrors. All students, regardless of their ethnicity, should be given access to curricula that not only open windows to events, people, and works of art from cultures different to their own, but provide mirrors to help them see themselves and their place in the wider context and history of the world.

In her vital book, *The Lost Girls: Why a feminist revolution in education benefits everyone*, Charlotte Woolley provides a set of questions to help teachers interrogate their curriculum to make sure it represents gender equity. Woolley has kindly allowed me to adapt these questions, for the purpose of auditing your curriculum provision:

> **Curriculum audit questions**
>
> - Does our English curriculum offer a balanced view of women and men, in characters and authors, across time periods and cultural backgrounds, and in all genres?
> - Do History students have opportunities to discuss a wide range of BAME figures throughout history?
> - Do we talk about BAME characters in the context of BAME history, thus developing a more subtle understanding?
> - Do we avoid treating people from ethnic minority backgrounds as 'other'? Are Black and White writers side by side in the curriculum?
> - Do we take opportunities to explore unconscious bias? For example, bias created by White privilege in language?
> - Do we explore emotions and feelings in detail, giving students the opportunity to use *their* own cultural vocabulary to express themselves thoughtfully and reflectively?
> - Do we offer plenty of chances for students to practise empathy and compassion in the way they discuss characters and non-fiction texts?
> - Do our non-fiction texts contribute to students' wider understanding of the people from backgrounds different to their own?
> - Do we have a fair balance of 'mirror' and 'window' stories in our curriculum?
> - Are students encouraged to write regularly and expressively about their own cultural heritage and lived experience?

Bennie Kara, a deputy head in the East Midlands, writes and speaks frequently about diversity in schools. I asked her if too much of the responsibility for diversifying the curriculum was put on teachers of English and History:

> While the English and History curricula naturally lend themselves to diverse narratives and allow for the mirroring of different cultures, positive

representation of Black figures is possible in a range of subjects if departments take the time to find some. An example might be in the study of a contemporary Black artist like Chris Ofili or looking at the contribution of Joseph Bologne in Music. Other examples include referencing immunologist Donald Palmer in Science, or Nira Chamberlain in Mathematics. Then it is the case that these figures are not an 'add on' during Black History Month, but an integral part of the narrative of a subject.

The emphasis on positive representation is important, as Kara explained further:

> It is important to note that these narratives cannot be solely focused on stereotypes and victim narratives. Positive representation provides an anchor for Black boys and GRT students to be able to define an identity outside of what is commonly presented about them in the media.

D. Involve parents of ethnic minority backgrounds

It is important to recognise that the parents of those students who tend to be excluded may not have had good experiences of school themselves, meaning they are less likely to play a role in developing positive attitudes towards – and relationships with – schools. GRT parents' perception of school is often informed by their own experiences. As Kalwant Bhopal notes in her 2004 study into GRT parent attitudes towards education:

> Many of their educational experiences were negative and this affected, to some degree, expectations of their children's experience of the education system.[29]

Relationships are two-way things. The issue of fractious relationships between GRT families and schools is no doubt compounded by teachers' bias towards families of GRT pupils. After all, if teachers are biased towards GRT pupils, that bias must, surely, also extend to GRT family members.

Schools have a responsibility to put the same care and attention into building relationships with the families of pupils as they do with pupils. Not always, but often, GRT parents have low literacy levels. Schools should be mindful of the language used in letters home, ensuring that vocabulary is suited for parents and carers who may struggle to read. Bear in mind that often, parents – and children of parents – who can't read are reluctant to tell schools that they can't. As Chelsea McDonagh bluntly told me: 'No kid is going to tell you their mum can't read.'

Remember that often, many families – particularly those from GRT communities – will have limited access to Wi-Fi. Invite parents into school and find an alternative system of communication that works best for them.

E. Employ more staff from ethnic minority backgrounds

The Timpson report made very clear the need for schools to employ a workforce that more accurately reflects the ethnic backgrounds of the pupils they support:

> To that end, it remains the case that some of the groups overrepresented in exclusion statistics are also underrepresented in the population of our school workforce. At present, one quarter of pupils in our schools are BAME yet the number of BAME classroom teachers is just 9%.[30]

Given that 'children from the relevant ethnic groups (Black-Caribbean, GRT) were much more likely to be excluded when they were in a small minority in a school,[31]' it's absolutely imperative that school leaders actively seek employees who reflect the backgrounds of the pupils they teach. Emmanuel Awoleyu explains:

> Having more BAME male educators normalises the idea of BAME men being educated. This is important for boys from ethnic minorities, but it is just as important for young boys to see BAME men doing good things in positions of authority.

This isn't necessarily because men make better role models than boys. Rather, it's about showing Black-African/Caribbean and GRT children that their school is a place that believes in empowering Black-African/Caribbean and GRT people.

One school I spoke to told me that each year, they offer a one-year contract of employment to an ex-GRT student, to work as a home-school link worker between the school and its GRT communities. This is a powerful way of bridging the gap between two communities who might otherwise remain divided by mutual hostility fuelled by misconceptions.

F. Make use of external providers

An assembly about Martin Luther King during Black History Month, whilst admirable in its intentions, is not enough. Schools need to think carefully about how they can engage and acknowledge the diverse cultures in their schools in ways that aren't tokenistic or a one-off. Irish Traveller Chelsea McDonagh told me that 'if you want to explore Gypsy, Roma or Traveller culture, then engage with Traveller organisations. Then you're not making bad mistakes.'

Awoleyu concurs with McDonagh's recommendation for the use of external agencies, even where financial constraints may prove a burden:

> Money is an issue, but what are your priorities? What things could schools *stop* spending money on to make space for things like this? There is a lack of role models and representation within schools for Black-African/Caribbean children, particularly Black-African/Caribbean boys and that's why programmes such as ours [The Reach Out Project] are important. We can provide

mentors who are advocates and guides for young people. Schools do not always have the funds or resources to support some of the groups within their school and that's why our programme has been so successful. We can support pupils who have often been marginalised and are now becoming disengaged with school and vulnerable to exclusions, paving the way for gang grooming and a life of crime. If schools do not feel they have the means to support their most vulnerable students, they should consider looking at external agencies whose expertise *can* support.

G. Think carefully about school trips

In my conversation with Awoleyu, we discussed how, often, the trips that schools take students on are whitewashed.[32] We take students to art galleries featuring portraits of White historical figures painted by White artists; we take them on reward trips to the cinema where they watch films featuring White actors made by White directors; we take them to the theatre to watch mainly White casts act out plays written by White playwrights.

Schools need to be looking into what cultural and artistic events are reflecting the artistic tastes and traditions of people from non-White backgrounds. Stacey Rye, the teacher in Birmingham who I mentioned earlier, told me:

> Spoken word events like poetry slams which come directly from hip hop culture are great. There is a powerful Black theatre culture and some incredible Black dance companies. Schools have to make the effort to see plays written by Black playwrights and performances by Black musicians – lots of people limit Black artistic output to rap and RnB. While I love both, that is not the limit of Black talent and creativity.

It may be that you are keen to diversify your trip provision but work in a school where the people that make decisions are mainly White. If this is the case, why not reach out to non-White parents and see what trips or experiences they recommend? Hire a parent representative as an advisor (or even better, a leader) on selecting trips that are representative of ethnic minority culture, heritage, and art. As Awoleyu explained to me, this not only ensures children of all ethnicities are exposed to a wide range of experiences, but has the dual benefit of strengthening relationships with ethnic minority families:

> In a majority White school, you must be careful to not marginalise parents from ethnic backgrounds. You must strive to have them feel included and valued. Invite parents in to lead on workshops/cooking sessions etc., especially if they are the minority population within the school.

H. Come down hard on racist bullying

Any school that doesn't come down hard on the racist bullying of ethnic minority pupils should be shut down immediately. It's hard to imagine a school that doesn't have strict sanctions in place for dealing with overt incidences of racist abuse such as name-calling, offensive jokes, or overt stereotyping.

But schools need to be aware that bullying isn't always overt. And it's not always dished out by pupils. Awoleyu explains:

> I never experienced bullying much from other students in school, but I experienced it from teachers in both primary and secondary school. Behaviours or acts that some may class as 'micro-aggressions' are sometimes just straight bullying. Refusing a child entry into your class because you don't feel like dealing with them today is a form of exclusion that gives you the same feeling you have when you are being picked on or bullied.

Rapper, journalist, and author Akala wrote about this in his book *Natives: Race and Class in the Ruins of Empire*.[33] He writes about his first teacher, who would only let him talk if the invisible 'magic button' on his chest had been poked hard first; of another teacher who told him 'I wish you were still there,' in response to Akala telling him what he knew about Jamaica; of one teacher who physically assaulted him and used the phrase, 'I admit to tapping him, but it's not because he is brown,' in a meeting with his mother.

I mentioned previously that explicit bullying in the form of racist name-calling is, rightly, never condoned by schools. However, GRT pupils and families would probably disagree with me. As Chelsea McDonagh explained to me, the racist slur 'pikey' is something that GRT children have to face daily:

> That's never stopped. It isn't always addressed. I think people don't think of Traveller groups as an ethnic group…I remember my brother got called a 'pikey' by a female in his class and he responded by calling her a 'slag.' She got a detention and he got excluded for a week. The Headteacher said he shouldn't have got upset because it wasn't offensive but that wasn't her call to make.

Whilst use of the term 'slag' is equally repellent, it's easy to see that the school's response here is disproportionate. Despite her brother's experience, McDonagh, who went to a different school to her brother, fared far better when it came to dealing with racism:

> At my school it was dealt with swiftly and that meant I didn't have to deal with it. It made all the difference.

A 2020 report from *The Traveller Movement*,[34] looking at the experience of GRT children in London, revealed that 26% of GRT boys have been bullied at school. Overall, 23% of students questioned said they would have liked to remain in school but couldn't because of bullying. Interestingly, 67% of GRT pupils (74% girls; 61% boys) claimed to have been bullied by teachers because of their ethnicity.

Clearly, schools need to do more to inform their staff about GRT culture, and the kind of bullying that GRT pupils specifically are victims of, in order to ensure that schools are places where these pupils feel included.

The final word

The start of this chapter began with some depressing exclusion statistics. These statistics may help to mask the fact that behind the numbers there are *children*. Children who, whether Black-African, Gypsy, Roma, Black-Caribbean, or Irish Traveller, are all victims of the same injustice. In all schools, the majority of exclusions could be prevented with a little more acknowledgement, a little more care, and a little more understanding.

Because of that, this chapter isn't really just about Black-African/Caribbean boys or GRT boys. It's about *all* children for whom feeling more included in school may have been a preventative measure in their exclusion. Of course, there are times when exclusions are necessary. But preventative measures can be taken, to ensure that boys – and girls – of all ethnicities are taught in such a way that social and educational exclusion – in the broadest sense of these terms – becomes a thing of the past and feeling included, valued, and happy becomes part of the here and now.

Notes

1 Department for Education. (2020). Academic Year 2018/19 Permanent exclusions and suspensions in England. Available at: https://explore-education-statistics.service.gov.uk/find-statistics/permanent-and-fixed-period-exclusions-in-england/2018-19 (Accessed: 9th December 2021).
2 The Traveller Movement. (2021). Gypsy Roma and Traveller History and Culture. Available at: https://travellermovement.org.uk/about/gypsy-roma-traveller-history-and-culture#differences (Accessed: 9th December 2021).
3 Ibid.
4 Essentialism is 'the view that certain categories (e.g., women, racial groups…) have an underlying reality or true nature that one cannot observe directly. This underlying reality (or "essence") is thought to give objects their identity, and to be responsible for similarities that category members share.' Gelman, S. A. (2005, May 1). Essentialism in everyday thought. Psychological Science Agenda. Available at: https://www.apa.org/science/about/psa/2005/05/gelman (Accessed: 21st November 2022).
5 Abrams, M. (2020). Gender Essentialism Is Flawed – Mirrors, windows, and sliding glass Here's Why. Available at: https://www.healthline.com/health/gender-essentialism#social-constructionism (Accessed: 13th June 2022).
6 Department for Education and Skills. (2003). Aiming high: raising the achievement of Gypsy Traveller Pupils. Available at: https://schools.essex.gov.uk/pupils/EMTAS%20Ethnic%20Minority%20and%20Traveller%20Achievement%20ervice/Gypsy_Roma_Travellers/Documents/Aiming%20High%20%20Raising%20the%20Achievement%20of%20Gypsy%20Traveller%20Pupils.pdf (Accessed: 9th December 2021).
7 Bhopal, K. (2013). 'This is a school, it's not a site': teachers' attitudes towards Gypsy and Traveller pupils in schools in England, UK. *British Educational Research Journal, 37*(3), 465–483.
8 This name has been changed.
9 Okonofua, J. A., & Eberhardt, J. L. (2015). Two strikes: Race and the disciplining of young students. *Psychological Science, 26*(5), 617–624.

10 In this chapter, I have capitalised the words 'Black' and 'White' to refer to ethnicity. Capitalisation of these words rightly recognises the important functions of 'blackness' and 'whiteness' in institutions and communities. Lower-case versions of the word would fail to honour the significant role that skin colour plays in society.
11 Gilliam, W. S., Maupin, A. N., Reyes, C. R., Accavitti, M., & Shic, F. (2016). Do early educators' implicit biases regarding sex and race relate to behaviour expectations and recommendations of preschool expulsions and suspensions? Yale University, Child Study Center. https://medicine.yale.edu/childstudy/zigler/publications/Preschool%20Implicit%20Bias%20Policy%20Brief_final_9_26_276766_5379_v1.pdf (Accessed 17th November 2022).
12 Ibid.
13 Goff, P. A., Jackson, M. C., Di Leone, B. A. L., Culotta, C. M., & DiTomasso, N. A. (2014). The essence of innocence: Consequences of dehumanizing Black children. *Journal of Personality and Social Psychology, 106*(4), 526–545.
14 Name has been changed.
15 Myers, M., McGhee, D., & Bhopal, K. (2010). At the crossroads: Gypsy and Traveller parents' perceptions of education, protection and social change. *Race Ethnicity and Education, 13*(4), 533–548.
16 Ibid.
17 Parveen, N. (2020). 'Not seeing ourselves represented': Union Jack row at London school shows divides. *The Guardian*. Available at: https://www.theguardian.com/education/2021/mar/25/not-seeing-ourselves-represented-union-jack-row-at-london-school-shows-divides (Accessed: 9th December 2021).
18 In haircutting, 'grades' refers to the length to which hair is cut using electric clippers. The lower the number, the shorter the haircut.
19 A haircut where hair on the sides is very short while hair on the top of the head is very long, popularised by hip-hop culture in the 90s.
20 The process of removing a child from their usual lessons, normally as punishment for a contravention of school rules.
21 The Traveller Movement. (2020). *Barriers in education – young Travellers in London*. Available at: https://wp-main.travellermovement.org.uk/wp-content/uploads/2021/08/TTM-Barriers-in-education_web.pdf (Accessed: 13th June 2022).
22 Cushing, I. (2020). The policy and policing of language in schools. *Language in Society, 49*(3), 425–450.
23 Bishop, R. S. (1990). Mirrors, windows, and sliding glass doors. *Perspectives: Choosing and Using Books for the Classroom 6*(3).
24 Black, Asian, and Minority Ethnic. Recent guidance from the Commission on Race and Ethnic Disparities advises against the use of the word 'BAME' as it emphasises certain ethnic minority groups and excludes other. I use the term here for consistency as it is what's used in the source I am citing. The guidance can be accessed here: https://www.ethnicity-facts-figures.service.gov.uk/style-guide/writing-about-ethnicity#:~:text=BAME%20and%20BME, We%20do%20not&text=In%20March%202021%2C%20the%20Commission,than%20as%20a%20single%20group (Accessed: 21st November 2022).
25 Centre for Literacy in Primary Education. (2021). Reflecting Realities: Survey of ethnic representation within UK children's literature 2020. Available at: https://clpe.org.uk/system/files/2021-12/CLPE%20Reflecting%20Realities%20Report%202021.pdf (Accessed: 9th December 2021).
26 However, this is a pleasing increase from the 7% of books in 2018 that featured BAME characters.

27 Chetty, D. (2018). Are only white people magic? *Independent Thinking*. Available at: https://www.independentthinking.co.uk/resources/posts/2018/april/are-only-white-people-magic (Accessed: 9th December 2021).
28 Bishop, R. S. (1990).
29 Bhopal, K. (2004). Gypsy Travellers and Education: Changing Needs and Changing Perceptions. *British Journal of Educational Studies*, *52*(1), 47–64.
30 Timpson. (2019). Timpson review of school exclusion. Available at: https://assets.publishing.service.gov.uk/government/uploads/system/uploads/attachment_data/file/807862/Timpson_review.pdf (Accessed: 9th December 2021).
31 Ibid.
32 'Whitewashing' is a term which, in this context, refers to the tendency to show content, or present an experience, which favours or caters to White people only.
33 *Akala*. (2018). *Natives*: *Race and Class in the Ruins of Empire*. London: Two Roads.
34 The Traveller Movement. (2020). Barriers in Education – Young Travellers in London. Available at: https://wp-main.travellermovement.org.uk/wp-content/uploads/2021/08/TTM-Barriers-in-education_web.pdf (Accessed: 9th December 2021).

References

Abrams, M. (2020). Gender Essentialism Is Flawed – Here's Why. Available at: https://www.healthline.com/health/gender-essentialism#social-constructionism (Accessed: 13th June 2022).
Akala. (2018). *Natives*: *Race and Class in the Ruins of Empire*. London: Two Roads.
Bhopal, K. (2004). Gypsy Travellers and education: changing needs and changing perceptions. *British Journal of Educational Studies*, *52*(1), 47–64.
Bhopal, K. (2013). 'This is a school, it's not a site': teachers' attitudes towards Gypsy and Traveller pupils in schools in England, UK. *British Educational Research Journal*, *37*(3), 465–483.
Bishop, R. S. (1990). Mirrors, windows, and sliding glass doors. *Perspectives: Choosing and Using Books for the Classroom 6*(3).
Centre for Literacy in Primary Education. (2021). Reflecting Realities: Survey of ethnic representation within UK children's literature 2020. Available at: https://clpe.org.uk/system/files/2021-12/CLPE%20Reflecting%20Realities%20Report%202021.pdf (Accessed: 9th December 2021).
Chetty, D. (2018). Are only white people magic? *Independent Thinking*. Available at: https://www.independentthinking.co.uk/resources/posts/2018/april/are-only-white-people-magic (Accessed: 9th December 2021).
Commission on Race and Ethnic Disparities. https://www.ethnicity-facts-figures.service.gov.uk/style-guide/writing-about-ethnicity#:~:text=BAME%20and%20BME,We%20do%20not&text=In%20March%202021%2C%20the%20Commission,than%20as%20a%20single%20group (Accessed 8th December 2021).
Cushing, I. (2020). The policy and policing of language in schools. *Language in Society*, *49*(3), 425–450.
Department for Education. (2020). Academic Year 2018/19 Permanent exclusions and suspensions in England. Available at: https://explore-education-statistics.service.gov.uk/find-statistics/permanent-and-fixed-period-exclusions-in-england/2018-19 (Accessed: 9th December 2021).
Department for Education and Skills. (2003). Aiming high: raising the achievement of Gypsy Traveller pupils. Available at: https://schools.essex.gov.uk/pupils/EMTAS%20

Ethnic%20Minority%20and%20Traveller%20Achievement%20ervice/Gypsy_Roma_Travellers/Documents/Aiming%20High%20%20Raising%20the%20Achievement%20of%20Gypsy%20Traveller%20Pupils.pdf (Accessed: 9th December 2021).

Gelman, S. A. (2005, May 1). Essentialism in everyday thought. *Psychological Science Agenda*. Available at: https://www.apa.org/science/about/psa/2005/05/gelman (Accessed: 21st November 2022).

Gilliam, W. S., Maupin, A. N., Reyes, C. R., Accavitti, M., & Shic, F. (2016). Do early educators' implicit biases regarding sex and race relate to behaviour expectations and recommendations of preschool expulsions and suspensions? Yale University, Child Study Center. https://medicine.yale.edu/childstudy/zigler/publications/Preschool%20Implicit%20Bias%20Policy%20Brief_final_9_26_276766_5379_v1.pdf (Accessed 17th November 2022).

Goff P. A., Jackson M. C., Di Leone B. A. L., Culotta C. M., & DiTomasso N. A. (2014). The essence of innocence: Consequences of dehumanizing Black children. *Journal of Personality and Social Psychology*, *106*(4), 526–545.

Myers, M., McGhee, D., & Bhopal, K. (2010). At the crossroads: Gypsy and Traveller parents' perceptions of education, protection and social change. *Race Ethnicity and Education*, *13*(4), 533–548.

Okonofua, J. A., & Eberhardt, J. L. (2015). Two strikes: Race and the disciplining of young students. *Psychological Science*, *26*(5), 617–624.

Parveen, N. (2020). 'Not seeing ourselves represented': Union Jack row at London school shows divides. *The Guardian*. Available at: https://www.theguardian.com/education/2021/mar/25/not-seeing-ourselves-represented-union-jack-row-at-london-school-shows-divides (Accessed: 9th December 2021).

The Traveller Movement. (2020). *Barriers in education – young Travellers in London*. Available at: https://wp-main.travellermovement.org.uk/wp-content/uploads/2021/08/TTM-Barriers-in-education_web.pdf (Accessed: 13th June 2022).

The Traveller Movement. Gypsy Roma and Traveller History and Culture. Available at: https://travellermovement.org.uk/about/gypsy-roma-traveller-history-and-culture#differences (Accessed: 9th December 2021).

Timpson. (2019). Timpson review of school exclusion. Available at: https://assets.publishing.service.gov.uk/government/uploads/system/uploads/attachment_data/file/807862/Timpson_review.pdf (Accessed: 9th December 2021).

3   Suicide and self-harm

> Although the content of this chapter is based upon many hours of extensive research, as well as interviews with leading authorities in the field of mental health, I, as author of this work, am not a qualified mental health expert. Anybody who is struggling with self-harm and/or suicidal thoughts should seek the help of, or be referred to, a qualified professional.
>
> This chapter has been read and checked by *Samaritans*.
>
> *Samaritans* offer free, non-judgemental support, day or night, 365 days a year. You can call them for free on **116 123**, email them at **jo@samaritans.org**, or visit **www.samaritans.org** to find your nearest branch.
>
> For young people who are struggling, *Papyrus* is a charity dedicated to helping young people struggling with suicidal thoughts. If you are struggling, you can contact *Papyrus* by phone, text, or email.
>
> **Phone: 0800 068 4141**
> **Text: 07860 039967**
> **Email**: pat@papyrus-uk.org
> They are open 9am–midnight, **every day of the year**.

The story

Written by Clare Milford-Haven

My son James – athletic, bright, charming James – underwent a minor operation on the 4th December 2006. Six days later, he came home from Newcastle University to spend time with his family. He seemed a bit quiet and a bit down – not his usual self. I suggested we go for a walk together with our dogs. We walked for about an hour and a half and during this time he told me that he didn't feel right, that he felt down and that his sex drive was reduced. I tried to reassure him that this was quite normal after operations, and that anaesthetics can make you feel a bit low and out of sorts. I told him to be patient and was sure that within a week or so, he would be back to his normal self.

After the weekend, James flew back up to Newcastle for the last four days of term. He called me to say he got back okay and was feeling a bit better. A few days later he called again to tell me he still felt 'not quite right.' Again, I did my best to try to reassure him that everything would be fine.

'Thanks Mum,' he said, 'You always make me feel better.'

What James neglected to tell me was that in actual fact, he was feeling so acutely anxious that, that very morning, he had visited the Newcastle Walk-In Centre to seek medical help. He was seen by a registered nurse who noted that James was concerned about the outcome of his recent operation.

She also noted that he felt suicidal.

Rather than keeping James there in a safe place and talking him through his concerns or calling the on-duty psychiatric registrar, he was transferred to A&E at the hospital next door. The priority level on James' report that morning was graded as '4.' On a scale of 1 to 4, 'priority level 4' is the least serious; patients graded a priority level '1' are a serious worry who require immediate treatment. James – a young man with suicidal thoughts – was given the same priority level as someone complaining of a toothache.

James walked out of A&E. Following the initial triage, which, as explained above, had resulted in his being graded as the lowest priority in the A&E department that morning, he didn't want to wait for up to four hours. He was an impatient, impulsive 21-year-old in considerable distress, and he needed to see someone straight away. The medical staff on duty at the hospital not only allowed James to walk out of the hospital in a suicidal state, but they also never contacted his family GP, whose details they took down on the report. Because of patient confidentiality, they also never contacted his next of kin, who happened to be me, his mother.

Two hours after James left the A&E department, he walked into another doctor's surgery near his house in Jesmond, Newcastle. He filled out a new patient registration form and saw a doctor who states that James never mentioned his earlier visit to the walk-in centre or A&E. James discussed his concerns about the after-effects of his recent operation. He apparently never made any reference to feeling suicidal. The doctor examined the area of the operation and said there was nothing to worry about and felt she had reassured him by the time he left the surgery.

The following day, on Thursday 14th of December, James was due to sit an exam and then drive home for the Christmas holidays. I expected him to arrive sometime around 10pm but by 4.30pm he was at home. I was surprised and asked about the exam. What had happened?

'I couldn't do the exam, Mum. I am not feeling right.'

This was the first time in 21 years that James had ever missed an exam.

James looked shattered. He told me he had lost weight, wasn't sleeping, and, above all, he wasn't happy. Immediately, I rang our family GP and expressed my concerns. The GP said that if things didn't improve in the next few weeks, he would prescribe a course of anti-depressants.

That night we had a family dinner and I noticed that James was quiet and not eating much, which was unusual. He was surrounded by all the people he loved – parents, siblings, cousins – but he seemed not to be enjoying any of it.

Normally, he was the life and soul of the party.

About two weeks later, on the 29th of December, James' GP *did* in fact receive a letter from the hospital in Newcastle. It turned out after all, that they had sent the report of James' visit to them, but they had sent it via second-class post, in the week leading up to Christmas, and to the wrong postcode.

It was a letter that arrived too late.

Two weeks previously, on the 15th of December 2006, my son had killed himself.

The tragedy of James' death cannot be separated from the disastrous clerical errors and miscommunications that might have prevented it. As a 21-year-old male, James was at higher risk than most of death by suicide. The idea that he could declare suicidal thoughts, to two separate medical practitioners on the same day, and no systematic process of intervention, prompted by communication between the different practitioners, be put into action is not only frustrating, but tragic.

What's interesting about James' story is that in many ways he *defies* the narrative; the narrative of male stoicism in the face of adversity and a reluctance to open up or lean on others during difficult times. James sought help. James spoke to people about his anxieties. And yet, still, it wasn't enough.

If we can take just one thing from James' story, it's that when dealing with issues of male mental health, a joined-up approach founded in strong communication links and consistency of practice is required.

The research

'Only very few'

During my research for this book, somebody told me that 'only very few' young people kill themselves each year. They weren't lying. Official statistics[1] for England, Scotland, and Wales show that in 2020, a comparatively small total of 264 people aged 10–19 died by suicide. 72% of these were boys.

Although 'very few' boys die by suicide each year, by the time these boys become men, suicide will be the biggest threat to their mortality: in England, *suicide is the single biggest killer of men under the age of 45*. They are three times more likely than women to die by suicide.

As teachers, we prepare students for the future. We teach students to work hard so that they have options. Students with good grades, emotional intelligence, and strong social skills are better able to successfully navigate a world that throws drugs, violence, and a myriad of other obstacles into the mix. Suicide is one of these obstacles. It is an obstacle faced particularly by those boys who one day will be men, and who sit before us in our classrooms. It is vital that teachers and schools accept this and make targeted attempts to prevent suicide from being seen as the most viable option for these boys who should one day become men. Men who believe that suicide is not just a viable option, but the *only* option.

Given its firm grip on male mortality rates, it would have been odd, in a book about boys' mental wellbeing, not to dedicate a whole chapter of this book to the topic of suicide. Equally strange, though, would have been to write a chapter that has no regard for the fact that suicide is no less devastating or no less a threat to the girls we teach and the women they become. As I mentioned in Chapter One, studies show that females are up to three times more likely to attempt suicide than men. And so, what follows is not simply boy-specific guidance. I may occasionally refer specifically to boys, but the advice contained within this chapter should be used as guidance for tackling the issue of suicide with all children, regardless of their sex as assigned at birth or gender identity. It's important to also remember that there is solid research to suggest that the harmful impact of bullying, discrimination, and stigma on transgender students means that they are more susceptible to self-harm and suicide.[2]

Teachers and child suicide

In 2017, *Papyrus*, a charity dedicated to preventing suicide in children, commissioned a YouGov poll of 804 teaching professionals on the topic of suicide. The study returned some concerning results:

- 1 in 10 teaching professionals said a student shares suicidal thoughts[3] with them at least once a term
- Only 53% of teachers said they felt they could support a child who shares suicidal thoughts with them
- Only 48% of classroom teachers, compared to 75% of senior leaders, felt confident in supporting children with suicidal thoughts

The study also identified several barriers that education professionals felt would stop them being able to support a child with suicidal thoughts:

- A lack of training (47%)
- Worries about making the situation worse (34%)
- Not knowing what to say (22%)
- Not knowing correct procedure (15%)[4]

This survey showed that despite these barriers, only very few teachers felt that providing support wasn't their duty: 2% felt it was down to parents and guardians, whilst 7% simply felt it wasn't their role. It is my hope that this chapter helps the majority of teachers who rightfully recognise that, however uncomfortable it may be, supporting children's mental health is an integral part of our profession.

Suicide and self-harm

Many teachers have had some experience, direct or otherwise, of child self-harm. It may be that they have been at the other end of a child's disclosure. For others, it will be something they've experienced in more abstract terms as part of statutory safeguarding training. For some, it will be hands-on experience of providing first aid and other frontline support following an incident of self-harm either in school or at home.

Dr Dennis Ougrin, of King's College London, is a consultant child and adolescent psychiatrist and one of the world's leading experts on adolescent self-harm. I spoke with Ougrin about the topic of adolescent self-harm and – in one hour – learnt more from him than I had ever learnt about self-harm over the course of my ten years in teaching.

'Self-harm is one of the single biggest predictors of suicide,' Ougrin informed me, 'and paradoxically, when we look at self-harm statistics in comparison with suicide statistics, the trends are reversed. Girls are much more likely to self-harm, which is strange given that males have a much higher representation in suicide mortality rates.'

Ougrin is correct. A recent study of self-harm and its links to suicide concluded that:

> …self-injury is as likely as suicide attempts to predict future attempts. Therefore, depressed adolescents with self-injury require the same high level of urgent assessment…and recent self-harm should alert us to a high risk for future suicide attempts.[5]

Another study, from 2016, says that the risk of suicide is increased by between 30 and 100-fold in the year following an episode of self-harm.[6]

Females are more likely to self-harm, with one study showing that 25.7% of females aged between 16 and 24 reported having self-harmed compared to 9.7% of males in the same age bracket.[7]

I can think of times when students have disclosed incidences of self-harm to me, and whilst my initial thoughts have always been about the wellbeing and safety of the child, thoughts that this child could potentially be at greater risk of suicide have rarely, if ever, come to the fore. Probably, this is because whilst a vague assumption about a link between suicide and self-harm is always there, lingering, it is nebulous, and rarely – if ever – has the evidence been presented to me as directly – and as seriously – as it should have been.

Why do young people self-harm?

Self-harm is defined as any act of self-injury, or self-poisoning, irrespective of whether the person carrying out the act wants to kill themselves. There are many reasons why a young person might self-harm. These include:

- They are suffering abuse
- They have experienced a traumatic incident
- They are struggling with family problems such as divorce
- They are being bullied
- They are struggling with a sudden change in their life such as a divorce, house move, or new school
- They are struggling with exam pressures or pressures from family members to achieve
- They have low self-esteem or body image issues
- They feel lonely and/or unloved
- They are suffering from feelings of guilt or failure

Gender differences in self-harm

Whilst all children, regardless of gender or sex, can self-harm, a study from 2018 of over 11,000 UK teenagers found that girls were over three times more likely to self-harm than boys. The study found that 'compared to boys, girls were two and a half times more likely to report negative moods and feelings; nearly twice more likely to report low life satisfaction; and four times more likely to report low self-concept.'[8] Given these devastating statistics, it is understandable that self-harm is often perceived as an almost exclusively female phenomenon – a quick Google image search of 'self-harm' reveals an overwhelming majority of photos featuring women and girls. However, another reason for the tendency to view self-harm as a 'female problem' could stem from the fact that we don't always recognise boys' self-harm *as* self-harm.

As youth mental health charity *Headstrong* explains, boys self-harm in very different ways to girls. Boys are far more likely to punch walls, or get into fights, which may be forms of self-harm. Often, however, when acts such as these *are* forms of self-harm, they are not recognised as such because they are simply perceived as acts of aggression. In actual fact, punching walls until the knuckles bruise, or getting involved in fights that result in school expulsion or punishment, could be ways of releasing feelings of failure or low self-worth. Headstrong also notes that:

Over-exercising, combined with under-eating, is another form of self-harm that can be overlooked in boys and praised by a society that sees an athletic and driven sports person.[9]

It's important that, when considering student self-harm, we remember that self-harm can manifest itself in different ways in boys. Boys who punch walls or faces may be doing so, not because they want to harm others, but because they want to harm themselves. It's important that we remember that destructive behaviour – particularly repeated destructive behaviour – can also be intentionally *self*-destructive. Boys who exhibit such behaviours require the same support and protection as girls found to be cutting.

In *BDT?* I espoused the 'need for a proactive approach that seeks to instil in boys a belief that talking about their feelings and emotions is the key for long-lasting mental wellbeing.'[10] Outdated expectations of male aggression are responsible for the more violent methods of suicide that men and boys often adopt when trying to take their own lives. For people who want to interrogate this in more detail, male violence is a topic I cover in Chapter Eight of *BDT?* The opening chapter of this book looks at dealing with male *expressions* of anger.

Prevention, intervention, and postvention

People acquainted with the literature on suicide and schools will know that suicide prevention is often divided into one of three categories: *prevention*, *intervention*, and *postvention*.

Postvention

Postvention refers to activities which reduce risk of suicide and promote healing after a suicide. *Samaritans'* **'Step by Step' programme** is a free service to help schools manage the aftermath of a suicide in the school community.

Information about the programme can be accessed by accessing the following link:

https://www.samaritans.org/how-we-can-help/schools/step-step

The precision, detail, and easy accessibility of the expert advice contained within *Samaritans'* 'Step by Step' programmes means that postvention is not something that this chapter will cover any further than it already has.

Suicide prevention charity *Papyrus* also provides a useful toolkit to help schools in their suicide prevention provision:

https://papyrus-uk.org/wp-content/uploads/2018/08/toolkitfinal.pdf

The free **Guidance Document** on this webpage should be looked at by school leaders, regardless of whether a suicide has occurred within their school community. The term 'postvention' is something of a misnomer – schools need to take pre-emptive action preparing for the aftermath of a suicide within the school community.

Intervention and prevention

Suicide prevention refers to the measures a person, people, or an organisation can make to reduce the risks of suicide occurring. Intervention refers to the direct efforts made to prevent a person or persons from trying to kill themselves. This chapter will attempt to offer solutions in these two areas.

The solutions

> The solutions below have been written largely with teachers, with little experience of mental health training, in mind. Teachers who are at the chalkface day in, day out, and who want to know how they can support students by helping to reduce the stigma associated with suicide and self-harm; teachers who may be the first person a child goes to with a self-harm concern or suicide disclosure.
>
> As soon as a child makes a disclosure, the teacher must report this to the Designated Safeguarding Lead (DSL) in their school. Teachers who are not trained in the area of mental health support should not be diagnosing or playing an active supervisory role in mental health intervention. Their responsibility is to listen to the child then recognise, respond, refer, and record a concern only.

A. If you think a child might be suicidal, ask them directly

If you think a child is suicidal, then you must ask them the following questions, directly:

> 1. Have you had thoughts about killing yourself?[11]
> 2. Have you thought about how?
> 3. Have you thought about when and where?

If the answer to all three of these questions is 'yes,' then the person is a suicide risk. An ambulance should be called, the DSL notified, and the student must not be left alone.[12]

It was only some weeks after learning of the above procedure myself, as part of my research for *BDT?*, that I suspected a child in my school (at the time) was suicidal. He seemed despondent and when I struck up a conversation with him, he said things that concerned me. After only a minute's conversation with the boy, I knew that I would have to ask him the first of the questions outlined above: *Have you had thoughts of killing yourself?*

My immediate feeling, as I realised I would have to ask this question, was one of reluctance and dread. I cared about this child, and I did not want to ask him a question that I knew could potentially expose him to awkward questions, hard truths, and the burden of upset family members. I remember clearly that in that split second – before I acknowledged that asking the question **was** the right thing to do – a series of objections that one might quite reasonably regard as selfish had raced through my mind:

- *What if, in just asking the question, I am planting an affirmative answer in the student's mind?*
- *What if, in just asking the question, I am going to cause upset to the child's family?*
- *What if, in just asking the question, I am going to inconvenience and hinder the smooth running of the school?*

Sadly, it turned out, that boy *was* having suicidal thoughts. He had thought about a method of suicide, and he had considered a possible time and place in which to do it. Immediately, I went to the headteacher, maintaining a supportive and friendly chat with the student as we went on a 'comfort walk.' Another member of staff watched the student as I went into the head's office and told him I was calling an ambulance. The head was supportive and called the boy's mother who came into school and joined him in the ambulance as he was taken to hospital.

The smooth running of the school *was* mildly interrupted that day. The question *did* lead to awkward questions, hard truths, and a trip to the hospital, all of which *did* cause considerable anguish to the boy's mother. But the boy received the treatment he needed and my asking of that question – *Have you had thoughts of killing yourself?* – was the first step in the journey of intervention services and support the boy has since received. I'm glad I asked.

B. Learn to recognise the signs of self-harm

It's important that teachers learn to spot the signs of self-harm. These may be visible in changes in the young person's behaviour. These changes may include:

- Changes in eating/sleeping habits
- Increased isolation from friends/family
- Changes in activity and mood, e.g., more aggressive than usual, unhappy, low mood – seems to be depressed or unhappy
- Lowering of academic grades
- Talking about self-harm or suicide
- Abusing drugs or alcohol
- Becoming socially withdrawn

- Expressing feelings of failure, uselessness, or loss of hope
- Risk-taking behaviour
- Wearing long sleeves at inappropriate times
- Spending more time in the toilet
- Unexplained cuts, bruises, burns, or other injuries
- Possession of razor (or pencil sharpener) blades, scissors, or knives
- Unexplained smell of Dettol, TCP, etc.
- Losing friendships
- Withdrawal from activities that used to be enjoyed
- Spending more time by themselves and becoming more private or defensive[13]

If you spot any one of these signs and have concerns that a child is self-harming, you should be open about your concerns. You should say something like:

> I've noticed that you have become easily angry today. Are things difficult for you at the moment?

If this does not lead to a disclosure, but you still have serious concerns, you can be more specific:

> I've noticed that you have some cuts on your arm and I know that this can sometimes be a sign of self-harm. Have you self-harmed?

Remember: as with suicide, asking a child about self-harm does **not** increase the likelihood that a child will self-harm. Any conversations of this nature must always be recorded and reported to the appropriate safeguarding personnel in the school. Never keep conversations like this to yourself, even if the student has not made a disclosure or asks you to keep a disclosure confidential.

C. Respond to disclosures appropriately

Responding to a disclosure

A disclosure of self-harm or suicidal thoughts can understandably be distressing, but it's important that teachers respond to disclosures appropriately. The following advice should help to ensure that teachers are giving vulnerable pupils the support they need in a safe way. Whilst the tips that follow are designed with classroom teachers in mind, some of the tips will be more relevant to members of staff who will be assisting the self-harmer beyond the initial disclosure.

- **Follow standard disclosure protocol**. As with any student disclosures, a few simple steps should be followed:

> - Do not promise confidentiality to students. They must know that it is your duty to pass their information on to someone who can support them and help keep them safe
> - Write down what the student tells you, in their own words. Record the location, date, and time of the discussion
> - Avoid asking leading questions
> - Pass on the information to the DSL as soon as possible
> - If necessary, take the child to a safe space where they can be supervised

- **Do not try to be a therapist**. Your job, as teacher, is to ensure that a child is safe and that any concerns you have about a child are passed on to somebody who is qualified to put the correct measure of intervention in place. So, whilst it is your responsibility to listen to a child's disclosure, it is **not** your job to offer advice or suggest methods of help to the child.

- **Try not to react strongly (but do be honest about your reaction)**. Often, self-harm injuries can be visibly shocking, even repulsive. Descriptions of self-harm injury can also be distressing. When a child shows you evidence of their self-harm, or describes it to you, do your best to hide your distress. This helps to reduce the shame and stigma the child may feel at having undertaken self-harm. However, it's also important that you are honest about any visual negative reaction if you sense that a child may have noticed it. A simple, 'I'm sorry – I felt shocked by that,' will suffice.

- **Don't give ultimatums or expect the self-harmer to stop immediately**. The last thing a self-harmer needs is to feel that they're letting somebody down. If a child reveals to you that they are self-harming, do not tell them they need to stop. Timelines and ultimatums are a pressure that self-harming children do not need. Secondly, it's important to remember that for many children who self-harm, the act of self-harm does make them feel better. Asking them to stop, without any replacement means of feeling better, could make things worse for the child.

- **Don't beat yourself up**. If you feel physically repulsed by a disclosure, that is okay. If you feel upset, angry, or emotionally drained by a disclosure, that is okay. Being a teacher does not make you impervious to any one of a thousand perfectly natural negative responses to something that any reasonable person would find upsetting. Seek help from the relevant support services if you need to.

I'd also ask any School Leaders reading this, to ensure that follow-up care and support is offered to teachers who witness self-harm, or deal with a disclosure.

- **Avoid 'no-framing.'** In 2020, Joseph Ford, from the College of Medicine and Health at Exeter University, and his team published research looking into the way doctors talk to patients about self-harm and suicide. The findings have interesting implications for teachers. The study showed that when doctors ask patients questions about self-harm and suicide, questions tended to invite a 'no' response. Take this question, highlighted in the research, asked by a doctor to a patient who has expressed feelings of depression:

> *But you've not had any thoughts of harming yourself or suicide or anything like that.*

As Ford explains:

> The phrasing of this question as a negative declarative statement with questioning intonation ('But you've not had any…') is clearly slanted in favour of a negative response.[14]

Other examples of 'no-framing' questions are:

> *You don't self-harm, do you?*
> *You've no plans to hurt yourself?*
> *I assume you don't intend to do anything dangerous?*

According to Ford and his team, such questions must be avoided as they can encourage people to lie when they give their answers:

> Questions about self-harm in primary care are overwhelmingly framed for a 'no' response. This makes it difficult for patients to answer affirmatively.[15]

Therefore, when we are having conversations with students about self-harm or suicidal intent, it is important we ask directly:

- *Do you self-harm?*
- *Do you plan to hurt yourself?*
- *Do you intend to do something dangerous which might put your life at risk?*

It's particularly important that teachers are aware of 'no-framing': because of their own desire to validate the child they may possibly, subconsciously, *seek* this type of negative response because the alternative may be frightening, or even overwhelming. We are the adults in this transaction and must ensure we have carefully considered our responses to the student who has trusted us with their disclosure.

- **Avoid stigmatisation**. Ford's study found that in doctors' discussions with patients, there was also a tendency for doctors to talk to patients about the impact that their self-harm or suicide may have on their family. For example:

Have you thought about how your family might feel if you were to die?

According to Ford, such statements only serve to make the patient feel guilty or ashamed of their feelings, and therefore less likely to want to talk openly and honestly about them:

> Invoking negative reasons not to end one's life such as the legacy it leaves for family is problematic when it exacerbates shame and low self-worth. Such negative stigma could be reframed by exploring patients' positive reasons for wanting to stay alive.[16]

Of course, it is important that teachers don't get involved in this type of discussion with any student who has disclosed that they are considering taking their own life or who has disclosed self-harm: a designated mental health professional should do this.

- **Express concern**. As Dr Peter Fuggle from the Anna Freud Centre – whose aim it is to help young students with mental health problems – explains, it is important that teachers talk about self-harm in instances where they believe it to be taking place, or when a child makes a disclosure. Fuggle states that if teachers notice evidence of self-harm, such as cuts on the arm, they should:

> express a little concern about that, in the way that you would be concerned about anything that looks like a young person's been harmed. The expressing concern is in many ways more reassuring to a young person than not speaking about it at all.[17]

This may seem obvious, but Fuggle's emphasis is on the fact that the expression of concern should be in line and consistent with the expression of concern for any sort of harm caused to a child. Fuggle is clear that the talk should be 'normal,' as dramatic proclamations of shock and concern do little to benefit the self-harmer. As Fuggle states, 'Don't panic. As much as possible, talk to the young person in an ordinary, interested, concerned way.'[18]

- **Ask students about their self-harm**. Dr Fuggle stresses the importance of asking students the question, 'Are you worried about your self-harm?' and following up with a question about whether they could benefit from talking about it a little bit more. Too often in these situations it's easy – and natural – to want to support the child by giving them lots of cautionary advice before directing them to the appropriate means of support, without actually asking the child about their feelings about their self-harm. These latter, more supportive, questioning conversations can often be illuminating and useful in helping the proper authorities to support the self-harmer.

D. Reframe your thinking on attention-seeking

In my experience, some people can be dismissive of acts of self-harm, criticising the person who has self-harmed for their 'attention-seeking.' Girls are often dismissed as 'drama queens' whilst boys' acts of more overt, aggressive self-harm are dismissed as violent behaviour or 'anger issues.'

Let me be clear: an act of self-harm, or a suicide attempt, is no less serious because the motivation behind it is a desire for attention.

I cannot understand how some people – particularly people working in schools – have come to believe that it could be so. For those people who use the term 'attention-seeking' dismissively, I recommend that they replace the phrase 'attention-seeking' with the phrase, 'something needs attending to.' Thus:

> Aaron cut himself because he was **attention-seeking.**
> becomes
> Aaron cut himself because **something needs attending to.**

The phrase 'attention-seeker' could be replaced with 'person who has a need that requires attention.' So:

> Jason cut himself because he is an **attention-seeker.**
> becomes
> Jason cut himself because he is **a person who has a need that requires attention.**

This simple language change can help to reduce the stigma attached to the phrases such as 'attention-seeker' or 'attention-seeking' that could potentially limit the support a self-harming or suicidal child receives. When students make disclosures to us, we can't necessarily make them feel less hopeless, isolated, lacking in control, or powerless. But we can give them the attention they need, and we can show them that somebody is listening.

E. Reduce access to means of self-harm and suicide

It may seem obvious, but schools should ensure that the environment is as safe as possible. Removing potential ligature points, restricting access to potential jump-spots, and locking away potentially harmful substances are essential mitigations in preventing self-harm and potential suicide.

As classroom teachers, ensuring sharp objects are safely away from children, whilst also monitoring children you know are at risk from self-harm while they use objects like scissors, can also be useful. While this may seem like hypervigilance (and near impracticable in some classrooms), the self-harming student can often feel like they are 'held in mind' by small adjustments like this which can be made in every classroom by every teacher. They may need us, as the adults in the room, to give them the sense of control which they feel is lacking. These seemingly minor actions can cumulatively help to support the student's need for attention and help them feel more listened to.

F. Create and refer to safety plans

For students who are vulnerable to self-harm and suicide, it is really important that they —and adults in the school – have access to a safety plan. Safety plans take about 20 minutes to create and help provide the student with a range of strategies to help them cope with thoughts of self-harm and suicide. They also alert adults to need-to-know information that could help the young person. Parents or guardians should be included as part of the creation process and a copy sent home. Self-harm safety plans should be reviewed regularly. An example is provided at the end of this chapter and may be copied, modified, or reproduced as desired.

G. Signpost support services

There is an abundance of free support services available to schools, teachers, and students who are experiencing self-harm and/or suicide. A comprehensive list can be found at **https://www.mind.org.uk/information-support/for-children-and-young-people/useful-contacts**. An abridged version is below, and it should be referred to in any in-school situation where suicide is a topic of conversation:

Campaign Against Living Miserably (CALM)	**0800 58 58 58** **Thecalmzone.net**	Provides listening services for anyone who needs to talk, including web chat options.
Childline	**0800 1111** **Childline.org.uk**	Support for children and young people in the UK, including web chat options.
Hope Again	**0808808 1677** **Hopeagain.org.uk**	Support for young people when someone dies.

Kooth	**Kooth.com**	Free online counselling service for young people. Counsellors available until 10pm daily.
Papyrus HOPELINEUK	**0800 068 41 41** **07860 039967 (text)** **pat@papyrus-uk.org** **papyrus-uk.org**	Confidential support for under-35s at risk of suicide and for those concerned about them. 9am–midnight.
Samaritans	**116 123** (freephone) **jo@samaritans.org**	Free 24/7 support for those who want to talk.

H. Teach about suicide responsibly

The Werther effect

It took Johann Wolfgang von Goethe just over five weeks to write his 1774 novel, *The Sorrows of Young Werther*. The novel, which details the eponymous Werther's doomed experience of unrequited love and eventual suicide, turned the 24-year-old Goethe, whom Lord Byron would go on to fawningly describe as the 'first literary character of his age,' into a celebrity overnight. Goethe's celebrity was second only to that of the fictional Werther he had created: all over Europe, young men started to dress in the same blue tailcoat, yellow waistcoat, trousers, and boots sported by Werther; people rushed out to buy merchandise in the form of porcelain figurines depicting famous scenes from the book; there was even a perfume – imaginatively branded as 'Eau de Werther'– produced in honour of Goethe's tragic hero. In 1806, when Napoleon ransacked Weimar after the Battle of Jena, Goethe's house was spared, such was the Emperor's admiration for the man who had created *Werther*.

And yet, in 1775, the authorities in Leipzig, Germany, were forced to ban sales of Goethe's novel. Denmark and Italy soon followed suit. The novel, authorities determined, was responsible for a number of imitation suicides (meaning copycat suicides), such as that of Christel von Lassberg who was found drowned in 1778 with a copy of *Werther* in her pocket.

In 1974, researcher David Phillips coined the term, 'The Werther Effect' to refer to what's known as 'suicide contagion.' Suicide contagion is the process in which people imitate the suicides of real people or fictional characters from books and films. Research shows that 'people who suffer with mental health problems, young people, and people who are bereaved'[19] are more prone to this phenomenon.

The risk of suicide contagion is a real one, backed up by significant amounts of research. Such is the seriousness of the issue, that most countries provide media guidelines detailing exactly how news outlets should report suicides in the media. In this country, it is *Samaritans* who provide the go-to guidelines for media suicide reporting. In fact, it is *Samaritans* who have meticulously scrutinised this chapter for any wording that could prove potentially triggering for people vulnerable to suicide.

I first came across *Samaritans'* media guidelines for reporting suicide some years ago, when it struck me that up and down the country, English teachers were teaching texts like *Romeo and Juliet* and *An Inspector Calls* – both of which contain graphic depictions and descriptions of suicide – with virtually zero knowledge of how to discuss suicide responsibly. Certainly, in my ten years of teaching English, I have never once received any instructional training on how to teach these texts in a way that takes The Werther Effect into consideration, or which is informed by any guidance from specialist organisations like *Samaritans* or *Papyrus*. There are educators in schools, such as pastoral Heads of Year and Designated Safeguarding Leads, who will, hopefully, have received specific training as to how to deal with disclosures of self-harm and suicidal ideation in schools. As part of this training, these educators should have received guidance as to how self-harm and suicide should be discussed. But rarely is this guidance disseminated to the wider staff body. Few classroom teachers – whatever subject they teach – know how to discuss suicide responsibly. Some may even find broaching the subject intensely difficult because of their own life experiences, yet rarely if ever is support and guidance offered to these colleagues with respect to the public discussion of suicide with a class of 25–30 teenagers.

In my conversation with Dennis Ougrin, I mentioned the fact that over a third of teachers (see above) avoid supporting children with suicidal thoughts because they worry that they will make the problem worse. He acknowledged the need for guidance on how classroom teachers should talk about self-harm and suicide in lessons:

> There is no doubt that teachers need to talk about self-harm and suicide, but they need to do it with strict rules and guidelines. Teachers who are worried about talking to children about these subjects, because they might do more harm than good, are right to be worried. Talking about self-harm and suicide the wrong way can indeed make things worse.

The need to talk about suicide (and self-harm) stems from the fact that a failure to talk about it only serves to stigmatise the thoughts of self-harm and suicide that a student might be experiencing. This could be catastrophic. It's very hard for a young person to be open and honest about thoughts of self-harm and suicide if they feel that suicide and self-harm are shameful topics that nobody is meant to talk about. However, there is a conflict between this need to talk and the reality that if not discussed correctly, discussions of self-harm and suicide could potentially be triggering for a vulnerable young person at risk. This conflict can be overcome, if we acknowledge that talking about self-harm and suicide can be a positive thing so long as we, as educators, discuss it within safe parameters.

What follows is a set of guidelines for teachers who are teaching content featuring suicide. These guidelines should be referred to by any educator teaching the topic of suicide, be it directly or indirectly, to young people in schools. Whilst I have endeavoured to make these guidelines as general as I can, the fact that *Romeo and Juliet* and *An Inspector Calls* are such an integral part of almost every secondary English curriculum across the UK means that I have made specific references to the teaching of these texts, to help the masses of English teachers who teach these texts daily, and with little or no training on how to address the suicides contained within them appropriately.

You should know that these guidelines have been read by *Samaritans*, and I have structured advice according to their recommendations. Andrea Vaughan, a doctoral researcher in applied linguistics at University College London, whose research focuses on the identification of the linguistic features of depression, anxiety, and suicidal ideation on social media and in suicide notes, has also acted as an advisor in the creation of these guidelines.

Guidelines for teachers: discussing self-harm and suicide in lessons

1. **Think about the impact of the topic of self-harm and suicide on your students**

    Lessons (or assemblies) that refer to self-harm or suicide could negatively impact students – particularly students who have experience of self-harm and suicide – so it's important that you take this into consideration before teaching. It may be that specific students need to be removed from the lesson for the period of the lesson where self-harm and/or suicide is discussed. If it's not possible to remove the child – for example, the child is studying *Romeo and Juliet* as part of their English Literature GCSE[20] – it's important that during the lesson, you provide information on where students with suicidal thoughts or emotional problems can access support. A simple PowerPoint slide, providing sources of national support – such as *Samaritans* – and local support serves as a supportive reminder that within the school there are adults who are willing to listen to students without judgement.

    The following can be copied and used in any suitable format for your lessons where suicide is a topic:

    > #### How to contact Papyrus Hopeline
    >
    > *Papyrus is a charity dedicated to helping young people struggling with suicidal thoughts. If you are struggling, you can contact them by phone, text, or email.*
    > **Phone: 0800 068 4141**
    > **Text: 07860 039967**
    > **Email: pat@papyrus-uk.org**

They are open 9am–midnight, **every day of the year**.
*For 24-hour help, Samaritans are here – day or night, 365 days a year. You can call them for free on 116 123, email them at **jo@samaritans.org**, or visit **www.samaritans.org** to find your nearest branch. Samaritans will not judge you or tell you what to do.*

2. **Exercise caution when referring to the methods and context of a suicide**

    Media-reported details of suicide methods have been shown to cause vulnerable people to imitate suicidal behaviour. With this in mind, *Samaritans* recommends:

    - **Avoid giving too much detail**. Care should be taken to avoid giving details of a method of suicide. Information about methods of suicide, such as describing someone as having died by overdose, can reinforce awareness of specific methods and increase perceptions of its effectiveness.

        Teachers should also be aware of literary depictions and descriptions of suicide. Whilst it's okay to read the scene in which Romeo kills himself using poison, it's not okay to talk to children about the type and amount of poison that he may have taken in order to kill himself or what effect it would have on his body.

        Some texts, such as J. B. Priestley's *An Inspector Calls*, describe specific details about the manner of suicide. In the play, the Inspector tells the Birling family, 'Two hours ago a young woman died in the Infirmary. She'd been taken there this afternoon because she'd swallowed a lot of strong disinfectant. Burnt her inside out, of course.' Whilst it's hard to avoid reading these comments in class, Samaritans advise focusing on sections of the text that mention suicide as little as possible.

    - **Take care when talking about unusual methods of suicide**. Incidences of people using unusual or new methods of suicide have been known to increase rapidly after being reported widely in the media. As such, teachers should take care when lessons necessitate the discussion of unusual methods of suicide, such as that in *An Inspector Calls*. Where a discussion does take place, emphasis should be placed upon the fact that suicide is preventable and that suicidal feelings can be very intense, but they do pass, and they are treatable.

    - **Remember that there is a risk of imitative behaviour due to 'over-identification.'** Students may identify with a person who has died, or with the circumstances in which a person (or people, as in the case of *Romeo and Juliet*) take their own life. For example, having romantic feelings for someone whom their parents disapprove of. In English lessons, this over-identification effect can be mitigated by:

        - Taking care to talk about characters purely as literary constructs, rather than real people

- Downplaying the similarities between the characters you are reading about or seeing on stage and the students in front of you
- Reinforcing the idea that support services which are available to people who struggle with suicidal thoughts do not exist in literary worlds like 14th century Verona, for example
- **Never say a suicide method is quick, easy, painless, or certain to result in death.** The nature of the double suicide in *Romeo and Juliet* may be the catalyst for a discussion on the methods of suicide chosen by Romeo and Juliet respectively. Such discussions should be avoided.

3. **Avoid over-simplification.** Approximately 90% of people who die by suicide have a diagnosed or undiagnosed mental health problem at the time of death.
   - **Over-simplification of the causes or perceived 'triggers' for a suicide can be misleading and is unlikely to accurately reflect the complexity of suicide.** Therefore, it's important when discussing a suicide, that teachers avoid the suggestions that a single incident is responsible for it. When teaching *Romeo and Juliet*, teachers should question and critique Shakespeare's assertion that the suicide of the 'star-cross'd lovers' was an inevitable twist of fate when, in actual fact, a long list of complex factors leads to the tragic outcome of the play.

4. **Avoid aftermath-blame talk**
   - **Framing suicide as a selfish act that ruins the lives of the loved ones of victims of suicides is harmful.** While understandable as an attempted preventative measure that may be necessary in moments where desperate individuals are making disclosures of suicidal intent, in general settings, such talk can only serve to make students with suicidal thoughts feel worse. They may feel burdensome or guilty, which can actually exacerbate suicidal intention.
   - **Harness the Papageno Effect.** There is also a small body of research evidence[21] which shows that sensitive portrayals of individuals demonstrating mastery over a suicidal crisis can have a protective influence. This phenomenon is known as the Papageno Effect, named after the lovelorn character from Mozart's 18th century opera *The Magic Flute*. Papageno decides not to kill himself after looking at alternative ways to solve his problems. Coverage describing a person or character seeking help and coming through a difficult time, rather than making a suicide attempt, can serve as a powerful testimony to others that this is possible. This content has been linked to falls in suicide rates. It is useful to focus on what people who have died by suicide could have done to protect themselves from suicide.

5. **Avoid glorifying suicide**
    - **Be careful not to promote the idea that suicide achieves results.** The deaths of Romeo and Juliet bring an end to the 'ancient grudge' between the Montague and Capulet families and peace is brought to Verona. This resolution, alluded to in the Prologue of the play itself, should be viewed critically, emphasising that it shouldn't take the death of two young people to forge a peace between two families led by adults. Again, you should also reiterate that the characters here are fictional.
    - **Avoid portraying suicide positively.** It could be that students are exposed to the idea of suicide as somehow noble and heroic. In history lessons, the death of Cleopatra, the acts of Japanese Kamikaze pilots, and the Roman act of 'falling upon the sword' rather than being taken by the enemy should be discussed critically, if at all.

        Baz Luhrmann's 1996 version of *Romeo and Juliet*, which moves the action of the play from 14th century Italy to modern-day America, is a staple of many English classrooms. Teachers use Leonardo Di Caprio's smouldering good looks, a pop music soundtrack, and the presence of guns to engage students in Shakespeare's most famous play. However, there are some significant differences between Shakespeare's version of the suicide scene in the play, and Luhrmann's modern interpretation: in Shakespeare's play, the two lovers kill themselves within the confines of a cold, dark tomb, referred to by Romeo as a 'detestable maw[22]…[a] womb of death.' On the blood-soaked stage (Friar Laurence makes three references to 'blood' or 'gore' in the opening six lines of his entrance into the Capulet tomb) upon which the young lovers kill themselves, already lie the corpses of Tybalt, killed by Romeo the day prior, and the sepulchred bones of Juliet's ancestors. Also on stage lies the newly killed and bloody body of Paris, slaughtered by Romeo just minutes before he and Juliet go on to take their own lives. The blood-soaked scene of chaos in which Romeo and Juliet take their own lives is miles away from that created by Luhrmann 400 years later.

        In Luhrmann's *Romeo and Juliet*, the bloody corpses of Paris and Tybalt do not intrude upon a scene Luhrmann has clearly intended to make beautiful. Instead, Romeo walks towards Juliet, who looks peacefully asleep, amidst a thousand flickering candles, the warmth of their light lending an ethereal beauty to a scene whose cinematography suggests the suicide to come is the ultimate act of romantic love.

        It's essential, if teachers must show this scene, which clearly glorifies suicide, that they talk about the *problems* of such a depiction with the students in the room. In my own experience, a comparison with Shakespeare's written scene can prove useful.

6. **Use the right language**

It's important that schools and classrooms are places where suicide is not stigmatised. Often, the language we use about suicide presents those who die by suicide as inherently bad, even criminal. For example, the phrase 'committed suicide' is still in common parlance even though suicide was decriminalised in the UK in 1961.

Of course, victims of suicide prior to its decriminalisation should never have been regarded as criminals, but the still-common use of the word 'committed' in the context of suicide suggests that those who kill themselves are – like those who commit murder, burglary, and arson – people who have deliberately made a choice to perform a criminal act.

Teachers should use the following table to guide them in how to talk about suicide.

Do use	Don't use
• A suicide • Taken his/her/their own life • Ended his/her/their own life • Die by/death by suicide • Suicide attempt • Attempted suicide • Person at risk of suicide	• Commit suicide • Suicide victim • Suicide 'epidemic,' 'wave,' 'hot spot' • Cry for help • A 'successful' or 'unsuccessful,' or 'failed' suicide attempt • Suicide 'tourist' or 'jumper'

The final word

Suicide and self-harm are some of the toughest issues that school-based professionals will encounter and need to respond to within their settings. But, as this chapter has illustrated, we cannot – and must not – shy away from discussing them directly, honestly, and responsibly.

Suicide and self-harm both have devastating and painful consequences for students, their families, and the school community. It is my fervent hope that the advice contained within this chapter will help all teachers, regardless of their level of training, to ensure that students stay safe not just as children but in their happy adult lives as well.

Self-harm safety plan

Self harm safety plan
Name:... **Date:**...........................
1) **I know I am likely to harm myself when**: (e.g., how would other people be able to tell? what do you think about when you feel really bad, how do you behave…?)
2) **The things that stop me from harming myself are**: (e.g., don't want scars…)
3) **When I feel like harming myself I want people to**: (name several people and what you would want them to say/do e.g., be reminded of things in 2 above)
4) **If I have harmed myself or think I might harm myself, it would be helpful to contact the following people**: (who to contact and how, what to say to them – think of as many options as possible)
5) **If I need medical attention (for an overdose or injury) or urgently need to see a specialist mental health worker**: I will call 999 and ask for an 'ambulance' or arrange for help to get to the nearest A and E Department. My nearest A and E Department is at:
6) **I will share this plan with the following people so they can help me stay safe**: (e.g., teachers, family members, friends, etc. List their names and contact details, think about how you will tell them about the plan and if you want anyone to support you with this)
7) **Any other relevant information?**
Signed: ....
Review date: ....

Notes

1. Samaritans. (2020). Latest Suicide Data. Available at: https://www.samaritans.org/about-samaritans/research-policy/suicide-facts-and-figures/latest-suicide-data (Accessed: 28th November 2021).
2. Almeida, J., et al. (2009). Emotional distress among LGBT youth: the influence of perceived discrimination based on sexual orientation. *Journal of Youth and Adolescence, 38*, 1001–1014.
3. The term 'suicidal thoughts' is often used interchangeably with the term 'suicidal ideation.' However, 'suicidal ideation' should be seen as distinct from 'active ideation.' 'Active ideation' is most concerning as this is where an individual has thought about methods or plans to take their own life.
4. Papyrus. (2018). Building suicide-safer schools and colleges: A guide for teachers and staff. Available at: https://papyrus-uk.org/wp-content/uploads/2018/08/toolkitfinal.pdf (Accessed: 28th November 2021).
5. Wilkinson P., Kelvin R., Roberts C., Dubicka B., & Goodyer I. (2011). Clinical and psychosocial predictors of suicide attempts and nonsuicidal self-injury in the Adolescent Depression Antidepressants and Psychotherapy Trial (ADAPT). *Am J Psychiatry, 168*, 495–501.
6. Chan M., Bhatti H., Meader N., Stockton S., Evans J., O'Connor R., & Kendall T. (2016). Predicting suicide following self-harm: Systematic review of risk factors and risk scales. *British Journal of Psychiatry, 209*(4), 277–283.
7. McManus, S., Hassiotis, A., Jenkins, R., Dennis, M., Aznar, C., & Appleby, L. (2016). Chapter 12: Suicidal thoughts, suicide attempts, and self-harm. In S. McManus, P. Bebbington, R. Jenkins, & T. Brugha (Eds.), *Mental health and wellbeing in England: Adult Psychiatric Morbidity Survey 2014*. Leeds: NHS Digital.
8. Hartas, D. (2021). The social context of adolescent mental health and wellbeing: Parents, friends and social media. *Research Papers in Education, 36*:5, 542–560.
9. Headstrong. (2020). Boys and Self-Harm. Available at: https://www.beheadstrong.uk/info/boys-and-self-harm (Accessed: 28th November 2021).
10. Pinkett, M., & Roberts, M. (2019). *Boys Don't Try? Rethinking Masculinity in Schools*. UK: Routledge.
11. It's important to note that the use of the word 'suicide' is not present in this question, to protect against the chance that the student may not be familiar with the word or concept.
12. Pinkett and Roberts (2019).
13. Rotherham Metropolitan Borough Council (No date). Supporting Children & Young People who Self Harm: Rotherham Self Harm Practice Guidance. Available at: https://rotherhamscb.proceduresonline.com/pdfs/self_harm.pdf (Accessed: 8th March 2022).
14. Ford, J., Thomas, F., Byng, R., McCabe, R. (2021). Asking about self-harm and suicide in primary care: Moral and practical dimensions. *Patient Education and Counselling, 104*, 826–835.
15. Ibid.
16. Ibid.
17. Anna Freud NCCF (2017, September 5). *Self Harm* [Video]. YouTube. https://www.youtube.com/watch?v=j3BUV6hhYiU&t=66s
18. Ibid.
19. Samaritans. (2020). Depiction of Suicide and Self-Harm in Literature. Available at: https://media.samaritans.org/documents/Suicide_and_self_harm_Literature_FINAL.pdf (Accessed: 27th November 2021).
20. General Certificate of Secondary Education.

21 Niederkrotenthaler, T., Voracek, M., Herberth, A., Till, B., Strauss, M., Etzersdorfer, E., Eisenwort, B., & Sonneck, G. (2010). Role of media reports in completed and prevented suicide: Werther v. Papageno effects. *The British Journal Of Psychiatry: The Journal Of Mental Science*, *197*(3), 234–243.

22 = mouth.

References

Almeida, J., et al. (2009). Emotional distress among LGBT youth: The influence of perceived discrimination based on sexual orientation. *Journal of Youth and Adolescence*, *38*, 1001–1014.

Chan, M., Bhatti, H., Meader, N., Stockton, S., Evans, J., O'Connor, R., & Kendall, T. (2016). Predicting suicide following self-harm: Systematic review of risk factors and risk scales. *British Journal of Psychiatry*, *209*(4), 277–283.

Ford, J., Thomas, F., Byng, R., McCabe, R. (2021). Asking about self-harm and suicide in primary care: Moral and practical dimensions. *Patient Education and Counselling*, *104*, 826–835.

Freud, A. NCCF. (2017, September 5). *Self Harm* [Video]. YouTube. https://www.youtube.com/watch?v=j3BUV6hhYiU&t=66s

Hartas, D. (2021). The social context of adolescent mental health and wellbeing: Parents, friends and social media. Research Papers in Education, *36*:5, 542–560.

Headstrong. (2020). Boys and Self-Harm. Available at: https://www.beheadstrong.uk/info/boys-and-self-harm (Accessed: 28th November 2021).

McManus, S., Hassiotis, A., Jenkins, R., Dennis, M., Aznar, C., & Appleby, L. (2016). Chapter 12: Suicidal thoughts, suicide attempts, and self-harm. In S. McManus, P. Bebbington, R. Jenkins, & T. Brugha (Eds.). *Mental health and wellbeing in England: Adult Psychiatric Morbidity Survey 2014*. Leeds: NHS Digital.

Niederkrotenthaler, T., Voracek, M., Herberth, A., Till, B., Strauss, M., Etzersdorfer, E., Eisenwort, B., & Sonneck, G. (2010). Role of media reports in completed and prevented suicide: Werther v. Papageno effects. *The British Journal Of Psychiatry: The Journal Of Mental Science*, *197*(3), 234–243.

Papyrus. (2018). Building suicide-safer schools and colleges: A guide for teachers and staff. Available at: https://papyrus-uk.org/wp-content/uploads/2018/08/toolkitfinal.pdf (Accessed: 28th November 2021).

Pinkett, M., and Roberts, M. (2019). *Boys Don't Try? Rethinking Masculinity in Schools*. UK: Routledge.

Rotherham Metropolitan Borough Council. (n.d.). Supporting Children & Young People who Self Harm: Rotherham Self Harm Practice Guidance. Available at: https://rotherhamscb.proceduresonline.com/pdfs/self_harm.pdf (Accessed: 8th March 2022).

Samaritans. (2020a). Depiction of Suicide and Self-Harm in Literature. Available at: https://media.samaritans.org/documents/Suicide_and_self_harm_Literature_FINAL.pdf (Accessed: 27th November 2021).

Samaritans. (2020b). Latest Suicide Data. Available at: https://www.samaritans.org/about-samaritans/research-policy/suicide-facts-and-figures/latest-suicide-data (Accessed: 28th November 2021).

Wilkinson, P., Kelvin, R., Roberts, C., Dubicka, B., & Goodyer, I. (2011). Clinical and psychosocial predictors of suicide attempts and nonsuicidal self-injury in the Adolescent Depression Antidepressants and Psychotherapy Trial (ADAPT). *Am J Psychiatry*, *168*, 495–501.

4 Talk

The story

People often ask me what it was that started me down the path of writing about boys in schools. To every person that ever asks, I give the same answer, because I know the *exact* moment I began to question the way teachers were engaging with boys in school; the moment I began to think about masculinity in schools, I guess.

It was a morning break time in the English department staff room way back in 2012, and awaiting me and my department colleagues, as we entered the room, was a gift from the library: the central work desk held a battered box with a torn piece of paper taped to the top of it. On this torn piece of paper was a hastily scrawled message in thick, faded-grey board pen: 'OLD LIBRARY STOCK. THOUGHT YOU MIGHT FIND USEFUL!'

Now there's nothing an English department likes more than books. And if those books are over 30 years old, with the majority of their pages missing, all the better. What a treat.

We sifted through the books, and, despite the librarian's hopeful note, we couldn't find a single book that could be conceivably described as 'useful,' if by 'useful' you mean something that could inspire a lifelong love of reading in teenagers who were unlikely to be thrilled by titles like *A History of the Calculator*, *Lake District Bird Spotting*, and *18th Century Pottery*.

But there was one book: *Banned Poetry for Teenage Boys*.

Ever a sucker for not-so-clever marketing ploys, I picked it up. 'Interesting,' I thought cynically, not having come across boy-targeted poetry before. I flicked through the book, glossing over poems about tricky homework, dreams of footballing stardom, and acne. Like most books written with the (very commendable) desire to inspire this this specific demographic with a lifelong love of reading, it appeared to have been written by somebody that had either a) forgotten what it was actually like to be a teenage boy or b) never actually been one.

It was – I confess – with some amusement that one poem caught my eye. I can't remember the exact title, but it was something like *The Minnow*. The poem described a boy, on holiday with his mates, frolicking around in the sea. The cold sea. Anyway, it just so happens that as the boy is frolicking, the female object of his affections appears on the shoreline and starts calling out to him, beckoning him to come out of the sea and join her. It is at this point that the boy becomes very aware of a part of his anatomy that had previously (before his foray into the cold sea) been a little bigger but was now – given the fact that the sea in which he frolicked was, as I have already mentioned, on the chilly side – a little smaller.

I can't remember how the poem ends *exactly*, but I do remember some clunky metaphors about a whale and a minnow.[1]

Years of gender socialisation mean that as a straight male, small or shrunken penises are Something I Need To Laugh About, and so I jokingly brought the poem to the attention of the other teachers in the department. And, it turns out, it wasn't just me that found the poem funny. Everybody did. Everyone found the poem hilarious. And I think it was at that moment that something inside me suddenly reacted, and changed.

I should have mentioned earlier that everybody else in my department was female and I was the only bloke. So sitting there, as the only person in the room who possessed a penis, whilst everybody who didn't have a penis laughed at the small penis of the poem, made me a little defensive.

How dare they all laugh at the fictional boy with the fictional shrunken penis in the fictional cold sea? Do they know what it's like to have a penis in a cold sea? Do they know what it's like to not have a 12-inch penis in a world where pornography exists? Do they know what it's like to have to force a laugh every single time somebody makes that bloody joke about big feet meaning big socks?

No. No they don't.

So, I said it:

'Do you know what? There might be some boys in this school for whom this is an issue. Like, some boys might be really anxious about issues such as the size of their penis.'

At this point, the laughter stopped. Bemused, puzzled, even affronted faces met mine. And then, one colleague looked me dead in the eyes and said the words I've never forgotten.

'You would say that. You're a man. All you think about is sex and the size of your penis.'

When the bell went for third period and everyone filed out the room, I remained seated, slightly dumbfounded. And then, as I got back to my classroom, it wasn't a box of unwanted and ignored books I thought of, but more a Pandora's box of unwanted and ignored problems. Unwanted and ignored *male* problems.

What struck me most that day was not the absolute cheek of the librarian, or the dreadfully poor fish-based metaphors.[2] What struck me most was the way that when I raised a legitimate concern that *could* be affecting the mental wellbeing of some of the boys in the school, it was instantly dismissed. And not just dismissed. Mocked. The Western narrative of male mental health has long focused on men's reluctance or inability to talk about the things that concern them. And what happened that day got me thinking: *What are we doing in schools to make boys feel that it's okay to talk? That their legitimate problems and concerns will not be mocked or dismissed, but listened to and understood?*

The research

Men and talk

It's a well-established fact that men are less likely than women to seek help and advice for their problems from doctors, therapists, family, and friends. A 2016 YouGov survey of 6,247 adults, commissioned by the Mental Health Foundation, found that of over 2,500 people in the study who had mental health problems, 28% of men admitted they had not sought medical help compared to 19% of women.[3] The same study also found that whilst a third of women who disclosed a mental health problem to a friend or loved one did so within a month, only a quarter of men did so. Also, whilst 25% of women waited more than *two years* to disclose a mental health problem to a loved one or friend, for men this figure rises to 35%.

Why don't men talk?

Ipsos MORI research,[4] commissioned by Movember[5] and conducted in 2019, investigated the reasons why men are less likely than women to talk about their problems. 4,000 men were surveyed across the UK, the USA, Australia, and Canada and here's what they found:

- Nearly half (48%) of men surveyed said that their masculinity was dependent on physical and emotional strength. Most men surveyed said that this pressure to be emotionally and physically strong came from society rather than from themselves. Also, the younger men are, the *more* likely they are to feel a need to appear masculine or 'manly'
- 38% of men avoided talking to people about their problems for fear of appearing 'unmanly'
- 41% of men expressed regret about talking about their problems to someone, with over half of these men saying that this regret means they would not open up again
- 43% of men wish that they could talk more about their problems

Despite these statistics – and the well-trodden narrative of male emotional mutism – the study also showed that a huge majority of men (76%) believe that talking can help when dealing with problems. The sad truth is that many men and boys realise that seeking advice *does* help, but the act of seeking help is at odds with expectations of what it is to be a man.

Children's emotional expression

There is considerable research into boys and girls and the way they express emotions.[6] Girls are more likely to display positive emotions such as happiness and gratitude than boys, with this gender difference becoming more apparent as boys and girls move into adolescence. Girls are also more likely to express negative internalising emotions – emotions directed towards the self – such as sadness, fear, sympathy, and shame, whilst boys are more likely to demonstrate externalising emotions – emotions directed away from the self – such as anger, disgust, or scorn. This difference is more pronounced at the preschool and middle childhood stages of development.[7]

Boys' talk

Despite the research available into the types of emotions boys display and despite the huge emphasis on getting men to talk as an answer to the male mental health crisis, there is little actual research into *how* boys talk about their emotions. What little research there is focuses on 'help-seeking' and the conditions under which boys are likely to seek advice for problems they are experiencing.

A small amount of research into the role that teacher gender plays in student help-seeking indicates that although students have no preference for a particular gender of teacher as far as academic attainment is concerned, there is a 'marginal preference for one gender over the other in relation to personal and emotional issues with boys preferring the involvement of male teachers and girls preferring the involvement of female teachers.'[8] The 'marginal' preference could be explained by the type of personal issue students have experienced: for an adolescent boy, telling a female teacher that you're worried about your upcoming exams is a little different to telling her that you're worried about the strange smell emanating from your genitals.

It's important to remember that teachers aren't the only source of advice available to students in school. Whilst the research into teacher–pupil relationships and emotional support is sparse, much has been done into looking at how students interact with each other when experiencing problems. In their paper, *Girls' and Boys' Problem Talk: Implications for Emotional Closeness in Friendships*,[9] Amanda Rose and her team sum up much of the research, which tells us:

- Girls disclose more problems to friends than boys do
- Girls are more likely to co-ruminate[10] than boys are
- Girls are more likely to respond positively to friends' problems than boys are
- Girls are more likely to offer verbally supportive strategies to friends' problems than boys are

By contrast:

- Boys are more likely to produce negative responses to problem disclosures from friends, such as minimising the problem or blaming the friend for the problem
- Boys are more likely to respond to a problem disclosure using humour

Whilst boys were more likely to respond negatively to disclosures, the study did acknowledge that:

> boys' friendships benefited as much as girls' friendships from problem talk and positive engaged responses. Based on these results, increasing positive engaged responses among boys may seem advisable.[11]

The study also stressed the emphasis on humour as a means of building close, supportive relationships between boys:

> For boys only, humour during problem talk increased friends' feelings of closeness. The appropriate use of humour in this context may prove to be a social skill that, if fostered among boys, could increase their experience of friendship closeness.

Clearly, the topic of boy talk is a complex one, made trickier by the lack of a focused research picture and the intricacies of the many types of talk that take place within a school. Where do we focus our efforts? On student–student talk or student–teacher talk? On formal talk or informal talk? One-to-one interactions or group talk? As with all the solutions on offer in this book, I have written the ones that follow with the (extra)ordinary teacher in mind. I have thought carefully about how teachers can best bring about cultural change with the little time and resources they have at their disposal. I have avoided repeating advice and suggestions made in the chapter on mental health from *BDT?* but would recommend readers refer to it for further suggestions as to how to help boys talk.

The solutions

A. Remind students of how to talk

I've never bought into the idea that a steady diet of video games and social media means that young people can no longer communicate effectively. If anything, I'd argue that social media has given a voice to people who struggle to be heard in other contexts. It was way back in 2017 when I wrote on this in my blog:

> …the one thing that makes social media an absolute necessity for me is the thought of all those quiet kids I grew up with when I was at school, who, although never uttering a word throughout the five years of secondary school, would surprise me every night with their social media status updates in which they lay bare their emotions: there were proclamations of love for people they

never had a chance with; there were dark hints at suicide; there were verbal jabs thrown with defiance at bullies, and there were joyful explosions of emotional insight into lives which, were it not for social media, I'd assumed were devoid of any feeling whatsoever, simply because these kids never actually *spoke*.

Social media allows people to speak where otherwise they may feel unable to do so. Thanks to social media, people don't wear their hearts on their sleeves anymore; they're wearing them on their screens. And that's a good thing. Because, when we talk about the things that hurt us or make us angry and when we talk about the things that make us feel good or make us tingle with excitement, we are expressing our humanity. Our humanness. People stand up and listen to that. And we all want to be listened to.

And yet, despite all this, it would be folly of me not to acknowledge that I *have* noticed, after the pandemic, a sort of regression in the way that many pupils are communicating. It's not that they've lost the ability to talk. But rather, when they do talk, it's as if they're talking like they talk on social media, as if some of the rules of 'real-life' talk have been abandoned. There seems to be less kindness, less eye contact, less waiting patiently before offering your say.

Any attempts at improving the way boys talk, and their willingness to talk, must begin with a reset of the rules for talk. I was particularly impressed with the work of Cirencester Deer Park School in trying to improve the way all students talk at school:

Case study: how we talk

Richard Clutterbuck, Deputy Head

We, along with many other schools, were navigating our way through the post-lockdown return to face-to-face schooling. And alongside the many issues of which I am in no doubt you are aware, we had noticed a shift in the way our pupils were talking to each other.

We knew that we needed to reset our expectations and re-train the pupils into the cultures which were automatic pre-pandemic. But we used the opportunity to reset the culture through the lens of pupil-to-pupil communication.

Our end goal is for our pupils to be kind to one another, exemplified through the way they communicate with each other daily. We want them to realise that some of their communication, often unconscious and automatic, is littered with unacceptable language and whilst they don't mean any harm by it (mostly), it is not their *intent* which is an issue but the reality of the words they use and the *impact* these words have on others.

We have created a poster (see figure 4.1, below) which represents our start, our change in approach in policy and practice. To model to the pupils what we want, to teach the pupils as though this were a curriculum with all of the benefits of evidence-informed research: make it routine, make it automatic, make it stick. So that we are kind in thought and deed. Our approach encompasses assemblies, tutor time, CPD[12] with scripts for teachers and support staff, links to the curriculum, 'calling out' writer's language in texts, communications with parents, feedback from pupils and staff, logging and reacting to pupils' reporting of the unacceptable language, and posters, lots of these posters.

We've created scripts to help staff, parents and pupils 'call out' the unacceptable but teach why it is wrong and model the right way. These have been invaluable in shaping our approach. Is it working? Yes. Slowly but surely we are seeing and hearing pupils acting upon our modelling and their own examples; pupils are coming forwards to report unacceptable language where before they would accept it, and we are seeing more staff embrace the scripting of How We Talk. It's only the start but we like the way the pupils are starting to talk.

How we TALK

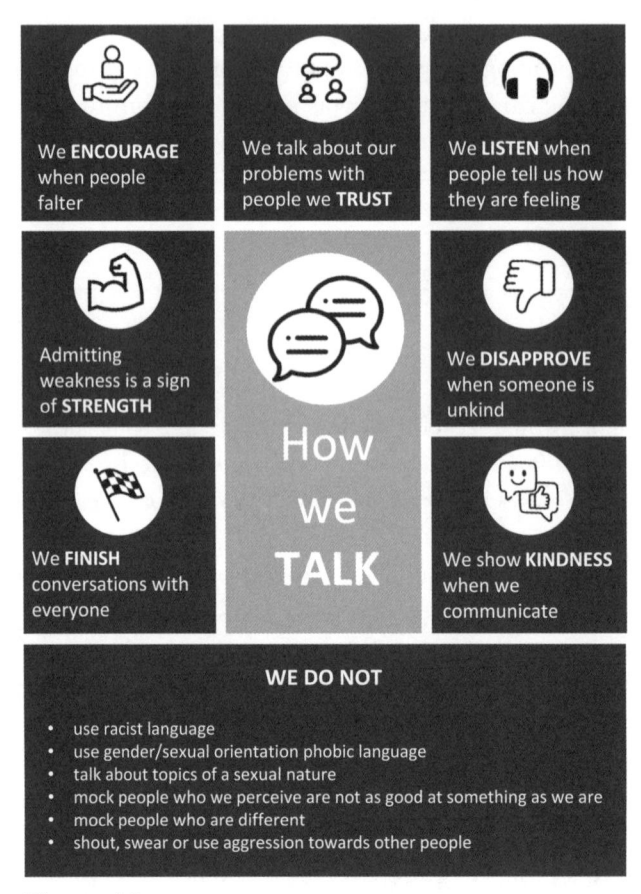

- We **ENCOURAGE** when people falter
- We talk about our problems with people we **TRUST**
- We **LISTEN** when people tell us how they are feeling
- Admitting weakness is a sign of **STRENGTH**
- We **DISAPPROVE** when someone is unkind
- We **FINISH** conversations with everyone
- We show **KINDNESS** when we communicate

WE DO NOT

- use racist language
- use gender/sexual orientation phobic language
- talk about topics of a sexual nature
- mock people who we perceive are not as good at something as we are
- mock people who are different
- shout, swear or use aggression towards other people

Figure 4.1

B. Normalise male emotional talk

In *BDT?* I wrote about the importance of modelling emotional openness:

> If we ever want boys to discuss their emotions honestly and frankly, we need to normalise the process of doing so…Normalising frank and honest discussion of feelings does not require dedicated assemblies or afternoon visits from external agencies. It is best achieved by getting the people pupils would *normally* expect to find in a school – teachers and support staff – taking the opportunities to discuss male emotion in *normal* school environments: classrooms, corridors and playgrounds.[13]

I then gave some examples of how this might look:

> - In history, the class are learning about the American civil rights movement. The teacher might say, 'As a man I always feel there's a real pressure to be physically aggressive in threatening situations. I really respect Martin Luther King for his ability to keep it together during his peaceful protests, even when other men were literally spitting in his face. How do you think he managed that?'
> - In PE, the class are studying performance-enhancing drugs in sport. The teachers says, 'I think that for men, there's a real pressure to always be the best at sport. I think that explains why so many men take to performance-enhancing drugs. However, it's illegal. What might be a better way of dealing with the negative feelings associated with the pressure to be the best?'
> - During playground duty, a student asks a teacher, 'How are you, sir?' The teacher replies, 'Actually, I'm having a bit of a down day today – I'm not feeling very positive. But that's okay; I'm going to see a friend later and talk things through – that usually helps.'

What's your weather?

Of course, assemblies and tutor times are also a really great opportunity to discuss emotions. I was impressed with a school in which I observed the use of 'What's your Weather?' to help students be open about their emotions. At this school, during tutor times, students take it in turns to tell the rest of the class about their 'weather.' The teacher begins by explaining what their own weather is like that day. For example:

> *My weather is cloudy today. I'm very busy at the moment and I'm a little bit worried about getting everything I need to do, done.*

Or

> *My weather is really sunny today. My nephew was born yesterday and so I'm really excited to meet him when I visit him in hospital later.*

Using weather metaphors to discuss your mood and emotions is great for two reasons. Firstly, it provides a concrete idea to attach to feelings, which can often be hard to describe. Secondly, it means that students who are uncomfortable with discussing their feelings can do so without having to mention any emotions or feelings explicitly.

You might think that older students will find this a bit corny, but once it becomes a part of the tutor time routine, even older students can find this process useful.

C. Help students to recognise emotional nuance

There has been some great work in recent years around vocabulary teaching in schools. Many schools now provide direct vocabulary instruction of Tier 2 vocabulary words[14] to students. People often think that expanding student vocabulary is only about improving the quality of their written work. However, wider vocabulary can help students to verbally express themselves more accurately. Look at these lists of Tier 2 words that are variations on 'sad' and 'worried:'

Sad	Depressed, Gloomy, Sombre, Glum, Melancholy, Wistful, Mournful, Grief-stricken, Pensive, Despondent
Worried	Anxious, Troubled, Tense, Fearful, Tormented, Distressed, Distraught, Apprehensive, Perturbed, Overwrought, Fretful

Being depressed is very different from feeling glum. Equally, feeling perturbed is quite different from feeling distraught. If we ensure that when we teach Tier 2 vocabulary, we include 'feeling words' too, we could help students to more accurately identify and articulate the emotions they are experiencing.

D. Set up talking groups for boys

Concerted efforts to normalise boys talking about their emotions can be really powerful. Many schools have utilised group talk sessions effectively. This case study details how Phil Denton and his team at St Bede's Catholic High School have harnessed group talk sessions to maximum benefit.

Case study: make talk your goal

Phil Denton, St Bede's Catholic High School

The Make Talk Your Goal programme involves leading speakers from the world of sport and the arts who help to promote conversations among our nation's boys and young men.

Make Talk Your Goal is headed up by Chris Kirkland, former England and Liverpool goalkeeper. Chris is a prominent campaigner for mental health awareness, having battled with his personal wellbeing for many years. This battle has been the feature of a BBC documentary, social media postings, and national media.

Chris teamed up with St Bede's after we noticed that boys were increasingly coming to talk to us during times of struggle, but only as they reached crisis point. They were seeking pastoral support, but only once they had reached the stage where they were desperate. We wanted to find a way to get boys talking about these issues before they reached these points of despair.

During the first group session, Chris talked about his own battle and opened up in a way that resonated with the boys. His persona and life as an ex-footballer gave a confidence to the other boys to share their own experiences with mental health and wellbeing.

Every single boy in the opening group discussion was open and honest about challenges they had faced; challenges which they had often not spoken about before to any member of staff at the school.

What follows is our five-step plan to developing a meaningful talk-based programme at your school.

Step one: walk and talk

Our programme began with a discussion involving the entire group. Chris kicked things off and invited a Q&A. He then posed some open questions to the group which allowed him to gauge the mental health of the collective (and of some individuals). Having seen Chris talk so openly, students were keen to open up also; their contributions were incredible in their honesty.

From this opening discussion, the boys set out on a nature walk for several hours with well-timed breaks. During the breaks, there was opportunity for snacks and chat. It is this last element which saw the boys build upon their opening discussion.

You don't need a professional footballer to run a session at your school. Any member of staff who has experience of male mental health struggles and is willing to talk frankly and openly about them, will do. This member of staff doesn't have to be a teacher. So long as they have received some input and CPD, and foundations have been agreed in advance, it might be a member of support staff, a member of kitchen staff, or a caretaker.

Step two: talking a good game

After the walk and talk, our boys enjoyed a football training session. There was a real mixture of abilities, which was deliberate. The session was led by Colne FC manager and Port Vale youth coach, Nathan Rooney. Nathan is positive and passionate. He talked to the boys about being part of a team and fuelling your mental health with positive relationships with your peers.

At your school, you don't necessarily have to get the boys playing football, just so long as you can get the boys in a team activity of some sort. The session needs to encourage supportive friendships to achieve a goal.

Step three: picture perfect?

A picture can tell a thousand words, as they say. Our programme utilises art therapy, delivered by St Bede's art teacher and qualified art therapist Helen Byrom. In a nutshell, the boys are encouraged, over a six-week process, to draw their own story and then talk about this either individually or in groups. This culminates in the drawing of masks that can replicate the facades we can sometimes hide behind during times of mental health challenge. This is part of the programme which takes the individual needs of the boys and starts to explore them in a bespoke therapeutic way.

Again, you needn't have an art therapist readily available to engage in a process of creative therapy. It may be that a member of your English department guides your group on a course of journaling their emotions. Perhaps a DT teacher helps boys to build sculptures to represent their feelings and pressures. What is essential is that each session encourages the use of open and honest talk as a necessary part of the creative process.

Step four: the final whistle

Our programme ends with another inspirational speaker. For example, the first group listened to Jamie Acton, a former rugby league star who had his career cut short by injury. His body-builder physique, coupled with his story of emotional vulnerability, is inspiring and engaging. Once again, the boys saw a male role model who was confident talking about mental health.

It's great if you can find someone from outside the school itself to come in and talk to the boys. It's particularly great if the speaker is someone the boys can relate to – or look up to – in some way. However, do consider people within school. There might be a history teacher with an extraordinary tale of triumph over adversity in your very school who would do the job supremely well.

Step five: post-match and the rest of the season

Once the programme is complete, we continue to support the boys through regular meetings, breakfast clubs and ongoing activities to encourage talking. The first group of participants will also act as role models for their peers and talk about their experiences to the next group of boys to get involved.

E. Teach boys how to listen

All areas of mental health support put a huge emphasis on the importance of talking. Talking, it would seem, is the answer. And yet, how easy is it to talk if people aren't listening?

41% of adult males have regretted talking to someone about a problem, and 53% of these men stated that this negative experience would prevent them from talking about their problems again. Of the men who expressed regret about being open about their problems, 45% said that they felt the person they were talking to did not respect them, or seem to care about their problem, whilst 30% felt that the person they were opening up to did not take them seriously.[15] This latter statistic should come as no surprise given that as children, males are more likely to respond to friends' disclosures of problems using humour.

Amanda Rose's research into the way boys and girls respond to friends' problems identified significant gender differences in the way boys and girls listen. Of the six types of positive responses identified, girls were significantly more likely to employ five of them (there was no gender difference for advice giving). These five types of positive response are:

1. **Support/agree**. Girls are more likely to explicitly state their support for their friends using comments such as, 'I think you did the right thing'

2. **Question**. Girls are more likely to demonstrate an interest in the problem using questions like, 'When did it happen?' to probe for more information

3. **Related experience**. Girls are more likely to link something in their own experience to the problem being disclosed. For example, 'I feel sad when she doesn't return my calls, too'

4. **Information/opinion**. Girls are more likely to display interest or investment in the problem being disclosed by offering new information about a problem. For example, 'And her parents let her stay out past midnight'

5. **Acknowledge/prompt**. Girls are more likely to convey that they are listening to the problem using statements such as, 'Uh-huh,' 'Oh,' or 'Keep talking'

How adolescent females come to learn to listen this way whilst boys do not, is no doubt down to gender stereotypes perpetuated by all those who play a role in children's development: parents, teachers, friends, and the media: children learn very early on that boys run, climb, tear, punch, and kick whereas girls care, talk, listen, and then care, talk, and listen some more.

PAIRS

We know direct instruction works.[16] If a child doesn't know how to balance equations, we tell them how to balance equations. We break the process up into small steps until the child can effectively balance equations independently. If a child doesn't know how to write a Haiku, plot coordinates, or execute a jump shot, we show them how. But too often in our schools, when it comes to those life skills that don't feature in any GCSE specification, we expect all children, regardless of their backgrounds and experiences, to be able to function as adults, and use adult skills, without any direct instructional guidance on how to execute those skills effectively.

I strongly believe that rather than telling boys and men that they simply need to talk more – something which is tantamount to a sort of victim blaming – we need to explicitly teach boys how to *listen*. After all, it's easier to talk when you know people are listening.

Take this hypothetical lesson plan, which can be used in tutor time, or in PSHE,[17] which looks to develop students' listening skills.

Lesson: listening with PAIRS

Preamble

This lesson explores the importance of listening skills in the school environment and the wider world. We'll be looking at what makes a good listener, and the session will give you the opportunity to practise good listening yourself.

Stage one (15 minutes)

Ask students to write a list of things that a good listener **does not** do. For example: *interrupts, appears distracted, makes light of the situation, gives terrible advice…*

Note: It should be stated explicitly that 'not making eye contact' should not be a feature of bad listening. Many students find eye contact difficult, even painful. It's much better to recommend that good listeners face their speaker, rather than try and engage in direct eye contact.

Get student feedback and create a whole-class list of 'features of a bad listener.' Try and draw out, if you can, those 'behaviours of bad listening' that research has shown boys will use when hearing friends' problems:

- Minimising the problem
- Blaming the friend for the problem
- Responding to the problem using humour

Then ask students in pairs to role play being 'bad listeners.' Student A must tell Student B about a problem they have. You can provide students with hypothetical problems, such as:

- Student A is worried about exams
- Student A is angry with a sibling for taking their things without asking
- Student A is struggling with their English homework

As Student A is telling them about their problem, Student B must then try and respond by using as many of the 'behaviours of a bad listener' as they can. Get students to switch roles. Have fun with it.

> Ask for volunteers to 'perform' in front of the class.
>
> **Stage two (25 minutes)**
>
> Ask students to write down what a good listener does. Ask them to separate their answers into two separate categories:
>
> - **Physical** *(nods, faces the speaker, doesn't fidget[18]...)*
> - **Verbal** *(asks questions, offers support, gives advice...)*
>
> Get feedback drawing a specific focus to the 'behaviours of a good listener' as outlined below.
>
> Ask students to write down the five 'behaviours of a good listener' using the **PAIRS** acronym:
>
> - **Prompt**. Good listeners convey that they are listening to the problem using verbal prompts such as, 'Uh-huh,' 'Oh,' or 'Keep talking'
> - **Ask**. Good listeners demonstrate an interest in friends' problems by using questions like, 'When did it happen?' to probe for more information
> - **Information**. Good listeners display interest or investment in the problem being disclosed by offering new information about a problem. For example, 'And his parents let him stay out past midnight'
> - **Relate**. Good listeners often link something in their own experience to the problem being disclosed. For example, 'I feel sad when he doesn't return my calls, too'
> - **Support**. Good listeners explicitly state their support for their friends using comments such as, 'I think you did the right thing'
>
> Now, using the same hypothetical problems above (or their own ideas) get students to practise being a 'good listener.' Get good listeners to then perform their role play for the class. Ask the other students to offer feedback as to what went well and what could be improved.

F. Harness humour effectively

I mentioned earlier on that Amanda Rose's study into the way boys and girls disclose problems recommends that teachers should foster boys' use of humour as a social skill, in order to 'increase their experience of friendship closeness.' As teachers, it's important that we model good communication. Teachers should show students how to communicate effectively: how to be courteous, clear, and concise. And, if humour is as important in building relationships, as the research says it is, perhaps we need to be modelling how to use humour appropriately too. Humour has additional benefits too. As noted in one major study, teachers':

> ...use of humour in the classroom has been linked to improved perceptions of the teacher, enhanced quality of the student/teacher relationship, [and] higher teaching evaluations...[19]

Given the importance of humour in developing relationships with boys, and the importance of strong teacher–pupil relationships in getting boys to talk about how they're feeling, perhaps it is time to change the content of our INSET days. After all, who needs a CPD session on *Effective Marking Strategies* when we can have *Effective Groucho Marxing Strategies?*

Thankfully, many teachers don't need humour-based INSET sessions to recognise the importance of humour in building relationships with pupils. Sadly, however, I believe that many teachers – and not exclusively male teachers – are using the wrong kind of humour, particularly with boys. In doing so, they are modelling the kind of humour that would make any boy reluctant to talk honestly and frankly about his problems for fear of being met with mockery, scorn, or sarcasm from other boys who have learnt how to use humour incorrectly partly through observation of so-called teacher 'banter.'

Banter

In *BDT?*, Mark described the word 'banter' as:

> a catch-all euphemism that covers the full gamut of ways that teenagers – especially boys – can humiliate each other: name-calling, mockery, malicious pranks, verbal and physical abuse.'[20]

And he isn't wrong. For many boys, banter like this is an essential component of the masculinity starter kit. Being able to dish out abuse to your friends shows that you're tough – not fazed by anything so 'girly' as affection between friends to stop you from engaging in witty repartee measured in value by how sexist, sexual, violent, or cruel it is.[21] But just as important as being able to give out vile banter, is having the ability to withstand it. Boys must never get angry, upset, or unsettled by the revolting abuse directed towards them or the people they love. To do so would demonstrate weakness. When so many boys' interactions with one another are centred around verbal violence like this, is it any wonder that so few boys – and the men they eventually become – find it difficult to be sincere, just for a moment, and open up about the fact that they might be struggling with something?

As teachers, we need to be showing students that banter like this, this *bad banter*, has no place in schools, relationships, or modern society.

Banter: why do teachers do it?

Professor Carolyn Jackson has done lots of research into boys' laddish behaviour and the way 'laddishness' features in teacher–student interactions. A study by Jackson, published in 2010, notes the way that male teachers often:

Locate themselves as 'properly masculine' by drawing on gender relations such as aligning themselves with 'the lads.' This can also facilitate the maintenance of discipline and control in the classroom as it can help them to get laddish, disruptive boys 'on-side.'[22]

Alarmingly, the study cites one male teacher who says:

> I know we're not supposed to touch kids, but [name of boy], he came in and I thumped him, playful thump. And, well, I'm one of the guys and I could get more out of him. And erm, joining in with the mickey-taking. They responded better to that…just gentle teasing, but in a sort of laddish way. I could get more out of them that way.[23]

Another teacher in the study talks about his banter with the boys:

> You say, 'right take your hat off, tuck your shirt in' and they kind of square up to you and you say, 'yes when you're big enough come back' and there's just a bit of banter like that.[24]

Such stories aren't limited to research papers where the more cynical among us might argue that stories such as these feature because researchers seek them out to prove their hypotheses as part of their own wider political or social agenda. I've been contacted by teachers telling me about similar stories of teachers – usually male – engaging in banter, usually in an attempt to get poorly behaved boys 'on-side.' One teacher told me:

> I was appalled at a pupil's account of how a male teacher (and a middle leader) asked if he was happy to have moved sets because the girls were 'better looking.'

Somebody else told me:

> We have a male member of staff who walks down corridors greeting boys by saying, 'Alright gangsters?' and other similarly awful things. He's big into being one of the 'lads' and acts as such. It's cringe, definitely, but also dangerous to the culture of the school.

Another teacher explained how banter with the boys was used by one male teacher to undermine a female colleague, something which happens more often than is acceptable[25]:

> The female head of geography teaches a group of tough Year 11 boys. One day, one of the boys asked her a question she didn't know the answer to. When she admitted this, the boys piled in on her. They said things like, 'That's rubbish, Miss. You should know.' It just so happened that the Head of Physical Education walked in at this point. His offering? 'Of course she doesn't know. She's a Geography teacher.'

I remember that one teacher once told me that he knew of a deputy head who, in response to a boy asking him if he had pubic lice, responded by saying, 'Yes, and I caught them from your Mum.'

The obvious problem with all of the teacher banter here – be it jokes about catching pubic lice off a student's mother, or insinuating something about a colleague's lack of intelligence – is that they show boys that humour which is sexist, cruel, or mocking in nature is an acceptable form of communication. In fact, teachers who engage in bad banter are what we can describe as 'cultural accomplices.' These are teachers who are simply reinforcing toxic cultural expectations of masculinity to curry favour with boys.

Banter and mental health

In November 2020, two Japanese researchers looked at the impact that teacher banter has on the mental health of students. Their study[26] distinguished between two different types of humour deployed by teachers towards students:

Aggressive humour: humour that 'targets students as groups or individuals and teases or condemns their opinions or mistakes'[27]

Affinity humour: humour such as 'laughing at and pointing out their own mistakes and failures, making fun of their own weaknesses, and telling nonaggressive jokes that make everyone happy'[28]

Intriguingly, the study found that aggressive humour is 'a predictor of maladaptive indicators of mental health' such as 'depression-anxious feelings, irritation-angry feelings and helplessness,' whilst affinity humour is 'a predictor of emotional well-being and self-esteem.'[29] That is to say, banter could literally be negatively impacting students' mental wellbeing. Sadly, boys' lives are full of bad banter: they're teased on the playground, the WhatsApp group, and on the internet. As they get older, they'll be teased in the office, at the pub, and on the stag do. As a man myself, it's no stretch to say that it can be relentlessly exhausting. Please, teachers! Let's be the one area of a boys' life where teasing and mockery are absent.

Harnessing humour to improve mental wellbeing

The study from Japan mentioned that humour that is 'nonaggressive' can have a positive impact on student mental wellbeing. It's true. Research has shown that very specific types of teacher humour not only lead to greater student recall of information later on, greater student intrinsic motivation, and greater student understanding, all of which are very useful, but *also* have a role in the creation of 'a beneficial class climate with positive teacher-student relationships and the perception of positive emotions.'[30] Yep. There are ways of being funny that make students feel better about themselves and, at the risk of sounding like David Brent,[31] I'm about to tell you all about them.

What students find funniest is humour that some researchers refer to as 'related humour.' Related humour is any humour directly related to the lesson content. Related humour can be conveniently broken down into ten subcategories:

1. **Props and different types of media to enhance learning**. Apparently, students enjoy it when teachers dress up for the 'theme of the class' (history teachers, be *really* careful here) or use props to aid understanding such as related cartoons or YouTube videos that were funny because they are outdated.

2. **Jokes**. Students like it when teachers use jokes related to the lesson content. Take, by way of example, this gem of my own creation, from a lesson on punctuation:

   You know who's going to win the best punctuation mark award this year? The colon. I can feel it in my stomach.[32]

3. **Examples**. Students like it when you make examples humorous. For instance – and I paraphrase from the research here – when maths teachers 'have used names in word problems that were humorous.' Right.

4. **Stories**. Students enjoy it when teachers use funny stories to explain concepts or reinforce learning. For example, I often tell students about the time I first learnt to use a semi-colon (it seems the source material of my comedy is limited to the very niche area of punctuation) and couldn't help but include them everywhere. Unfortunately, none of my friends knew what they were and kept thinking I was trying to wink at them in the middle of text messages. (You sort of have to be there, for this one…)

5. **Cynicism**. Apparently, teachers who are cynical about course materials such as textbooks, or information videos, are the source of great hilarity to students. This is a great opportunity to legitimately let loose on those textbooks from the 1970s – or possibly even the 1870s – that have been collecting dust in the book cupboard.

6. **Stereotypes**. Pot shots at student behaviours are apparently very much welcomed. You know – 'all teenagers are lazy,' 'all teenagers hate homework,' 'teenagers don't know the meaning of hard work' etc.. Apparently, teasing them about the slang they use is also funny, but I'd be careful here. Become well-acquainted with Urban Dictionary before you say *anything* you hear students say.

7. **Student teasing**. Rather confusingly, although student teasing is one of the most disliked types of humour used by teachers, it comes number seven on the list of most-liked types of humour too. But only so long as it's 'related to the material.' An example from the study was 'using a student in a demonstration that was

humorous and harmless.' I think you could get away with asking the kid with the loud voice to step up to the board because 'they like the spotlight.'

8. **Teacher performance**. Students love it when teachers perform. Examples from the study include a teacher running around the classroom as he got excited about topics. Slightly strange. Another teacher did the voice of Christopher Columbus as he spoke about voyages to America. Acceptable. One student from the study talked fondly of the time his 'teacher did a rap about math.' Abhorrent.

9. **Role playing/activities**. Getting students to play parts is always fun. Whilst I think it's totally fine to get students playing electrons, protons, and neutrons in Chemistry, getting students to play the roles of sperm and the egg in Biology is probably very totally not okay.

10. **Creative language usage**. The use of puns, humorous mnemonics, and funny names – the study talks about one entertainingly comic teacher who refers to bacteria as 'little beasties' – are all acceptable forms of humour.

So, there you have it. Go, be funny, and see your students thrive academically *and* emotionally.

G. Use *I Feel, I Need* cards

I Feel, I Need cards are inspired by something I saw a few years back when I went to visit James' Place in Liverpool. James' Place was founded by Clare Milford-Haven and Nick Wentworth-Stanley following the loss of their son, James, to suicide. The centre provides therapy and a safe, comfortable place for men in the midst of suicidal crisis. For many men and boys, talking about their emotions honestly and openly is difficult. It's even more difficult to speak when they are in a heightened emotional state. I was impressed, then, when I observed at James' Place the use of cards that enabled men at risk of suicide to articulate their thoughts and feelings clearly and effortlessly, without the need for speech. I have adapted the idea for use in schools here.[33]

How to use *I Feel, I Need* cards.

1. Photocopy the cards on the next page. Cut them out and laminate them if you can

2. When engaging in a conversation with a child in distress, or a child you are concerned about, show the child the cards one at a time and ask the child to select the cards that best reflect their own feelings and needs

Please note that you are welcome to copy or reproduce this resource yourselves. Statements can also be modified according to the age, learning, and emotional needs of your learners.

I feel sad	I feel thirsty	I feel angry	I am not eating	I have a headache	I feel tired	I feel drained
I can't sleep	I feel confused	I feel scared	I am sleeping a lot	I feel like my heart is racing	I feel sweaty	I feel sick
I feel shaky	I feel like I need to cry	I feel worried	I feel like I can't think straight	I feel like I will cry	I feel like I have a lump in my throat	I feel dizzy
I feel hungry	I feel frustrated	I feel I am overeating	I have aches and pains	I am pulling my hair out	I feel lonely	I don't want to be around people
I want to hurt myself	I want to punch something	I am having thoughts about killing myself	I am struggling to breathe	I feel like I need to scream	I have no motivation	My chest feels tight
I feel hot	I feel cold	I need to talk to a friend	I need to take a walk	I need to draw	I need to write	I need a fidget toy
I need space	I need to say sorry	I need to speak to another teacher	I need to cry	I need a quiet space	I need something to hit	I need to phone home
I need a drink	I need to eat	I need to read a book	I need medical attention	I need my safety plan	I need to report something to the police	I need help in managing my emotions

The final word

I've spoken to a huge number of boys, over the years, about what makes it so difficult for them to talk. 'It's weird, talking about your emotions to your mates' one boy told me recently 'and if you did, everyone would just take the mick.' I've heard countless variations of this statement and each one is a damning indictment on the fragility of the masculinity many boys strive for. When we think about mental health, it's upsetting to think that there are thousands of boys in our schools right now, dealing with problems and anxieties they can't discuss for fear of being mocked.

We must make concerted efforts to normalise male emotional talk. However, we can't assume that the skills required are something they'll learn by osmosis. We must teach them to talk. We must teach them to listen. And, more importantly, they need to know that we're listening.

Notes

1 For any keen anglers reading this book, the inaccuracy of placing a *freshwater* fish in a setting where it would not survive anyway is less significant, in this anecdote, than the abovementioned clunky metaphor about the comparative sizes of the fish concerned.
2 Except whales are mammals. Move along now…
3 Mental Health Foundation. (No date). Survey of people with lived experience of mental health problems reveals men less likely to seek medical support. Available at: https://www.mentalhealth.org.uk/news/survey-people-lived-experience-mental-health-problems-reveals-men-less-likely-seek-medical (Accessed: 6th March 2022).
4 Movember. (2019). Perceptions of Masculinity and the Challenges of Opening Up. Available at: https://cdn.movember.com/uploads/images/2012/News/UK%20IRE%20ZA/Movember%20Masculinity%20%26%20Opening%20Up%20Report%2008.10.19%20FINAL.pdf (Accessed: 11th March 2022).
5 Movember is an annual fundraising event where the growing of moustaches, often sponsored, raises awareness of men's health issues such as prostate and testicular cancers, and men's suicide.
6 Here, I am talking largely about the experiences of neurotypical children. The research into anger, and how to teach and talk about emotions, with neurodivergent children is out there and I urge anybody who teaches autistic children in a mainstream setting to seek it out.
7 Chaplin, T. M., & Aldao, A. (2013). Gender differences in emotion expression in children: a meta-analytic review. *Psychological Bulletin, 139*(4), 735–765.
8 Martin, A. J., & Marsh, H. (2005). Motivating boys and motivating girls: Does teacher gender really make a difference? *Australian Journal of Education, 49*(3), 320–334.
9 Rose, A. J., Smith, R. L., Glick, G. C., & Schwartz-Mette, R. A. (2016). Girls' and boys' problem talk: Implications for emotional closeness in friendships. *Developmental Psychology, 52*(4), 629–639.
10 Co-rumination is a psychological term for the practice of discussing and rehashing problems excessively, whilst dwelling on the negative feelings associated with them. Co-rumination can have both costs and benefits for the problem-holder.
11 Rose, A. J. (2016).
12 Continuous Professional Development.

13 Pinkett, M., & Roberts, M. (2019). *Boys Don't Try? Rethinking Masculinity in Schools.* UK: Routledge.
14 Tier 2 vocabulary words are words that most adult readers would know. They appear regularly in complex written texts although not so much in spoken communication. Examples are: haste, vendor, ubiquitous, and talisman.
15 Movember (2019).
16 Kirschner, P. A., Sweller, J., & Clark, R. E. (2006). Why minimal guidance during instruction does not work: An analysis of the failure of constructivist, discovery, problem-based, experiential, and inquiry-based teaching. *Educational Psychologist*, 41(2), 75–86.
17 Personal, Social, Health, and Economic education.
18 Again, know your audience. There will be some students with developmental conditions like ADHD who actually focus better on what is being said when engaged in a physical activity like doodling on paper or fiddling with an object. Don't make them feel alienated with your explanations of these categories.
19 Bekelja Wanzer, M., Bainbridge Frymier, A., Wojtaszczyk, A. M., & Smith, T. (2006). Appropriate and inappropriate uses of humor by teachers. *Communication Education*, 55(2), 178–196.
20 Pinkett & Roberts (2019).
21 In *BDT?* Mark cites one study in which a boy was heard saying to another boy, 'Your mum's been raped so many times she puts a padlock on her fanny.'
22 Jackson, C. (2010). 'I've been sort of laddish with them…one of the gang': teachers' perceptions of 'laddish' boys and how to deal with them. *Gender and Education*, 22(5), 505–519.
23 Ibid.
24 Ibid.
25 For more on this, refer to *BDT?*
26 Tsukawaki, R., & Imura, T. (2020). Students' perception of teachers' humor predicts their mental health. *Psychological Reports*, 125.
27 Ibid.
28 Ibid.
29 Ibid.
30 Bieg, S., & Dresel, M. (2013). Student perceptions of teacher humor forms and their relationship to instruction characteristics, learning indicators and student motivation and emotion. Available at https://www.researchgate.net (Accessed 10th March 2022).
31 David Brent is the name of the main character from British TV show *The Office*. He is renowned for his embarrassing attempts to inject humour into the everyday running of the paper merchant's office which he is manager of.
32 The follow-up joke about the semi-colon and how you 'sort of feel it in your stomach' is also good. Although, both of these jokes might put you in a comma.
33 Special thanks to Twitter user @_Mrscompton, who went ahead and made suggestions for card content after seeing a talk in which I described use of the cards.

References

Bekelja Wanzer, M., Bainbridge Frymier, A., Wojtaszczyk, A. M., & Smith, T. (2006). Appropriate and inappropriate uses of humor by teachers. *Communication Education*, 55(2), 178–196.

Bieg, S., & Dresel, M. (2013). Student perceptions of teacher humor forms and their relationship to instruction characteristics, learning indicators and student motivation and emotion. Available at https://www.researchgate.net (Accessed 10th March 2022).

Chaplin, T. M., & Aldao, A. (2013). Gender differences in emotion expression in children: a meta-analytic review. *Psychological Bulletin*, *139*(4), 735–765.

Jackson, C. (2010). 'I've been sort of laddish with them...one of the gang': Teachers' perceptions of 'laddish' boys and how to deal with them. *Gender and Education*, *22*(5), 505–519.

Kirschner, P. A., Sweller, J., & Clark, R. E. (2006). Why minimal guidance during instruction does not work: An Analysis of the failure of constructivist, discovery, problem-based, experiential, and inquiry-based teaching. *Educational Psychologist*, *41*(2), 75–86.

Martin, A. J. & Marsh, H. (2005). Motivating boys and motivating girls: Does teacher gender really make a difference? *Australian Journal of Education*, *49*(3), 320–334.

Mental Health Foundation. (n.d.). Survey of people with lived experience of mental health problems reveals men less likely to seek medical support. Available at: https://www.mentalhealth.org.uk/news/survey-people-lived-experience-mental-health-problems-reveals-men-less-likely-seek-medical (Accessed: 6th March 2022).

Movember. (2019). Perceptions of Masculinity and the Challenges of Opening Up. Available at: https://cdn.movember.com/uploads/images/2012/News/UK%20IRE%20ZA/Movember%20Masculinity%20%26%20Opening%20Up%20Report%2008.10.19%20FINAL.pdf (Accessed: 11th March 2022).

Pinkett, M., & Roberts, M. (2019). *Boys Don't Try? Rethinking Masculinity in Schools*. UK: Routledge.

Rose, A. J., Smith, R. L., Glick, G. C., & Schwartz-Mette, R. A. (2016). Girls' and boys' problem talk: Implications for emotional closeness in friendships. *Developmental Psychology*, *52*(4), 629–639.

Tsukawaki, R., & Imura, T. (2020). Students' perception of teachers' humor predicts their mental health. *Psychological Reports*, 125.

5 Friendships

The story

In a best friend I look for loyalty and trust. It's important that you feel confident with them. I'll always have their back. I'd do anything for my boys.

Noah, aged 16

I want friends who don't take themselves too seriously. I want friends who take the mick, but who also listen when you need them too. It's hard to be emotionally available but if someone is a true close friend, you can show how seriously you care about them by listening to their serious problems. The ones they've trusted you with. Keeping secrets secret is also a great way of showing you're a good friend.

Hassan, aged 19

Fear of judgement means I can't talk openly about my problems to my male friends. I feel that girls are better able to open up about issues but also better in offering support.

Scott, aged 19

I don't have best friends. I have lots of close friends, but I can't talk openly about problems with them. It's awkward. As for showing affection – no! You can't do that. Maybe a hug, but anything else would just be awkward.

Rodney, aged 15

Trust and respect are really important in friendships. I want a friend who isn't a nob, but there are a lot of nobs out there. Also, boys don't connect with boys the same way girls connect with girls. And that's okay for me, because I don't want to tell people about my problems and then have people pity me.

Tavinder, aged 15

From a friend, I want someone who cares about me. Someone who is always there for me. Whenever I know that my friend is angry or if something bad has happened, I always talk to them to make them feel better.

Mick, aged 12

The problem with being a boy is, you can't be honest and talk about your feelings. You always have to put a face on. Everything is about banter and if you ever dare to show affection, you're called 'gay,' and ridiculed.

Chineme, aged 14

In friendships I want support, trust, and respect. And hugs.

Paul, aged 12

The research

Emotional and physical closeness with others are essential to our mental wellbeing.[1] Friendships not only protect us from loneliness, but they increase our sense of belonging, happiness, and self-worth. Friends provide us with encouragement, advice, and security. Friendships help us to cope with the faecal matter that life occasionally decides to hurl in our direction at blistering speeds.

A longitudinal study of 1,103 French participants concluded that 'individuals with no friends were approximately twice more likely to experience internalising symptoms (depression, loneliness, anxiety) compared to those who had at least one childhood friend, even after controlling for socio-demographic factors, childhood psychological difficulties, and parental characteristics.'[2] The same study also found that 'a larger number of friends did not appear to confer an added benefit; rather, having one good friend in childhood was enough to reduce the odds of psychological difficulties in young adulthood.'[3]

Male friendships

Some people believe that male friendships differ from female ones. They believe that boys and men poke fun at each other, tell stupid jokes, and absolutely abstain from any show of emotional vulnerability whatsoever for fear of appearing 'girly' or 'gay.' Females on the other hand, from an early age, talk and listen to one another. They support one another. Instead of mocking jibes, they offer shoulders to cry on. Their eyes project support and sympathy rather than uncomfortable, debilitating awkwardness. In female friendships, emotional vulnerability isn't just welcome – it's vital. Vital because to talk about feelings and emotions is to demonstrate absolute trust in someone. And what's friendship about if not absolute trust?

Stereotypes aside, the reality is that many boys and men – who'd have thought it – are emotional beings who desire the same physical and emotional intimacy often thought to exist exclusively within female friendships. No, really.

Professor Niobe Way at New York University has been studying boys' friendships for a long time. In her TEDMED presentation, *Why 'boys will be boys' is a myth – and a harmful one at that*,[4] Way draws upon 15 years of interviews with boys to explain what it is boys want from friendship. She talks about three key 'themes' of young male friendships:

1. **Boys like to share secrets**. According to Way, boys value having somebody they can trust enough to disclose private information with

2. **Boys believe that friendships are essential to their mental wellbeing**. Boys are able to explicitly state their recognition of the fact that having somebody to talk to is good for them

3. **As boys get older, they struggle to maintain close relationships**. Sadly, once boys get to around aged 15 and onwards, they find it harder to hold onto the types of relationships that they value so much as younger adolescents

Where does it all go wrong?

As Way explains, 'Boys are very explicit about their desire for emotional intimacy with other boys…They want emotional connection.' However, Way continues, 'As they get older, their language shifts. The vulnerability goes out of their language. Anger and frustration come into it. They become macho…about not caring about having meaningful friendships.'[5] Way cites a fear of appearing 'gay' as a reason for the breakdown of close male relationships in late adolescence:

> It is only in late adolescence – a time when, according to national data, suicides and violence among boys soar – that boys disconnect from other boys. The boys in my studies begin, in late adolescence, to use the phrase 'no homo' when discussing their male friendships, expressing the fear that if they seek out close friendships, they will be perceived as 'gay' or 'girly.' As a consequence, they pull away from their male peers and experience sadness over the loss of their formerly close friends.[6]

This sadness stems from a recognition that something has been lost, and despite the tendency to avoid close relationships as they get older, boys still want the same things from friendships that had, prior to their initiation into macho culture, been permissible for them:

> Boys want to be able to freely express their emotions, including their feelings of vulnerability; they want others to be sensitive to their feelings without

being teased or harassed for having such desires. They want genuine friendships in which they are free to be themselves rather than conform to rigid masculine stereotypes.[7]

Judy Chu is a lecturer at Stanford University and her own research into boys' friendships echoes this link between a failure to form meaningful relationships and the fear of appearing gay. She explains how the boys in her study:

> ...tended to regard their peer group culture as presenting certain obstacles to their development of close friendships. These context-related obstacles include, for instance, the need to protect their vulnerability, prove their masculinity, and preserve their integrity when among their male peers.

Chu explains how in many friendship groups, masculinity is defined by its rejection of femininity. As a result, boys tend to exaggerate their masculinity and suppress any behaviours or emotions that might be perceived as feminine. This rejection of femininity extends to the rejection of boys who don't conform to the heterosexual masculine ideal:

> ...the threat of being called gay (i.e., having one's manhood called into question) did appear to be a primary motivation for conforming to (or at least not deviating too much from) masculine norms of behaviour.[8]

Chu goes onto explain the dilemma that many boys face: the conflict of wanting close, intimate relationships that they rightly recognise as advantageous to their mental and emotional wellbeing with the need to always appear macho. The fact that boys generally perceive their male peers as, 'judgemental, insensitive, and potentially hostile' means that it is unsurprising that many boys make concerted efforts to protect themselves by restricting outward expressions of emotional vulnerability.

Homophobia as a bonding tool

Worryingly, some researchers suggest that homophobia can actually be something which heterosexual boys bond over. Associate Professor of Sociology at the University of Oregon, C. J. Pascoe claims that:

> Through homophobic banter, jokes and harassment, straight boys define their masculinity in ways that are hostile both to gay boys and to straight boys who don't measure up to a particular masculine ideal. Insulting each other for being un-masculine, even for a moment, reinforces expectations of masculinity and also provides space for straight boys to forge intimate ties with one another, while affirming to themselves, and to each other, that they are not gay.[9]

True Bromance

The landscape of boys' friendships isn't completely bleak. In fact, rays of friendly sun do shine through the dark clouds of fragility-induced homophobia. Perhaps the warmest of these metaphorical rays is the 'bromance' – a close, homosocial, non-sexual relationship between two men.

When I first heard the word bromance – a portmanteau of 'bro' (as in brother) and 'romance' – I was appalled. 'This ludicrous word only serves to fetishize loving, heterosexual male friendships and we must stop using it,' I pontificated, self-righteously, when I spoke about boys at schools and education conferences up and down the country. In retrospect, as somebody who is currently enjoying the benefits of several bromantic relationships,[10] my criticism of the semantics at play prevented me from looking at bromances critically. Thankfully, there are researchers out there – researchers like Stefan Robinson, Eric Anderson, and Adam White – who, instead of getting on their soap box, prefer to examine, scrutinise, and evaluate social phenomena with intelligence and rigour. Their paper, *The Bromance: undergraduate male friendships and the expansion of contemporary homosocial boundaries* provides fascinating insight into the shifting sands of male friendships. Interviews with 30 British undergraduates suggest that, despite what Chu, Pascoe, and Way have observed, some males are managing to find close, intimate friendships with other males as they get older.

The components of 'bromantic' attachment

For the men in the study, bromances were characterised by a greater degree of emotional disclosure than regular friendships:

> All participants suggested that bromances differ from friendships through the level of emotional disclosure that is permissible to one another. This included sharing secrets and confiding exclusively with their bromantic friend(s). They were clear that a bromance offers a deep sense of unburdened disclosure and emotionality based on trust and love.[11]

Close physical intimacy was an integral part of the bromances in the study. Twenty-nine of the 30 participants said that they had cuddled in bed with another man. Others described kissing, casual nudity, and even shared sexual encounters[12] as important factors in their relationships with other men. Interestingly, these moments of physical intimacy were completely devoid of any sexual feeling – both physical and emotional – between the men involved. The men in the study were comfortable in displaying physical affection for their friends in what researchers call 'their social world.'

Benefits of bromantic relationships

The researchers were keen to point out the benefits of bromantic relationships to the mental wellbeing of those within them:

> The overarching implication of our research, beyond defining and situating the bromance in the context of contemporary masculinity, hinges on the im-

pact that these bromances may be having on men's emotional well-being. We are encouraged to see that these men are engaging on a deep emotional level with their bromances to better their, and their significant others', emotional well-being. We recognize that sharing emotional and physical closeness with others serves an important purpose in maintaining one's mental well-being.[13]

Male friendships, then, are complicated. Very complicated. Let's try and make things a little simpler, shall we?

The solutions

A. Normalise loving, male relationships

The emotional openness present in bromantic relationships should be something we want for all our boys. One way we can make it easier to resist traditional, toxically masculine culture's attempts to marginalise, penalise, and stigmatise those men who want intimate male relationships is to make loving male relationships the norm. The best way to do this is to assume that every social interaction that takes place is being watched and internalised. Male teachers: compliment your male colleagues. Talk lovingly about your friends, your children, your siblings, and your parents. If you can, bring your own children into school and unabashedly smother them with affection. Hug a colleague! Praise and salute male emotional vulnerability wherever and whenever you can.

B. Champion the bromance

In their bromance study, Stefan Robinson and his team stress the importance of recognising bromances as an important tool in the male mental wellbeing toolkit:

> Mental health practitioners should recognize bromances as legitimate influential relationships in the everyday lives of young men. For instance, these men often suggested that they could only fully discuss concerns over their health and sexual lives with their bromances, not with their families or romantic partners. Practitioners should recognize the implicit benefit of these relationships, having almost unbound limits in what can be disclosed. For those who are dealing with depressive symptoms or social anxieties, bromances may offer a way forward and a coping strategy.

Teachers aren't mental health practitioners, nor are we able to force bromantic relationships, but we can certainly do a little to promote them. Here are a couple of ideas.

Expose students to literary bromances

The literary men that boys encounter in school aren't great examples of male kindness. Take the staples of many schools GCSE English Literature provision, for example. Whilst Ebenezer Scrooge comes good at the end of *A Christmas Carol*, he only does so because of the quite concerted efforts of three supernatural life coaches. For the majority of the novella he is – let's face it – a bit of a numpty. Macbeth isn't great either. He kills lots of people. In *An Inspector Calls*, the one good man in the play who isn't a womanising, greedy, sexual abuser – the Inspector – turns out to be probably mythical anyway. An analysis of the 'Relationships' cluster in one major exam board's literature poetry anthology revealed not a single poem dealing with male-to-male friendships. Students studying the 'Conflict' cluster, however, will read nine poems describing male-on-male violence.

In order to combat the glut of male toolishness that pervades the GCSE curriculum, it's important that at Key Stages 1, 2, and 3[14] we expose children to texts that include close, emotionally intimate, and enriching male relationships. There are plenty of books out there brimming with bromantic relationships. Sam and Frodo. Holmes and Watson. Benji and Reggie. The list below offers some nice suggestions:

Primary-aged readers	**Secondary-aged readers**
• **The Boys** by Lauren Ace • **Songs for our Sons** by Ashling Lindsay • **A Porcupine Named Fluffy** by Helen Lester • **Harry and the Dinosaurs Go to School** by Ian Whybrow • **On Sudden Hill** by Linda Sarah and Benji Davies • **Nen and the Lonely Fisherman** by Ian Eagleton • **A Boy Like You** by Frank Murphy • **After the War** by Tom Palmer	• **The Bubble Wrap Boy** by Phil Earle • **The Scar Boys** by Len Vlahos • **A Separate Peace** by John Knowles • **The Kite Runner** by Khaled Housseini • **Harris and Me** by Gary Paulsen • **The Bombs That Brought Us Together** by Brian Conaghan[15] • **The Outsiders** by S. E. Hinton

Teach a bromance lesson

This short lesson – which can be used as a tutor time activity or part of a wider PHSE lesson on friendships – explores the concept of bromance and encourages students to discuss male friendships.

Lesson: bromances

Preamble

This lesson introduces students to the concept of 'bromance' and encourages students to think about their own friendships.

Stage one (10 minutes)

Give students the following statements. Ask students to put them into either one of two categories: THINGS I CAN DO WITH MY BEST FRIEND(S) and THINGS I CAN'T DO WITH MY BEST FRIEND(S)

- Trust them with a deep secret
- Tell them I love them
- Hug them
- Kiss them
- Tell them about a problem I was having
- Listen to a friend when they tell me about a problem
- Tell them I value their friendship

Get feedback from the class and use feedback as a starting point to discuss any possible gender differences that are apparent. Are boys' best friends mainly other boys? Are certain things acceptable in female-female friendships, but not in male-male friendships? Why do you think this might be? Might any category placements change as students get older?

Stage two (15 minutes)

Introduce students to the word 'PORTMANTEAU.' A PORTMANTEAU word is formed by combining two other words. For example, Jeggings – a cross between the word 'jeans' and 'leggings.' Ask students to guess which words the following portmanteaus are made of.

1. Hangry (*Hungry, Angry*)
2. Brexit (*Britain, Exit*)
3. Brunch (*Breakfast, Lunch*)
4. Glamping (*Glamour, Camping*)
5. Bromance (*Brother, Romantic*)

Display the word BROMANCE on the board. Give students the definition of BROMANCE and ask them to write it down: *A bromance is a relationship between two men that is close but not sexual.* You may wish to ask students at this point if they are involved in a bromance or bromances. Girls and non-binary students might want to say whether they know of any boys in bromances.

> Now display the following on the board:
>
> ### BROMANCE
> *Brother, Romance*
>
> Ask students to list how being in a close male-to-male relationship might be like being somebody's brother or romantic partner. Students might say: *It's founded on loyalty, you stick by each other no matter what, you look out for each other, you love the other person, you tell them your secrets, you tell them about your problems, you listen to them, you are physically affectionate with them, you are open with them.*
>
> **Stage three (10 minutes)**
>
> Discussion. Ask children to think about a) what barriers there are to forming bromances in school and b) what are the advantages of forming bromances in school?
>   Potential barriers might be *ridicule, people questioning your sexuality, lack of confidence, not having formed a connection with a friend yet.*
>   Advantages might be *emotional support, confidence, somebody to trust, somebody to share similar interests with.*
>   Discuss how barriers might be overcome.

C. Teach boys to listen

Boys crave emotional intimacy. In the statements that open this chapter, many boys identified that what they want from a friend is somebody they can go to for support. The problem is that many boys find listening to other boys' problems or worries quite difficult. In Chapter Four, on Talk, I explain how we can use the PAIRS acronym to teach boys to be better listeners, and I assert that it's a lot easier to be emotionally available to somebody who knows how to listen, with care and attention.

D. Talk to boys about friendship

It may be the case that boys are struggling to maintain friendships and want to talk to a trusted adult about them. What follows is a guide to talking to boys about their friendships. It is based on the work of expert in boys' friendships, Niobe Way.

1. **Talk to boys**. The simplest way to learn about boys' friendships is to talk to the boys themselves. Perhaps due to a misconception that boys don't like to talk about their emotions, teachers are often reluctant to talk to boys about things directly linked to feelings such as male friendships.

2. **Ask open questions**. Boys are far more willing to talk about their friendships than you'd think. Open questions such as, 'Can you tell me about your friendships?' or 'How are your friendships going?' are really useful because they're not

leading and can provide real insight into what the boy you're speaking to is most concerned about.

3. **Normalise loneliness**. Many boys feel a pressure to be popular. Feelings of loneliness can be wrongly perceived as a failure of masculinity. Boys can feel that they're the only one who feels lonely and that everyone else is really popular, but in actual fact many boys experience loneliness. Boys need to be told explicitly and directly that loneliness is a perfectly normal human emotion. It can be useful to ask them, 'Have you ever felt lonely?'

4. **Respond to their vulnerabilities appropriately**. Never react to a boy's disclosure or comments in a way that makes them feel odd or unusual. As far as the boy is concerned, they need to feel that what they're telling you is something you've heard a thousand times before.

E. Look for opportunities to create connections

As Kwame S. Sakyi and her team acknowledge in their 18-year longitudinal study into the impact of childhood friendships on later adult mental health:

> …having at least one friend early in life is protective of internalizing symptoms in young adulthood, which is a crucial time when individuals establish their family and professional lives. *Therefore, children who do not have friends may require special attention, whether they experience concurrent psychological difficulties or not.* Additionally, family and school characteristics that help children foster friendships from early in life should be supported.[16] [My emphasis].

Teachers must use whatever available resources they have to encourage friendships between pupils. There are several ways they can do this.

1. **Regularly change seating plans**. If students are always sat next to the same person for a whole year, you could be preventing them from forging meaningful connections with other members of the class. Try changing your seating plan every half term to ensure that students have the opportunity to work and engage with a greater number of pupils. If teachers of every subject took this approach, the number of possible connections for any given pupil over the course of a whole school year, or a whole school career, increases dramatically.[17]

2. **Use group work effectively**. Getting students to work collaboratively alongside each other, particularly with students they wouldn't normally talk to, is another way we can open up a world of connections to children. Personally, I hate group work and that's because I'm not very good at implementing it effectively. What I want when I do group work is students working together like a slick, well-oiled corporate, even conglomerate machine. What I actually get is 10% of students doing 100% of the work and 90% of students arguing about who's going to be spokesperson.

My failure to implement group work effectively is attributable to a number of factors:

1. I was told to use group work in lessons, without ever being told *how* to use it lessons

2. I was told that learning had to be fun and active and group work was sold as a sure-fire way to make lessons fun and…erm…active

3. Students think group work is fun, but students also fail to fully distinguish between work talk and social talk. I wrongly assumed that students could make this distinction

4. I tended to let students choose who they worked with

5. I was led to believe that in groups, students would learn automatically via a deductive process. In groups students would discover key concepts and learning, by simply 'bouncing off' one another

6. I assumed that students would automatically know how to agree and delegate roles, problem-solve, accept 'corporate responsibility' where needed and mediate within the group as required, then allocate tasks, working within strict time limits to meet their objective

Luckily, for me, Durrington Research School has spent some time looking at what makes group work effective. In their summary of Robert Slavin's paper *Co-operative learning: What makes groupwork work?* they offer the following tips to effective groupwork:

i. When setting up group work, spend time considering the aims. If it's to improve student learning, then a structured, team-learning approach is most likely to be the best way forward. This would still require considerable input from the teacher through direct instruction, explicit modelling and feedback

ii. Where the aim is to improve all students' learning then think carefully about how you will create individual accountability. Slavin seems to highlight individual quizzing or assessment, with the scores accumulated for the group, as particularly beneficial for the learning of all students

iii. Support colleagues in reflecting on and discussing how they set up group tasks. This may help to generate some purposeful activities that can be shared and developed and avoid group work lessons where, for some students, very little learning occurs[18]

James Crane's blog on effective group work in practice summarises the main elements of successful group work:

i. Classroom culture and a cohesive group dynamic where students regularly work collaboratively, and feedback and teamwork are pillars of the culture

ii. Careful planning and strong subject knowledge – knowing the different elements of a task and how these have to come together to produce the final product, be it a sports game, performance or even a piece of writing. In effective group work where learning takes place, individual students are not responsible for just one element but for all of them

iii. Individual accountability – Simply put, this is achieved through individual assessment at the end of the task coupled with the individual outcomes affecting the final assessment of the whole group[19]

3. **Engage children in connection projects.** School projects which foster shared experience and connection are a great way to help facilitate friendships. One such project, known as *The Listening Project*, was created by Niobe Way and Joseph D. Nelson in an attempt to combat what they term the 'crisis of connection' – the growing emotional distance that occurs between boys as they get older – evident in many US schools. The project teaches students interview skills, with the end goal being that these students make meaningful connections with classmates. Students also prepare to write a biographical essay about their chosen interview subject at the end of the course. In-depth information about the project is freely available via a quick Google search[20] but I have written a summary for you below. The project needn't solely be used with boys. Some might say that the COVID-19 pandemic has induced a crisis of connection for all our students, and so what follows should be useful for any student regardless of their gender or sex.

The listening project

(Adapted from **The listening project: Fostering curiosity and connection in Middle schools**[21] by Niobe Way and Joseph D. Nelson.)

Sessions one–four: learning about interviewing

Introduction to interviews

In the first two sessions students are introduced to the concept of interviews. For some students, this may well include an explanation of what an interview actually is as many students, particularly Key Stage 3 students, may have little or no awareness of this process. They are then asked two specific questions:

1. **Why conduct interviews?**
2. **What could one learn from an interview?**

Students are encouraged to go with their intuition and are encouraged to provide reasoning for their answers through the use of the follow-up questions such as, 'Why do you think that is true?'

Teachers or course facilitators then provide their own answers to these questions. Teachers also discuss with students how to create an environment that will make an interviewee feel comfortable and forthcoming.

Modelled interviewing

In the second session students interview their teacher, with the help of another teacher who is not being interviewed. The primary aim of the assistant teacher-interviewer is to model 'engaged curiosity' strategies such as eye contact, head-nodding, asking follow-up questions, and asking for elaboration. The teacher-interviewee must also model honesty and openness in response to being interviewed. This is to help students recognise the type of responses they're looking for later in the project sequence when they get to interview a fellow student.

Eliciting a range of experiences

Students are taught that eliciting either only positive or only negative experiences provides limited understanding of the interviewee. The trainee student-interviewer is then encouraged to draw out both positive and negative stories from the teacher-interviewee. When the teacher-interviewee proffers both challenging and negative stories, they are showing students the sort of breadth they should expect from their interviewees when they play the role of interviewer later on in the course.

Gold nuggets

Gold nuggets are stories that 'reveal emotional complexity, depth, and vivid detail' and that enable an interviewer to fully visualise the experience being related. Way explains that gold nuggets are distinct from bronze or silver nuggets which have potential for gold, but which lack depth and detail.

For example, an interviewee might reveal that they were once a bully. This is a bronze or silver nugget. It only becomes a gold nugget once they go on to explain the reasons they were a bully and how they feel, looking back, about being a bully.

After the practice interviews, students are encouraged to give each other tips on how to 'mine' a gold nugget from an interviewee.

An added benefit of practice interviews

Practice interviews also enable students to make connections based on what the teacher-interviewee has revealed. For example, the teacher-interviewee may reveal that they always feel nervous in large social situations. It may be that a student onlooker also suffers from social anxiety and reveals this to the class: *Me too! I hate large crowds*. In turn, another student in the class, who also suffers within social situations, now has something they can use to connect with the student who has just made the revelation.

Skills practice

In sessions three and four, students have to pick two other people in the school with whom to practise their own interviewing skills. They're asked to pick somebody they don't know very well. It might be a teacher, the caretaker, or a member of support staff. This is to help build new connections and make students feel more connected to the life of the school. It may be necessary to model an approach and allow 'rehearsal time' for those students unsure how to speak to a member of staff they are unused to interacting with.

Feeding forward

Teachers who took part in the session one and two interviews give individual feedback to students about their initial practice interviews. Students are encouraged to consider this feedback as they conduct the next phase of interviews.

Sessions five–nine: preparing for interview

Selecting your interviewee

In sessions five and six, students are helped to select who they want to interview for the biographical essay they will need to write at the end of the project. Students must choose someone they have a close relationship with, but a portion of their interviewee's life must be unknown to them. Many children choose family members such as grandparents, but they're welcome to choose other trusted adults in the school building.

Question selection

Students must choose questions carefully. They are encouraged to think about and avoid questions which could be limiting in terms of the response they elicit. Students are also encouraged to think about questions – and a method of questioning – which allow the interviewee to open up, and potentially reveal some gold nuggets. Students are encouraged to select questions that are of interest for them. Depth rather than breadth of information is the aim, so questions mustn't be too far-ranging in their scope.

Students then share questions with each other and give feedback. They then edit and redraft their questions based on the feedback given.

The interviews

Sessions seven, eight, and nine are dedicated to processing the series of interviews which students have now recorded, via digital recording device or smart phone, outside of class time. Students record three interviews in total, ensuring that they are recorded between each of the three transcription sessions, and not all at once. This is because after each interview, students will listen to what they have recorded, in small groups.

> Again, students and teachers offer feedback on interview technique which students must then address in their next interview. Prior to each session, students must also transcribe their interviews verbatim.
>
> More often than not, the initial interview lacks the depth of the successive interviews. This is because the interviewer hasn't probed the interviewee for golden nuggets. Getting feedback after each interview addresses this problem.
>
> ### Sessions 10–14: biographical essays
>
> *Essay writing*
>
> The final sessions are focused on students reviewing their transcripts and selecting gold nuggets for use in their final biographical essays.
>
> Students are given feedback from other students and teaching staff about their gold nugget stories and students then begin writing their biographical essays. The emphasis of these final sessions is on how to write a biographical essay of quality.
>
> *Final presentation*
>
> In the final session students present their essays to the rest of the class and feedback is given. Many schools have some sort of bulletin or magazine that gets published regularly. It's great if students taking part in this project could submit their interviews for publication.

According to Way and Nelson, their *The Listening Project* succeeds in its aims of fostering connection between pupils:

> [The project] achieves its goal of nurturing curiosity, empathy, trust, perspective-taking, and critical thinking skills by teaching the students how to listen closely and ask meaningful questions. The goal is to gain insight into another person and see her or him outside of the constraints of a stereotype. The students and teachers who have participated in our Listening Project report learning new things about themselves and each other that enhance their sense of connection to those in and outside of school.[22]

You can't say fairer than that.

The final word

Recently, I was interviewed for a podcast. The interviewer, a mother of a young son, told me she was overwhelmed by the issues her son would face as he got older. As we talked about male friendships she looked genuinely pained as if she had just realised, with crushing agony, that her son was inevitably destined for a life of mickey-taking, emotional isolation, and a lack of meaningful connections.

She needn't be so worried. Men and boys are reconnecting with each other again. Look at the bromance phenomenon: up and down the country boys are leaving school and making friends with whom they can talk openly and frankly about their feelings, worries, and vulnerabilities. Some of them are even cuddling. Heterosexual men are cuddling. And now you've read this chapter you're free to go out into the classroom and prepare boys for a life of meaningful relationships because you know that the boys you teach aren't the emotionless husks many people believe them to be. No. Instead, they're individuals who thrive on robust and profound connections.

Notes

1 Hruschka, D. (2010). *Friendship: Development, ecology, and evolution of a relationship* (Vol. 5). Berkeley: University of California Press.
2 Sakyi, K., Surkan, P., Fombonne, E., Chollet, A., & Melchior, M. (2014). Childhood friendships and psychological difficulties in young adulthood: An 18-year follow-up study. *European Child & Adolescent Psychiatry*, *24*(7), 815–826. doi: 10.1007/s00787-014-0626-8
3 Ibid.
4 Way, N. (2018). *Why 'boys will be boys' is a myth—and a harmful one at that*. [Presentation]. TEDMED.
5 Jama. (2017). How Adolescent Boys' Need for Friendship Affects Their Mental Health. [Podcast]. Available at: https://edhub.ama-assn.org/jn-learning/audio-player/18009128 (Accessed: 1st June 2022).
6 Way, N. (2013). The hearts of boys, *Contexts*, *12*(1), 14–23.
7 Ibid.
8 Chu, J. (2005). Adolescent boys' friendships and peer group culture. *New Directions For Child And Adolescent Development*, *2005*(107), 7–22.
9 Pascoe, C. J. (2013). Homophobia in boys' friendships, in Way (2013).
10 Unlike traditional social convention regarding romantic relationships, in bromantic relationships multiple partners are an acceptable norm.
11 Robinson, S., Anderson, E., & White, A. (2017). The Bromance: Undergraduate male friendships and the expansion of contemporary homosocial boundaries. *Sex Roles*, *78*(1–2), 94–106.
12 Threesomes with a female in which the two bromance friends had no sexual contact.
13 Ibid.
14 Primary school education and the first years of secondary school, up to age 14.
15 Adapted from Conaghan, B. (2016). Male friendship in teen books – yes, really. *The Guardian*. Available at: https://www.theguardian.com/childrens-books-site/2016/apr/15/male-friendship-in-ya-teen-books-brian-conaghan (Accessed: 2nd June 2022).
16 Sakyi, K., Surkan, P., Fombonne, E., Chollet, A., & Melchior, M. (2014).
17 Be aware that for autistic or neurodivergent pupils, seating changes may need to be handled sensitively and with care. The same goes for the approach to encouraging the pupil to explore and develop new working partnerships.
18 Using Group Work for Effective Learning. (2019). [Blog]. Available at: https://researchschool.org.uk/durrington/news/using-group-work-for-effective-learning (Accessed: 2nd June 2022).

19 Crane, J. (2019). Group Work in Lessons: Bright Spots [Blog]. Available at: https://classteaching.wordpress.com/2019/03/06/group-work-in-lessons-bright-spots (Accessed: 2nd June 2022).
20 Search 'Niobe Way The Listening Project' and you'll find it.
21 Way, N., & Nelson, J. D. (2018). The Listening Project: Fostering connection and curiosity in middle school classrooms. *The Crisis of Connection: Roots, Consequences, And Solutions*, 274–298.
22 Way, N., & Nelson, J. D. (2018).

References

Chu, J. (2005). Adolescent boys' friendships and peer group culture. *New Directions For Child And Adolescent Development*, *2005*(107), 7–22.

Conaghan, B. (2016). Male friendship in teen books – yes, really. *The Guardian*. Available at: https://www.theguardian.com/childrens-books-site/2016/apr/15/male-friendship-in-ya-teen-books-brian-conaghan (Accessed: 2nd June 2022).

Crane, J. (2019). Group Work in Lessons: Bright Spots [Blog]. Available at: https://classteaching.wordpress.com/2019/03/06/group-work-in-lessons-bright-spots (Accessed: 2nd June 2022).

Hruschka, D. (2010). *Friendship: Development, ecology, and evolution of a relationship* (Vol. 5). Berkeley: University of California Press.

JAMA. (2017). How Adolescent Boys' Need for Friendship Affects Their Mental Health. [Podcast]. Available at: https://edhub.ama-assn.org/jn-learning/audio-player/18009128 (Accessed: 1st June 2022).

Pascoe, C. J. (2013). Homophobia in boys' friendships, in Way (2013).

Robinson, S., Anderson, E., & White, A. (2017). The Bromance: Undergraduate male friendships and the expansion of contemporary homosocial boundaries. *Sex Roles*, *78*(1–2), 94–106.

Sakyi, K., Surkan, P., Fombonne, E., Chollet, A., & Melchior, M. (2014). Childhood friendships and psychological difficulties in young adulthood: An 18-year follow-up study. *European Child & Adolescent Psychiatry*, *24*(7), 815–826.

Using Group Work for Effective Learning. (2019). [Blog]. Available at: https://researchschool.org.uk/durrington/news/using-group-work-for-effective-learning (Accessed: 2nd June 2022).

Way, N. (2013). The hearts of boys. *Contexts*, *12*(1), 14–23.

Way, N. (2018). *Why 'boys will be boys' is a myth—and a harmful one at that*. [Presentation]. TEDMED.

Way, N., & Nelson, J. D. (2018). The Listening Project: Fostering connection and curiosity in middle school classrooms. *The Crisis of Connection: Roots, Consequences, And Solutions*. 274–298.

6 LGBTQ+ masculinity in schools

The story

I always knew I was never going to write this chapter.

Instead, here, you will find stories written by frank, inspiring, and in some cases remarkably brave LGBTQ+ educators. These experiences, narrated with eloquence and poignancy, illustrate the struggles and prejudices confronting LGBTQ+ young people and adults in education and in wider society. Any research I might choose to present, and my own lived experience as a white, heterosexual male from a working-class background, cannot possibly provide the same clarity as these accounts. Therefore, I provide a brief reflective commentary at the end of each story. I suggest how we might learn from the experiences and reflections of these contributors, and improve how we shape the future for the LGBTQ+ young people in our care.

Sir Ian McKellen outed me...at school!

Alex Foster

I started a French and German degree in 1996 and for me, university offered two key opportunities: to get on the internet for the first time, and to come out and live as my real self – a young gay man. Being out had not been possible at school or sixth form, although a family night watching *Four Weddings and a Funeral* had allowed me, hands shaking, to broach the subject with parents who were more supportive than I had expected.

University allowed for those first, faltering steps into gay pubs and clubs, a first few fumbles at relationships, and, through the LGB Society (as it was then), some top-notch bona fide gay sex education which, of course, had been illegal for me at school under Section 28.[1]

Post-degree, and now in my 20s, I worked in Adult Education and also served eight years as a local councillor. Having come out at university, I didn't need to go in again. I could be an out gay man in council, in politics, and at work. At one high point, I even got some local TV and radio coverage as I campaigned against the ban on gay men giving blood. A long-term relationship and a civil partnership followed, before a sudden political realignment led to me losing my council seat – and livelihood – quite abruptly, one May.

As a consequence, I returned to my modern languages background and became a teacher again, but this time in the secondary school sector. Modern Foreign Languages was a shortage subject, so it wasn't particularly hard to get accepted onto a PGCE[2] course and I began training the September after the election defeat.

My university course included optional seminars for trainees identifying as LGBT (as it now was), and I went along, keen to see how to promote LGBT inclusivity in the classroom. 'It's common for Languages teachers to describe their families in the target language,' I said. 'Should I use this as a chance to come out to classes?' This was not seen as a great idea, so I shelved the plan.

A year later, I was in a classroom of my own, beginning my teaching career and, for the first time in my adult life, firmly back in the closet, at least professionally. My colleagues knew I was gay, but the children I taught did not. And really, as an NQT[3] with enough trials and tribulations to endure, it didn't seem wise to paint another target on my back. The consensus seemed to be that being an openly gay teacher in a secondary school was a scab that needn't be picked. Despite this, my school was a fair way along its journey in covering LGBT topics in PSHE, and we were a Stonewall[4] partner. We used their resources in the classroom and towards the middle of my first year, we were fortunate enough to have Sir Ian McKellen come in as a guest speaker for the whole school.

For the only time in my nearly ten years at that school, the entire school body met in the one room. More than 900 students and 50 teachers all gathered in the sports hall to hear Sir Ian. I was concerned I would not be able to get my tutor group to behave, but once he began speaking, he soon held the entire student body in rapt attention. He spoke unamplified, yet you could have heard a pin drop. He told a story about a homophobic attack – a murder in London – bringing his words from piano to crescendo, and when he described the 'CRACK' as a man had his head stamped in, every person there felt – quite viscerally – that injury. Every face grimaced. Then, in the neat structure of the speech, he took our horror and turned it into an exhortation to show greater kindness to each other, especially our LGBT friends and relatives, and ended on a glorious Gandalf joke: if you don't revise for your exams…you Shall Not Pass.

After the students were dismissed, Sir Ian held a separate, smaller meeting for school staff, and it was here he laid his cards out. 'If there are gay members of staff,' he said, 'you really have a duty to be out at work. Can you imagine how useful that would have been to you as young gay people in your own time at school, had Section 28 not prevented it?'

Reflecting on my own school days, there had been rumours about teachers who might be gay, but when push came to shove, the poor pastoral approach to homosexuality during my time as a pupil meant that coming out now, as a member of staff, was somewhat daunting. I particularly recall one incident where someone had written the home phone number of another boy in my year on a toilet wall. His parents were far from impressed by the calls they received. I was summoned to the deputy head who was investigating the incident. Had *I* written the number as a joke? Did I know who might have done? 'No,' I said. 'I don't know his number. Also, the hurtful things they say about him, they say about me too.'

'Oh dear, young man. Not to worry; it's probably a phase...'

Galvanised by Sir Ian, I broached the subject with my headteacher. I asked if I should be out, in class. 'Why not?' he asked. Whilst my PGCE mentor at university had thought it a terrible idea, my headteacher was prepared to be supportive. And so, without a great deal more soul-searching on the subject, I began the process.

Straight people don't always immediately appreciate that coming out isn't a single life event that happens once at some distant point in the past, but rather something you do again and again in your life with each new person you meet. In the school community, I found the lively rumour mill amongst the students meant it didn't take a lot before *everyone* knew. In class and tutor time, a few judicious references to 'my husband' were all it took for most students to twig. 'I do hope you're not using "gay" as an insult in your gay French teacher's classroom?' was also a useful phrase, but not one I needed to use often.

Things have moved on a great deal in the years since I was at school. Now, everyone knows a gay uncle or aunt; several children live with both mothers. Many students are out themselves and there are growing numbers of trans and queer young people who feel no need to be closeted teens. Even the curriculum is slowly catching up: *une famille homoparentale* is a vocabulary item in the French GCSE specification and there's a gay wedding depicted in the new online textbook.

A few incidents over the years stick in the memory. A troubled Year 8 boy once challenged me by asking loudly, 'Oi, Sir! Does your wife like it when you wear pink shirts?' I didn't even need to respond, as the students turned on him. 'Oh, come off it, mate. Don't you know? Sir's gay!'

For most of my decade in the school classroom, being out at work was simply not a big deal. Everyone knew and nobody cared. In PHSE, during discussions about homosexuality, the children were amazed that people in the not-so-distant past used to be virulently homophobic. Having said this, I recognise that I was very lucky to work in a school where both the staff and student bodies were very forward-thinking in their attitudes towards homo- and transsexuality, and where being an openly gay, or even trans, student did not automatically earn you a beating. It was and is a school where several students are openly out; a school where students can safely request to be addressed by their chosen name, and this is not criticised as being odd or inappropriate.

I was able to be a role model to two young people in my school who were beginning to explore their own gender identity. One student, assigned male at birth, began socially transitioning in Year 11, wearing a skirt and skilfully applied makeup to class. This student was determined to wear a dress to Prom and spoke of little else in the weeks leading up to the event. Once in the venue, there was a small crisis of confidence, so we had a

> bit of a chat around projecting confidence we didn't necessarily feel: 'You bought this *amazing* dress, you need to have an amazing night in it! Deep breath, shoulders back and fake it till you make it!'
>
> Another student confided in me that they saw themselves as trans and although I felt my involvement was little more than signposting and safeguarding, when I saw their parent at parents' evening, they were overwhelmed with gratitude 'for all I'd done.' A bigger question is whether a pupil coming out is, in and of itself, a safeguarding issue at all?
>
> My teaching experience was confined to a single school, so I am reluctant to generalise, but my feeling is that staff and student bodies in most places are far more forward-thinking in their attitudes to sexuality than they were in the Section 28 days. Unsurprising, in the context of the evolution of wider society's views and that young people are broadly further ahead than older generations.[5] There are some hints that Year 7 students' understanding of people's gender is making it easier to teach them gender in French grammar – and I don't think the sudden understanding of what a pronoun is can be *entirely* attributed to Michael Gove's Key Stage 2 grammar reforms.
>
> Ultimately, what I'd wish for all staff speaking to young people with any sort of gender or sexuality concerns is to possess the wit to avoid mentioning anything at all about 'phases.'
>
> But if you're the sort of person who's read this far, I'm sure you didn't need me to say that.

Commentary

I've always felt a little torn on the subject of teachers being out publicly. On one hand, I think that more openly LGBTQ+ adults in schools can only be a good thing. As Alex and others will testify, and as I have seen first-hand, they serve as role models who make LGBTQ+ students feel seen and safe.

On the other hand, I recognise everybody's right to privacy. I appreciate that years of prejudice and intolerance and discrimination can make coming out very difficult. I can fully understand why many LGBTQ+ educators would ask, *Why open myself up to more abuse?* I don't believe coming out should be a duty.

I would urge all school leaders to think long and hard – and formalise it in the form of policy – about what they can and will do to support LGBTQ+ colleagues in coming out and staying out, should they choose to do so. Equally, this should be balanced with policy on ensuring the privacy of those LGBTQ+ colleagues who wish to keep their sexuality private.

Ultimately, however, I'm on the side of McKellen. I mean, he is Gandalf after all…

The impact of establishing an LGBTQ+ group at school

Gemma Astley and Matt Stone

There's a real buzz in the air. A cluster of dedicated and confident young people is designing posters for the new LGBTQ+ group; a polite excitability simmers through the adults working in the school. Most colleagues feel this new group will be something positive. Nonetheless, some perhaps inevitable questions start to arise from the wings. *What will the parents say? What if there is a community backlash? Should we do things more subtly so as not to stir controversy?*

The policy is clear: Heolddu, a school located in the town of Bargoed in South Wales, is an inclusive school. Everyone is welcome here. This is our message, and we will not change it. We explain to everyone that any community backlash or parental concerns will be met with a response indicating that our school expects positivity towards this support group, not criticism or censure. It's both a relief and a reassurance to hear other staff echoing these words in their own classrooms, too.

As a vision statement, *'Everyone is welcome here'* begins to look – and sound – a little hollow as a vision statement alone. Actions, after all, speak louder than words. Unconscious bias is palpable in our school; it flows through the corridors. The students feel it. They accept it. Any meaningful change therefore requires a focus on the school culture and a critiquing of heteronormative and cisgendered norms. Without a thorough and careful understanding of how to 'normalise' being LGBTQ+, and without ensuring this becomes part of the culture of the institution, other interventions – although helpful – are unlikely to make a significant difference to the experiences of young people who identify as LGBTQ+. However, there is a robust body of research that indicates the positive mental health benefits of LGBTQ+ clubs in schools.

Starting our own LGBTQ+ student group was easy. The students did most of the organising, alongside some trusted adults who acted as facilitators for the necessary privacy and space for students to be themselves, or to be allies of their peers. Now, we meet weekly, every Tuesday, after school, in our nominated safe space. We display Pride flags to remind LGBTQ+ pupils that they are safe. We have participated in a range of activities and have invited guests to come and talk to us about their own experiences. Having such role models is an important part of adolescent development. It's important for our LGBTQ+ young people to see other people, like them, in society so that they feel represented, inspired, and motivated to be their best selves.[6] Our guests have included ex-pupils who are now highly successful sports people; the local authority lead for LGBTQ+ and filmmakers who have been shortlisted for the LGBTQ+ film festival in Cardiff Chapter Arts Centre. Other days are more sedentary, but no less valuable. We eat cake and drink hot chocolate. We talk about things – regular things, like family and pets and school trips. It's fun, it's non-judgemental and, most importantly, it's comfortable. In these moments, students find the confidence to talk about the things that they struggle with.

In the safety of the LGBTQ+ student group, many share stories about self-harming and depression. Anxiety is a hot topic too. We empathise because these emotions are something we have all experienced. We talk about strategies that help. A huge bugbear is the changing rooms for Physical Education (PE) lessons. We provide gender-neutral facilities – the disabled toilets – but the students quite rightly point out the fact that being part of the LGBTQ+ community is *not* a disability. A solution is proposed: students ask to wear PE kits to school on PE days to avoid having to change. This is accepted, and is a small, but welcome, compromise to the unwaveringly high standards of uniform that have always been a source of pride to the school community.

Referrals are made where more specialist support is needed, and we also employ an LGBTQ+ counsellor to support the young people. Their needs are unique, and yet heartbreakingly common in the LGBTQ+ community. We get angry together, but a positive outcome of this anger is that we then collaborate to design lessons to be shared with all students to celebrate Pride and LGBTQ+ history month. The technology teacher makes pronoun signs for teachers' doors to show support. We hold LGBTQ+ Awareness non-uniform days. We've commissioned a mural to show our support. Slowly, the group keeps growing.

Students in classes speak about their families – families that are the same, but different too. There is hope, respect, love, and kindness in the air. We see students who are not 'out', looking a little more comfortable in their own skin, briefly. The group isn't just focused on itself. It's about the whole school; about respectfully bringing all people together without prejudice and bias. It's not long, however, before unkind and hurtful words from some students are heard in lessons. Staff think they are being supportive by shouting or sending them to the leadership team for detention, but this doesn't help these students to learn about their prejudice or give them a chance to reflect and change. People are on pins. It's confusing and awkward. People want to support, but they are unsure how.

In response, the LGBTQ+ group sets up sessions after school for pupils who have phobic views and may have questions to ask. Some turn up. They clearly do want to learn. As a consequence, tough but supportive conversations take place. The LGBTQ+ students are willing to sit in restorative sessions and tell students about their experiences. This helps.

As far as we have come, we also accept that our school might not yet be fully ready for the change we wish to see. Maybe one day it will be. There are people who live a lifetime of lies for fear of judgement by others. There are those, tragically, who are not with us anymore, because they felt so strongly that they did not belong in this world. There are people who hide their true selves from the world, who shrink themselves in order to make others more comfortable.

We are so proud of our LGBTQ+ students. We are so proud of them all. The students who are learning, the students who are allies, the students who are out and proud, the students who are questioning and the staff who are still unsure but trying hard to do their best. We are proud because we are moving, edging ever forward towards a school where everyone is welcome and where our actions speak louder than our words. We are doing it together.

Our group is a small group, but it matters. It really matters.

Commentary

This is a searingly honest account of running an LGBTQ+ club in schools. Instead of virtue signalling, it reminds us that schools are chaotic places where positive intentions don't automatically result in positive outcomes. Staff struggle. Students struggle. But they struggle together, and in striving for better – rather than striving for 'perfect' – the mental wellbeing of young people is improved.

This story reminds us that LGBTQ+ clubs are not just places for LGBTQ+ students and allies to hang out. Rather, they're an essential tool in supporting the mental wellbeing of those young people who frequently feel marginalised, targeted, and othered.

This a club that looks outwards. It's a club that is working, not for itself, but for the whole school. The club doesn't berate; it educates. It doesn't judge those whose values don't align with their own. Instead, it understands that talking through prejudicial beliefs and challenging them restoratively – a skill we know that boys and men need a little help with – is a powerful means of changing people's beliefs.

LGBTQ+ education in schools: a marathon, not a sprint

Brendan Bartram

Some people have a strong awareness of their sexual orientation from a very early age. This wasn't my story – an admission that has often been greeted with surprise by friends. Why didn't I realise? It's anyone's guess of course, and a question even I can only partly answer through retrospective self-scrutiny.

Growing up in the working-class Midlands of the 1970s was certainly not growing up in a world that felt open to any discussion of sexuality. At home, the only visible manifestations of 'gay men' were the few camp comedians occasionally on television. And, by definition, these characters were figures of fun and ridicule, not relatable role models. These ideas were reinforced at school – not formally via the curriculum, where homosexuality remained completely invisible (though this omission itself conveyed a message of course), but in the playground. From a very early age, it seemed that homophobia played a central role in the performance and assertion of working-class male identity. As such, homophobic taunts, insults, and bullying were an ordinary part of my early school life.

Looking back, I'm sure I wasn't the only pupil singled out for such treatment. I'm also sure that those six-, seven-, and eight-year-olds didn't know that I actually was gay. They knew I was shy, sensitive, and gentle, so at a time – and in a world – where gendered behaviour was strongly coded in terms of binary opposites, such qualities in a boy meant it was open season for cries of 'poofter,' 'bender,' and worse. This story is, of course, the common story of many gay men who grew up at that time. Teachers must have been aware of what seemed, to me, routine behaviour, but I never remember any attempts to counter or correct it – the hidden curriculum in operation once again perhaps. Against this fiercely hetero-normative backdrop, being gay was simply not possible – at least for me. Of course, I can't remember consciously articulating this, but I was certainly aware that the pressure was on in every sense to conform, to deny inner doubts and repress internal questions.

Skipping forward many years to the early 2000s, beyond the horrendous 1980s 'gay PR damage' of Thatcher's Section 28 and tabloid coverage of AIDS, the landscape had finally begun to look rather different. Social attitudes towards homosexuality had changed significantly, and representations of sexual difference were both far more conspicuous and considerably more positive. This changing external climate, I feel, allowed my own internal world to begin to shift. The urgency to come out, and to face the personal and social disruptions this process inevitably involved, became overwhelming. My professional environment by this point – a modern university – was also very much an accepting environment. That said, a number of pre-coming-out conversations with colleagues come to mind; remarks about an aborted cinema trip to see *Brokeback Mountain* ('Well, it is disgusting what they do, isn't it…?'); 'I'll tell you who's a gay-boy in that department…;' 'No, he's not gay, he's a proper, red-blooded male…!'). Clearly, shifting societal attitudes was still something of a work in progress.

Surrounded by a strong social support network, however, coming out was – in the end – not the mental health trauma I had feared but, like any transition, not without its difficulties. I came out to close colleagues first at work, though remained broadly guarded with others and with students for many years. It's difficult to throw off years of internalised fears and prejudices, and remarks like those quoted above linger long in the psyche. I was struck by the sense of sadness expressed by many to whom I came out that it had taken me so long (aged 40). I can't deny that the hostile, homophobic climate of the 70s and 80s must have played some part in that, but for me this is not the tragic trope of the homosexual living a life of long denial. I came out when *I* felt ready. I had been questioning (the original Q of LGBTQ) for a long time. So, late by some standards no doubt, but it was on my terms and in my time. Who dictates the timescale anyway? I came out at the point where I felt I had developed the interior resources, certainty, and mental resilience to negotiate the social, personal, and sexual upheaval involved. It was right for me.

So where do these brief personal reflections lead me? Clearly, I can only applaud the huge efforts of schools, the media, and other organisations to normalise and celebrate sexual difference. The 2020s are, thankfully, a long way from the 1970s. Huge improvements have been made in many areas of social and educational life, yet further work is of course still required. Homophobic hate crimes remain persistent, and we are often reminded, particularly via the efforts of certain national newspapers, the occasional failed actor, and with increasing visibility on social networking sites, that public attitudes are not universally positive.

> Have we, however, pushed too clumsily in some ways? I'm worryingly aware of professional conversations with some pupils who have expressed a growing fatigue and irritation with what they see as LGBTQ+ fixations in their schools and in the media. Such conversations have led me to wonder whether well-intentioned efforts to redress past wrongs and imbalances may in some cases inadvertently create new pressures and even confusions, particularly in the current climate where the politics of identity loom so large, and have seemingly become so charged and divisive. I realise it's difficult to distil these personal musings into concrete recommendations. I hope, however, that they might serve as a basis for wider reflections and professional conversations on how educational institutions approach the pace, scale, and place of LGBTQ+ awareness-raising initiatives and how well – and sensitively – such initiatives embrace notions of personal readiness and receptiveness for teenagers who may be questioning.
>
> Yes, broader societal and awareness-raising issues around LGBTQ+ are essential, but reassuring 'Q-individuals' that it's okay – and indeed vitally important – to take their time with and on their own journeys is equally pressing.

Commentary

Brendan writes eloquently about the experience of growing up in a time and environment where homosexuality is stigmatised. Whilst, as Brendan acknowledges, times have moved on, we needn't be under the illusion that homophobia no longer exists within the confines of our school gates. It most certainly does.

Because of this, it's great that there are thousands of schools trying to combat homophobia and transphobia as they also try to make LGBTQ+ students feel included. Brendan's closing comments on these efforts are thought-provoking. He asks if schools are guilty of pushing LGBTQ+ awareness too far, too soon, for some of our young people and he emphasises the need for educators to acknowledge that not all journeys are the same. Whilst for some LGBTQ+ students and their allies, efforts to make them feel included will be beneficial, for others it could bring enormous pressure. We need to be mindful that – because of a whole host of different contextual and intersectional factors – different students will need different strategies for support, at different times. Not all students will know exactly who they are by the time they leave school. We mustn't make them feel like they have to.

> ### Being in school forced me out of the closet
>
> *Thomas Cope*
>
> I attended a comprehensive school a five-minute walk away from my home in a suburban town in close proximity to Gloucester in the southwest of England. Several pupils that I knew also transitioned to this school from my primary school in the year 2000, although I didn't retain many of these relationships. As an adolescent, I stammered, had

two large protruding front teeth, didn't like football, and felt uncomfortable about my mixed heritage. Consequently, my mission at school was to make myself as unobtrusive as possible.

Conversely, I recognised my sexuality from a young age. I adored Dean Cain[7] in *Lois & Clark: The New Adventures of Superman*. I read with curiosity news stories about gay celebrities like Stephen Gately, George Michael, and Will Young. There was one boy within my year group who presented quite effeminately. I therefore told myself not to associate with this boy, out of fear of what this would tell others about myself. 'Gay' was commonly used as an insult, meaning 'bad' or 'weird.'

I successfully, albeit awkwardly, flew under the radar for my first three years at secondary school. By Year 10, I made a best friend and formed a new friendship group, different to those I had spent my first three years with. For the first time in years, I felt content. We would have sleepovers, play wrestling games on the PlayStation, smoke, drink, and go to house parties. I instantly fell for my best friend, convincing myself that he felt the same and was also just trying to fly under the radar.

Before the explosion of social media that we know these days, MSN Messenger[8] was everything. If you weren't making plans to walk the streets for a couple of hours after school, you were making plans to 'meet up' on MSN Messenger with the people you spent all day with. My best friend explained to me that I should initiate online conversations with 'Safe!' as opposed to 'Hey!' Was my gay showing and was he subtly supporting me to continue to fly under the radar?

A boy – to be known here as 'G' – added me onto MSN Messenger towards the end of Year 10. My memory of the details of this experience is patchy, buried in a box with other aspects of my teenager years. He was in my year at school, although in none of my classes. I sat next to his best friend in Maths; however, our friendship groups were separate, and we had never had a face-to-face conversation. I don't remember feeling an attraction to G specifically, although I was still enamoured with my best friend, who had replaced Dean Cain in my affections. Nonetheless, G and I started speaking on MSN Messenger about mundane topics, as we all did. At some point, as we both had exit passes, we arranged to spend time together over the lunch hour at my house.

Prior to our online conversations, I had no idea that G was gay. I don't ever remember either of us telling each other we were gay over MSN Messenger, although it was implied. I was fearful that if written explicitly, it could be used against me, and I certainly wouldn't have felt confident coming out in the school I was in. Also, G was not effeminate like the boy I had distanced myself from. Had *he* viewed *me* as gay prior to our MSN Messenger exchanges? G must have seen something in me, something that I had spent years trying to hide. Was it my overly gelled hair? Did I walk or talk like a gay person? Anybody who was different was targeted, and I can imagine most secondary schools in the early noughties were similar. Did my preference for wearing jeans and a t-shirt as opposed to a tracksuit let me down – or, rather, show me up?

G and I spent multiple lunchtimes at my house over the next few weeks and engaged in activities which were mostly of a sexual nature. We instigated this type of relationship during the first visit and this continued, probably to cover up that we had nothing else in common. Once we had explored what we were willing to explore, the relationship fizzled out. We stopped talking online and did not see each other whilst in school – easy in a comprehensive with over 1,000 pupils.

A couple of months later, G came out to his close friends. His being gay soon became common knowledge. Shortly afterwards, a few of my friends asked if *I* was gay. It transpired that G had told his friends about our conversations and lunchtimes together. I felt disgusted for allowing this to happen. I had spent years trying to fit in and not draw attention to myself; however, my teenage urges had now put me in a position in which someone was able to destroy everything I worked so hard to achieve.

I told my best friend that it was a lie, and that G was making it up. I was worried that if I told the truth, I would lose both my best friend and the security of this platonic friendship that I had come to enjoy. He was angry on my behalf, convincing me to go with him to G's house to confront him. A tentative confrontation took place on his doorstep; ultimately, a fairly one-sided confrontation in which G said nothing. That was the last time we spoke. I fumbled through my final year at school, avoided classes by gaming the registration system, and dodged any references to my being outed. My close friends believed me, and this was all I cared about.

I was 15 at the time, and only vaguely aware of the fact that, from a legal standpoint, I had engaged in sexual activity as a minor[9] – an aspect which, had school found out, would automatically have triggered a phone call home to my mother, most likely from a safeguarding perspective. This, in turn, would have led to very uncomfortable conversations at home; conversations I was not ready to have. At the time, I don't believe I would have approached a member of school staff to explain the situation and ask for advice or support independently. I was very worried about it getting back to my family.

I *would* have liked a member of staff to recognise a change in my behaviour. I was previously a very conscientious pupil, but soon became a serial truant. This, like my being gay, went totally under the radar. The size of the school meant I was able to miss half of my lessons each week without anyone detecting it. I knew I needed to register in the morning and then after lunch. The ideal situation, for me, would have been that an empathetic adult in the school *noticed*, and was prepared to approach me in a supportive manner to ask what was going on. Had a member of staff approached me, I would possibly have given them some indication about what was happening, likely in a vague or euphemistic manner, but I would have said *something*, nonetheless. I did feel that I was going through it very much alone, and I was not mature enough to deal with the situation. I needed someone to problem-solve with me. I couldn't do anything other than keep my head above water, and I achieved this through lying about what had happened. I needed to know that I didn't have to go through it alone, with some promise of confidentiality, although I don't think this would have been possible then.

> Looking back, I still harbour some animosity towards G for outing me. Ten years or so ago, I was tempted to contact him over Facebook to ask why he did it, although I stopped myself. I was just not ready to open a dialogue about this with him.
>
> My fears of being associated with homosexuality and presenting as feminine were very deep-rooted, shaping my teenage years. I've learnt now that there isn't a 'gay' way of walking, talking, or dressing, but it *was* a very real fear I had. As I visit schools as an adult, I take comfort in seeing 'LGBTQ Safe Space' stickers,[10] alongside feelings of regret that this comfort wasn't available to me in the early noughties. I would like to think that were I to have my time again, I would access these safe spaces discreetly, although I can't say this with any certainty. The culture in my school, as a pupil, was very different to the schools I've worked in as an adult. I do know that I would have felt anxious about other pupils seeing me access a safe space and the conclusions they would come to. Likewise, at the time, I was convinced that were I to seek support from school staff, my family would then be told that I was gay.
>
> How valid these concerns really were, I do not know. What I *do* know is the energy I spent flying under the radar meant that I denied myself a lot of enjoyment in my teenage years.

Commentary

As a heterosexual man, I can't imagine what it must be like to have gone through what Tom did, during his time at school. And yet, I would hope that now as a teacher, I can be there for pupils, like Tom, who need my support.

Schools need safe spaces. That much is clear. But Tom's story is a reminder that safe spaces aren't needed just for the students who are openly LGBTQ+. Schools need to think about how they can provide safe spaces for those students who are not yet ready to come out, or for those who are questioning their sexuality but not wanting people to know that they are. Headteacher Mark Pritchard told me that in his school, his LGBTQ+ club is known as the 'Q & A' club. Q & A stands for 'Queers and Allies,' meaning that attendance at the club needn't necessarily signify that you are in fact LGBTQ+ yourself. This could help students who are reluctant to be out to attend without worry. Equally, the name of the club also enables students to discuss attendance at the club with parents and family without any direct reference to LGBTQ+, should they prefer.

The ideal situation is that all schools are safe spaces in their entirety. A firm stance on sanctions for homophobic abuse, and the outing of students, in the way that G outed Tom without his consent, would be a vital step in a wider move to making any school a safe space.

Embrace your vulnerability: LGBTQ+ educators should be true to themselves

Tom Mackenzie-Chalmers

I am gay. These are words that I have never had to say, at least out loud, in my professional life. Despite this, I am openly gay in my school – to staff since my first day, and, more recently to pupils. I also haven't ever chosen to say the words, 'I am gay' to come out at school, although there is no problem with doing so. Circumstances, created along the way, have created opportunities for me to be my true self in school: firstly, my relationship with my now husband; secondly, the recent adoption of our son. My story is about how I came out in school and how my journey, as a gay pupil, then university student, then primary school teacher, along with a little prod in the right direction from another educator, helped me to do so.

My personal experience is narrated against the context of the recent protests outside primary schools in Birmingham. These created a highly toxic climate for many LGBTQ+ educators and protestors were unrelenting in their pressure to remove mentions of LGBTQ+ relationships and people from the curriculum. The Relationships, Sexual Health, and Parenthood[11] resource in Scotland has been met with hyperbolic outrage by political opponents and some parents, with some demanding that all mentions of LGBTQ+ people be removed from the resource. I've received many letters from parents not wanting their child to be in the room while I am teaching the lessons in this scheme of work about LGBTQ+ people. That's difficult to digest.

Even now, the volume and age of young people coming out is a regular discussion topic on social media platforms such as Twitter, with suggestions that teaching children about LGBTQ+ people is *causing* them to be gay. As if the mere discussion of LGBTQ+ issues serves as some kind of insidious recruitment tool. Not only is this ridiculous – Sex Education lessons didn't make me straight, just as learning about the Olympics couldn't make me an athlete.

The point is, of course, that we live in a hetero-normative world and LGBTQ+ education is *not* contributing to a rise in LGBTQ+ people. What is great is that it *is* allowing more people to be out, to express themselves and not feel ashamed of who they are.

The protests I mentioned above are increasingly reminiscent of Margaret Thatcher's damaging Section 28 law which forbade local authorities from 'the promotion of homosexuality.' This created a generation of young LGBTQ+ people whose experience of education rarely provided them with role models or the faintest idea about how to look after their sexual health. It also caused problems for many teachers, who had to repress their own natural instincts towards both liberality and inclusivity, in order to avoid accusations of 'promoting' LGBTQ+ as a perfectly acceptable life choice, should that be a young person's stated inclination. The environment of distrust surrounding gay people, created during Section 28, often leads to gay people hiding their true selves in primary schools for fear of parental backlash.

So what does all of this mean for me, and for my journey?

Upon returning from parental leave after the adoption of our son, a child in my new class asked, 'But who is looking after your little boy now?'

A great question. For most teacher-parents, it's a simple answer. For a gay teacher, however, the answers to such questions are not so straightforward. Similar questions include, 'Do you have a girlfriend?' 'Who do you live with?' and, on more than one occasion, when spotted by pupils while out walking with my husband, 'Is that your friend?'

You see, I didn't ever practise a cover-up response to these kinds of questions, despite their frequency. It doesn't feel good to lie and deny your own existence and so having a go-to, rehearsed answer which did exactly that seemed inauthentic.

Often accompanying the desire to give a rehearsed response are the underlying reasons for anyone, anywhere, *not* to be out: fear of rejection; shame and trauma avoidance; the unknowns in status and perceptions that go along with change. Schools are places that many LGBTQ+ people associate with experiences of bullying and fear. In fact, Stonewall reports that 45% of young LGBTQ+ people are bullied and 68% of LGBTQ+ 18- to 24-year-olds experience depression.

As a young gay pupil, I didn't come out at school either, in order to keep safe, to be accepted and, consequentially, to protect myself from the kind of difficulties outlined above. As an adult, I realised I was trying to avoid similar changes in my status. I aimed, above anything else, to be respected by learners and accepted by parents. In other words, what every teacher wants: just to be able to get on with my job and teach.

So who *was* looking after my little boy, then?

At this point, no fanfare was required for me, no announcement. I just answered the students' questions honestly. But why? Probably because our recent adoption of our son meant that the denial of my new family seemed like a mortal sin. But serendipitously, just two days before, I had listened to a Scottish Educators Connect podcast that helped to change my instinct to tailor responses around this issue. This podcast is written and presented by Anita Le Tissier and James Cook, who are both openly LGBTQ+. Their podcast on LGBTQ+ issues in Scottish education has profoundly challenged my outlook. Anita tells of how an interaction with a young LGBTQ+ person allowed her to recognise that she had a responsibility to provide young people in her school with an LGBTQ+ role model. Anita stressed how vital it is that young people understand how unimportant sexuality actually is when it comes to assessing someone's character. It is, as Anita says, 'the least interesting thing about me.'

This rang true with me. I grew up without LGBTQ+ role models, who I felt would have helped validate my existence as a young gay person. I don't want any other young gay people to grow up without validation. I also don't want to contribute to a world which is 'straight-washed' – where non-LGBTQ+ people don't experience gay people because of a fear of offending young people and their parents by merely existing.

My own school experience hardwired me to close off, and the educational climate I've discussed only compounded this instinct. Being visible has now become important for me, for young people, and for my family. Being vulnerable is equally important, and

> that is not something that men are great at; vulnerability and masculinity traditionally don't go hand in hand. Embracing vulnerability feels unfamiliar – there might be unkind comments, disrespect, or even rejection – but it's an essential step in the right direction for being myself, being visible, and being true to my family.
>
> All those things can only make me a better educator.

Commentary

Tom and his husband have recently adopted their first son, and this has profoundly changed his attitudes to the importance of being openly 'out' with his students. His story compels me to observe the paradoxical nature of being a gay primary school teacher. On one level, primary teachers are in the wonderful position of teaching pupils at an age where they are less likely to be tainted by societal prejudice, with whom they can normalise homosexuality and LGBTQ+ acceptance. And yet, with teaching younger pupils comes the fear of being accused of indoctrination and, at its most extreme, the conflation of being homosexual with dissolution and depravity.

I would hope that if any LGBTQ+ adult working in schools receives the sorts of negative treatment from parents that Tom describes, a robust response from the school is promptly delivered to the offending parties. A school's failure to deliver on this would serve to perpetuate the stigma attached to homosexuality and I'd urge anybody working in such a school – LGBTQ+ or otherwise – to seek alternative employment as soon as possible.

There's much to take from Tom's story, but what stands out is that being openly gay isn't simply about being openly gay. In Tom's case, being openly gay isn't the defining characteristic of his personality. Just as it *never* is for heterosexual teachers. Rather, being openly gay gives him the chance to be his authentic self: a husband, a father, and an educator. To be Tom.

> ### Embedding LGBTQ+ literature in the curriculum
>
> *Louise Belshaw*
>
> When I first qualified as a teacher in 1998, Section 28 was still in place. I had a buzzcut and I was not immune to the odd homophobic comment. As my career progressed, I discovered that homophobia was quite commonplace in schools, and it was rare to encounter anyone who was openly gay. By the time I was working in my fourth school, however, progress had been well and truly made. There were all kinds of LGBTQ+ pupils out, open, and happy to be themselves. This was made even better by the number

of other, often straight, pupils equally as happy to defend and advocate for them. I felt lighter and hopeful for these young people entering secondary school.

In 2017, I was appointed to Head of English in a school in a working-class town in the North-West of England, in one of the largest boroughs in Lancashire. Some of the school's surrounding areas were in the top 10% most deprived in England, although the borough did boast higher than average Progress 8[12] attainment. This was where I received my first wake-up call. A mere 30 miles away from my previous school was an educational establishment where it was not just difficult to be openly gay, it was impossible.

Fear was prevalent. Fear of being different, of being singled out. Fear of what the future held and, sometimes, of violence. One pupil in Year 9 had been subjected to persistent verbal abuse which eventually escalated into a group of peers beating him up and stealing from his bag. Eventually, one of the perpetrators was expelled for continuous homophobic abuse, but it carried on more subtly in other areas and in other year groups.

Three years later, in late March 2020, my faculty and I – like many others – found ourselves isolated, journeying along a very steep curve of 'remote learning.' We set about rewriting our curriculum, a process which would involve much collaboration. We wanted our novel choices to be fresh, current, and relevant to our pupils. If I could not singlehandedly change the culture of the whole school, we could – together – at least begin to tackle some of their firmly held and prejudiced beliefs through what we loved best: literature. A professional discussion group on a social media platform was created. We began to read a variety of books from the Carnegie Medal[13] finalists of 2020 and, over time, we all began to love *The Black Flamingo* by Dean Atta. Not only was it beautifully written in a modern, accessible format, but it dealt with themes of personal identity, self-exploration, and sexual identity. It was perfect.

Being a realist, I knew I would have to convince my line manager and the headteacher of its value. Fortunately, there was no resistance, just compromise. We agreed it would be taught to pupils towards the end of Year 9, and that a letter to parents warning of sensitive content would be sent home prior to students reading the book in classes. To support it further, we collaborated with the head of PSHE and ensured that the RSE curriculum was tailored to cover content also relevant to the novel: drugs, decision making in higher-risk situations, sexual preferences and relationships, equality, diversity, and consent. When the letters went home, I braced myself, but in the end, we only had *one* parent request for their son to be removed from lessons, and alternative provision was given. I spent a few anxious weeks leading up to teaching the scheme where I would imagine conflicts, frustrating conversations, and all manner of potential scenarios where pupils expressed bigoted, homophobic comments and the kind of responses I could give. My team, meanwhile, took it in their stride and eventually we started to teach the book.

> The reaction of pupils took us all by surprise. By focusing on themes like identity, race, and sexuality, Dean Atta had given us a way to connect with everyone we taught. We began by presenting pupils with society's stereotypical views on gender, encouraging pupils to question and discuss. Using Atta's '*I come from…*' poem, we asked pupils to explore their own identity through poetry and what made them who they were. I was able to share these with the author himself, then relayed his glowing praise to the pupils back in the classroom.
>
> As the scheme progressed, it was clear that many pupils were receptive, others quiet, but mostly curious. Some classes were very quiet and reluctant to discuss openly but would approach the teacher later with comments or questions. We then started to have real 'moments.' One boy from a deeply religious background was troubled by the content. His attitude was one of confusion. 'Why do gay people have to come out at all?' and 'Was this really a suitable book to be read in school?' The staff handled questions like this with understanding and patience. Despite my early and deepest fears, there were still no confrontations resembling those I had imagined. The Year 9 boy I mentioned earlier, who had been subjected to frequent homophobic bullying, wrote three sides on the bullying of Justin Fashanu[14] before proudly coming out himself on the final page.
>
> While in some classes discussions flourished, in others they did not. In an effort not to lead discussion too much themselves, some teachers felt that pupils lacked the confidence to lead and offer their views, whilst some were shocked into silence.
>
> This was our first time teaching this particular text and we are now empowered and galvanised to go on to address some of these issues. We intend to encourage more silent debates and include more personal writing within the scheme. The scheme provides invaluable insights into a range of different cultures, including LGBTQ+. More importantly, it allowed us to challenge prejudice and misconceptions and gave a voice to pupils often sidelined – or immobilised – by homophobic culture in school.

Commentary

In Chapter Two I wrote about texts as mirrors and windows. *The Black Flamingo* is one such text. It allows LGBTQ+ students to see themselves, much like the story's protagonist, placed centre stage. For other students, texts like this open a window to the life of someone who might not be like them, but, just possibly, could be someone they might like. It helps them to reflect and ask questions.

It's not just English teachers who can diversify their curriculum. Whether you teach history, science, or maths, the life stories of LGBTQ+ people are found everywhere, and it's our job to seek them out and use them not only to inspire and engage students, but because of their inherent educational value also.

Coming out as a trans female in school

Becky, South-West England

I knew from a teenager that I felt differently to other boys. I hated my name but couldn't say why. I always looked longingly at women and their clothes, and I struggled to feel happy when good things happened to me. It took me a few years to realise that I was transgender but by this time I was in a healthy (and heterosexual) relationship, so coming out didn't seem like a viable option. I never felt a relief when I realised I was trans when I was younger, since I had to hide myself away for fear of what I thought society's reaction would be. I hate that I had these thoughts for so long and internalised everything rather than being brave enough to speak about it.

Fast-forward a few years. I decided to become a teacher to feel like I was doing something worthwhile for me and the world. I did my teacher training and found a school where I felt at home and the staff were very welcoming. I began working and was known by my deadname[15] for two years, feeling that this school was one of the only places I felt comfortable and happy, largely because of my colleagues.

All went along smoothly until one day, by chance, my wife discovered I was trans. I spent several months in a deep depression until we both realised that me transitioning was the best thing for both of us. For a few months, I felt very alone and listless. I decided that as enough people in my personal life knew that I was trans, it was now time to start with people at work. The first person I told was a learning support assistant – let's call her 'T' – whom I had got to know well. We were speaking about a student who I was helping; a non-binary Year 11 student who I will call 'J'. I asked T, 'Do our counsellors also help staff who know they are trans and have been hiding it for more than years?'

The next day T rushed into my classroom and gave me a massive hug. That's the point when I knew I could make it and wouldn't have to be alone. If nothing else, I had T.

The next person I told was a fellow maths teacher – to be known here as 'L' – who ran the LGBTQ+ club. I helped her out one day and afterwards, I told her I was trans. She would go on to become my biggest ally at school that year. She convinced me that the next person I needed to tell should be my head of department. She pretty much dragged me into his office and held my hand while I shook, cried, and just about got the words out. I am so glad she hauled me into that little room. My head of department and I then discussed how to tell the team. I wanted them to know who I was so, together, we wrote a speech and agreed that he would deliver it. He was so supportive throughout, sharing my story with the rest of my colleagues at the end of our next department meeting. I sat, hoping throughout that the ground would swallow me up.

I needn't have worried.

One colleague came up to me to put me in touch with her trans cousin. Another asked me about my pronouns and how I came up with the name Becky. Several more texted me that night to tell me how brave I was and that they were there to support me. I had the backing of my whole department. Actually, the word 'backing' doesn't begin to cover the extent of the support they offered, and 'department' doesn't do justice to the way I felt about these people now. They were more than a department. They were family.

One day, the student I mentioned earlier – J – and I were talking about body image issues. J already had a clue that I was LGBTQ+ so when I mentioned I was trans, their face lit up. This moment is etched on to my memory forever. They finally had someone who knew what they were going through. Finally – someone who could support them who *really* understood.

I told a few more trans students over the next few weeks and the overall response was the same; they felt that they had someone to represent them, and they felt seen. I was a teacher who was not just an empathetic ally, but an adult who had experienced a similar journey that they were now on. I will never forget these moments. It's why I teach – to help the students to grow and to support them.

The principal at the school was supportive from the moment she heard my story. She let me choose my own timeline, choose how staff were informed and everything else that goes into transitioning openly. I didn't feel pressured at all. This is how staff should be treated. She made it so easy and was so laid back about it. She also saw the change in me and how, as time went on, I became happier and more confident.

The lowest moment of my coming-out year was during a Year 8 class one Tuesday morning in July. The class came in very excited about something; there were lots of giggles and stares and I couldn't work out what was going on. I had recently come out on Facebook, so it took me a few minutes to realise the two things were related. I felt very unnerved too, as I had the sense I couldn't control what was going on in my class. At break time I went into the department office. Several colleagues came in and asked if my Facebook security settings were set to 'Private.' They were, but someone in that Year 8 class had somehow seen my profile photo and my name, and worked out I was trans. They had posted a screenshot of my profile to their own social media story thread, and it had gone around the school like wildfire.

I experienced so many emotions for the rest of the day. My head felt loud. Unbearably loud.

By the end of the day, L had convinced me that what had happened with Year 8 was actually a good thing. The classes she had taught that day were obviously talking about it, but were all very positive, wanting to know how to address me, wanting to ask questions, and generally not wanting to get it wrong. At that point, I realised that all the student had really done, in outing me, was speed up my own coming-out timeline by about a fortnight. It was July, and I was returning to school in September as myself, so was planning to tell students at the end of term anyway. Although I hated being the current 'hot topic' of conversation around school, I knew that things would have settled down by September, so it would be easier for me in the long term.

The principal subsequently sent an all-staff email confirming the students' rumours and outlining the school's support for my transition. After this, I received several supportive messages from colleagues.

> It was now time to take stock of where I was. All the staff knew, most of the students knew and, by extension, their parents now knew as well. I thought it best to tell my classes directly, so they knew it was okay to ask questions of me. Of course, they had questions, which I answered as honestly as I could. I had an amazing response from them all. They sat completely silently whilst I told them who I really was and most of them started addressing me as 'Miss' straight away. I had worried about the student response and how they would react, but I needn't have. Students mostly have such an open-minded worldview that they accepted me without judgement.
>
> When I finally came to the decision to transition last year, I felt such relief as I realised I *could* have a chance at happiness. Previously, I had arrived at a point where I thought the only two options available to me were either transition or suicide. And with the prospect of transition being so daunting I had tried and – so, so luckily – failed on the second option. I realised that I could make the first choice – to transition – and try to be happy with my body, and my life. Starting my transition was the best thing I have ever done. I have felt emotions I have never even known existed. I have felt loved and wanted. I know that helping my LGBTQ+ students to find themselves is my calling in life.
>
> I absolutely don't regret coming out and I can't wait to go back to school in September. As myself.

Commentary

Becky's story is an inspiring one. It's a story about Becky's personal experience of transition and the positive impact this process continues to have on her mental health and wellbeing. It's also a story about effective school leadership and effective school communities. Becky's school principal, her head of department, and her colleagues gave Becky a vital source of support in one of the biggest moments of her life.

While Becky has been lucky, we should not ignore the fact that students can bully teachers. Some students will take it upon themselves to target teachers, as well as other students, for homophobic abuse.

Becky's school leaders let her control the narrative and that's what true allyship is about. It's not about stamping out fires, containing situations, or paying lip service to inclusivity. It's about making LGBTQ+ colleagues, pupils, and parents feel included, valued, and loved through actions, rather than words in policy documents. Not everybody is going to be as lucky as Becky, but hopefully this story will make trans people realise that if their school isn't a place where they can *come out*, it's probably time to *get out*.

For the students of LGBTQ+ teachers like Becky, her bravery means that, hopefully, one day, homophobic abuse will become a thing of the past. As we have seen elsewhere in this chapter, supportive leadership teams are vital in helping to shift attitudes and make schools places where everyone can be themselves. Just like Becky.

A whole-school approach to raising inclusivity and tackling homophobia

Laura Evans and Faheem Khan

At Woodbridge High School, an ethnically diverse secondary comprehensive in East London, nothing is more important to us, as senior leaders, than making sure our students feel safe, valued, and celebrated. Perhaps this is because our senior leadership team (SLT) members themselves are hugely diverse – including proudly visible members of the LGBTQ+ community. We have lived experience of racism, sexism, and homophobia.

With over 1,800 students on roll, any widespread policies to support the wellbeing of our cohort need to be based on more than anecdotal feedback from a minority of voices – not all of whom will necessarily represent those students who are most vulnerable. We have found anonymous online surveys to be an invaluable tool in gaining insight into the student experience. We schedule them throughout the year with a clear focus (anti-bullying, wellbeing, or equality) and can compare responses from key demographics. Our most recent survey had responses from over 50% of our student body.

Much of what we do is therefore informed by our diverse cohort. We have empowered students to have a voice and to use that voice. We have established a range of student-led support groups that come together to form our Equality Council, which directly contributes to school strategy. Whether it's our gender-neutral uniform, staff training, our Pride month celebrations, or our new gender-neutral toilets, we do it because LGBTQ+ students tell us it will improve their school experience. We release a 'you said, we did' recap regularly, to show that the surveys do result in change. Embedding these feedback loops throughout the year has meant that our school is – in many important respects – one led by the students, where staff listen and facilitate change where necessary. Students believe us when we say we will listen.

It is incredibly useful to see how areas of focus have improved – or not – year by year, and the surveys have allowed us to pick areas for development that we might otherwise have overlooked. Our first ever wellbeing survey highlighted a real disparity between the experiences of students who identify as gay (mostly positive) and those who are transgender (more negative). This showed us the importance of a more differentiated approach rather than a blanket focus on 'LGBTQ+-phobic behaviour.'

We are rightly proud of our LGBTQ+ work. We do a lot. We know it's important for students to feel seen and heard. A good balance exists between education and celebration. We ensure there is LGBTQ+ representation in the curriculum and have LGBTQ+ staff act as role models. We host student conferences for LGBTQ+ History Month and celebration events for Pride month. It is a privilege to be recognised as a Beacon School by the Local Authority in this area and be chosen to help other schools to support their LGBTQ+ students. As part of this, we host borough-wide events bringing together LGBTQ+ and their allies, the last of which was attended by 225 students from 18 different schools. The day included networking opportunities for like-minded young people to meet, inspiring LGBTQ+ guest speakers, workshops guiding students to create inclusion action plans for their schools, signposting to local LGBTQ+ support groups, and even some fantastic drag performances led by ex-students.

Woodbridge's 'Equality Manifesto' has been created with our students. It is a set of values and shared language around what equality means at our school. This is displayed in classrooms, students' planners, used in PSHE lessons, referred to in assemblies, and in our communication with parents. It's a dynamic and relevant document that we all own and are proud of.

One of our pledges in our equality manifesto is 'We support, not shame.' Our aim is not to make people feel bad about topics or characteristics they may know less about, but to encourage safe spaces for intelligent debate and support individuals who want to find out more about the experiences of others. If a student exhibits homophobic behaviour, we put them on a course that might include 1-1 sessions with key members of staff on 'homophobia and the law,' 'homophobia and mental health,' and our school ethos. Parents are also invited to engage in the same content.

We know that bullying can take place anywhere and that certain groups of students (including LGBTQ+ students) are more at risk of being bullied. We have worked with the Anti-Bullying Alliance to produce an anti-bullying policy that works for us and explicitly references the support the student who has been bullied will receive and the sanction and education the student who displays bullying behaviour will receive. We log if bullying incidents are motivated by any protected characteristic and consider if wider work with friendship groups or year groups is necessary.

Student leadership has been a huge factor in bringing our anti-bullying work to life. We worked with The Diana Award to train our anti-bullying ambassadors: students who organise whole school events to raise awareness/promote inclusivity and manage disclosures of potential bullying as the first step in a whole-school response. We worked hard in our recruitment drive to ensure the demographic of our anti-bullying ambassadors was reflective of our cohort. It was important to us that every student in the school felt they had someone that could at least empathise with their own lived experience of a particular race, gender, or sexuality, while recognising that lived experience is unique to that person, not the collective.

While we were incredibly proud to receive the Gold Award from the Anti-Bullying Alliance as recognition of the work we have done to show improvement in the wellbeing of students and reduction of bullying, our work is never done. We constantly look for new ways to support our LGBTQ+ students. We must do more to support our trans students, ensure we provide more LGBTQ+ role models from ethnic minority backgrounds, and further develop our work on intersectionality.

For us, it all starts with our school ethos: *Kindness, Respect, Diversity, and Excellence*. Everything we do is informed by this. We regularly tell our students that the most important thing they can do is to be kind to themselves and kind to others. We believe that if you get this right, the rest falls into place. We are clear that if we can do it here, any school can. Anywhere.

All any school needs is a champion. That champion could be you.

Commentary

When I first read this essay, I was stunned. There's a lot that schools can learn from this account. This school has listened to the experience of LGBTQ+ people in school and has made practical changes that other schools might shy away from. Gender-neutral uniform *and* gender-neutral toilets, Pride celebrations, a systematic process of garnering student opinion on issues such as inclusion, and the offer of parent education are things that many schools would consider brave. However, for Woodbridge High School, what once was brave, is now the norm.

The final word

What comes through in almost every story is the damage done by the Section 28 legislation. This legislation deprived tens of thousands of LGBTQ+ pupils of the opportunity to see themselves reflected in the literary and cinematic characters their schools could stock or show. It forced an entire generation of teachers into the closet. It denied an entire generation of LGBTQ+ young people the opportunity to be comfortable with their own identity, safe in the knowledge that there were adult role models to learn from and emulate.

As a result, we find ourselves in relatively uncharted territory. Educators like the ones who share their stories here aren't learning from those who have come before them. They're pioneers and role models for a new generation of LGBTQ+ students. Like we saw in our final story from Woodbridge High School, they are taking brave steps.

We must be braver too.

Notes

1. Section 28, introduced by Margaret Thatcher's Conservative government in 1988, and not abolished in England and Wales until 2003, refers to a series of British laws that prohibited the so-called 'promotion of homosexuality' by local authorities. The statute also stipulated that schools should not 'promote the teaching in any maintained school of the acceptability of homosexuality as a pretended family relationship.'
2. A Post-Graduate Certificate of Education is the course that most secondary school teachers undertake to qualify to teach in schools.
3. Newly Qualified Teacher.
4. Stonewall is an organisation advocating for the rights of LGBTQ+ people.
5. *Sexual orientation and attitudes to LGBTQ+ in Britain.* IPSOS survey. (2020). Available at: https://www.ipsos.com/en-uk/sexual-orientation-and-attitudes-lgbtq-britain (Accessed: 28th July 2022).
6. https://www.barnardos.org.uk/blog/why-young-people-need-famous-lgbtq-roles-models
7. Dean Cain played the role of Clark Kent/Superman in the hit 90s show *Lois and Clark: The New Adventures of Superman.*
8. MSN Messenger was an online instant messaging platform, popular with young people in the early part of the 2000s.

9 I discovered, after the fact, that the age of consent for homosexuals was only reduced to 16 (same as for heterosexuals) in 2000 (see The Sexual Offences (Amendment) Act 2000). This was only a few years before this part of my story occurred.
10 Introduced in the 1990s, these are stickers which announce to students, without the need for any discussion, that the school, or a designated space within the school, is LGBTQ-friendly and supportive. They are widely available to purchase on several internet sites.
11 More information can be found here: https://rshp.scot
12 Introduced in 2016, Progress 8 is an accountability measure which determines students' progress from starting points across eight subjects at GCSE by comparing students, nationally, who have similar prior attainment at Key Stage 2. Progress 8 replaced the previous 5 A*–C measure which was used, crudely in many cases, to compare the performance of schools without considering the prior attainment of the students in question.
13 The Carnegie Medal is an award conferred by the Chartered Institute of Library and Information Professionals. It recognises, annually, one outstanding new English-language book for children or young adults.
14 Justin Fashanu was a Black professional footballer who, after coming out publicly in 1990, faced immense criticism and a huge backlash from the media, the wider Black community at the time, and even from his own brother. He died by suicide in 1998.
15 'Deadname' is the term used by some trans people to refer to their birth name, following the trans person's name change upon transitioning. 'Deadnaming' is when someone, intentionally or not, refers to a person who is transgender by the name they used *before* they transitioned. Deliberately deadnaming a trans person – in other words, refusing to use or acknowledge their trans name – is considered to be an act of invalidation or even harassment of trans people.

References

https://www.barnardos.org.uk/blog/why-young-people-need-famous-lgbtq-roles-models
Sexual orientation and attitudes to LGBTQ in Britain. IPSOS survey. (2020). Available at: https://www.ipsos.com/en-uk/sexual-orientation-and-attitudes-lgbtq-britain (Accessed: 28th July 2022).

7 Sport and physical activity

The story

Physical Education in school basically consisted of football and only football, and from Year 8 onwards I just refused to take part because of the humiliation. Humiliation which came from the teachers laughing and making snide, often horrendous comments to me, along with the other lads in my class, about my sexuality. In one lesson, I distinctly overheard one Physical Education teacher say to another: 'I bet if there was a dick in the middle of the field, he'd run towards it.'[1]

Sachin Patkar

I had a Physical Education teacher at school who singled me out a few times, especially in rugby. I was small and he named me, 'The Big Fairy.' This led to humiliation in the changing room, alienation from any kind of social group beyond the small group of friends I had, and a fair amount of self-loathing around my own body image.

Billy Batchelor

I developed an absolute hatred of football in school because it was for 'the lads.' I used to dread those sessions because I could not handle the changing room 'banter' of homophobic comments and harassment, which were always ignored by the teacher.

Mikael Garson

I was never sporty, and Physical Education was almost always something competitive – football, basketball, and the like. I was regularly called a 'gay-boy' by the other boys as I floundered about, trying my best. The male Physical Education teachers never did anything to stop it and once or twice they told me that I needed to 'man up,' or that my efforts were pathetic.

Scott Ong

These stories, relayed to me on Twitter in response to an appeal for stories about damaging experiences of Physical Education whilst at school, will be familiar to many of us. To others – whose athletic physiques and sporting abilities protected them from the bullying and abuse dished out to those who weren't so gifted – they will be completely alien. But, as I found out during the research for this chapter, the misconception held by many a former non-sporty boy (or girl), that Physical Education lessons are essentially hell on earth, is being tackled – pun fully intended – head on, as this case study demonstrates:

Case study: the Boys Move initiative

Written by Paul Beeson, Deputy Head of Lower School and Physical Education Support Leader, Herne Bay High School

Herne Bay High School was offered the chance by the Youth Sport Trust to be part of a new Physical Education (PE) initiative focused on the substantial mental health and wellbeing concerns surrounding boys in today's social climate. We jumped at the chance. In our initial sessions, designed to assess the problems the boys – mostly from low-income households in the coastal town where we're based – were facing, it soon became clear that their main issues were a lack of drive, depression, anger, and apathy. The task in front of us seemed gargantuan but, nevertheless, we worked with the Youth Sport Trust (YST) to develop a pilot for the Boys Move initiative, which is now being rolled out nationally.

The success of the original pilot means that we have continued with the project. Each year, we identify a target group of young males who are at real risk of making some potentially life-changing bad choices and we work with them, using the power of physical activity, to help them better understand the options available to them and hopefully make better choices. Our groups typically consist of around ten boys who meet weekly to cover the programme that has been designed, reviewed, and updated to meet their specific needs.

The kinds of sessions the boys engage in are as follows:

Dodgeball

Here, students write something that 'triggers' or annoys them on a dodgeball. The game then commences and at random points it is paused. During the break, a ball is chosen, and the topic written on it is discussed as a group. How could this trigger/annoy someone? How may they react? What advice would we give them to make a better choice during their reaction?

Tug of war

Students are divided into two teams, with one team symbolising things that positively impact our mental wellbeing and mood, and the other representing those things that negatively impact our mental state. We discuss what these positive and negative things might be. For example, a positive thing might be a good night's sleep, or a joke with a friend. A negative thing might be an argument with a friend, or feeling frustrated with homework. Then an adult or two joins 'Team Negativity' and this team wins. Inevitably, this leads to a discussion around life's fairness – or lack of it – and how sometimes things happen which are out of control. The discussion moves to what we can do to overcome the curveballs (as well as the dodgeballs) that life throws at us, and we try and angle the conversation towards the importance and effectiveness of asking for help. Students are then encouraged to ask for help and as they do so, the adults in the session come to the positive side and Team Positivity wins, demonstrating the benefits of asking for help and sharing the load. Perhaps it's corny, but it gives many of the boys a palpable experience and a visual representation of the effectiveness of asking for help when faced with problems in the future.

Laser tag

We are extremely lucky to have laser tag sets at our school. However, you don't need a big budget to harness the benefits of this activity. Traditional touch tag can be used as well. In this session, students create an indoor arena in the space, turn the lights down, and play laser tag. Sometimes we put disco lights on! As the game is happening, the adult session facilitator projects onto the main screen a collage of the types of social media images which place pressure on young people and the way their bodies 'should' look. The game is paused periodically, and the pictures are discussed. *How do the people in the images look? Is this realistic? What pressure do images such as these put on young people?* The game continues and later is paused again. *If these images are having a negative impact, why do we still look at them? Are we surrounded by them on television, in magazines, and on social media? How do we get away?* Again, play continues. Finally, we stop and discuss the game of laser tag we have just had. *The room was dark, and everyone played and participated. The targets and guns worked the same for everyone regardless of how they looked and dressed. If we can experience success and joy like this, and recognise and understand this, how can we transfer it to our everyday life? How can we take this confidence with us and get rid of – or minimise – the negative pressure that the media forces on us?*

Walk and talk

These sessions are a little more tailored to meet participants' individual needs and tend to be on a one-to-one basis. Students walk around the site with an adult and discuss their week, their feelings, sometimes even the weather – it really can be anything. During the session, we try to advise the student of some coping strategies that they could try. We also review how previously discussed coping strategies have worked in practice. Ultimately, the aim of this session is simple; it is to teach that a problem shared is a problem halved.

> Students can initially be slow to discuss how they're feeling, with a preference for engaging in the activities, but as the weeks go on and relationships build, meaningful conversations begin, and this is where the real difference happens.
>
> **Case study commentary**
>
> *The argument, or at least the perception, might be that it is problematic for these students to miss other lessons to participate in this initiative, or, even worse, that they are having low expectations foisted upon them because they are 'let off' academic subjects to go and do a bit of sport. But this misses the point. The much bigger picture is that these boys are building their resilience to engage with school and to reduce potentially damaging thoughts and feelings – the impact of which will be far greater on their longer-term success than one or two missed maths or history lessons.*
>
> *The Boys Move initiative at Herne Bay High School is wonderful in the way that it makes the link between physical activity and mental wellbeing so explicit. It's a shame it's not something happening in all schools because there is a long-established link between physical activity and improved adolescent mental health.*

The research

Physical activity and mental health in children and adolescents

A large-scale US study of over 35,000 children and adolescents aged six to 17 from 2019 looked at the impact of physical exercise on children with anxiety and depression. The study found that:

> Children and adolescents who engaged in no days of physical activity had significantly greater odds of having an anxiety diagnosis than those who met the physical activity guideline of daily engagement in physical activity…
>
> …Likewise, a lack of participation in any physical activity or extracurricular activities was associated with a greater likelihood of depression for adolescents, compared to those who engaged daily in these behaviours.[2]

Traditionally, studies have shown that it is daily 'moderate' to 'vigorous' exercise that is required to reduce the likelihood of anxiety and depression in children and adolescents. However, this same 2019 study discovered something new:

> engaging in *even occasional* physical activity might be important to reduce the likelihood of anxiety and depression for adolescents. In other words, some physical activity, although not daily or longer than 60 min, is better than none for mental health outcomes [my emphasis].[3]

A six-year longitudinal study in the UK, published in 2020, looking at the mental wellbeing of adolescents aged 12, 14, and 16, has also highlighted the positive benefits that just 'light' exercise can have on wellbeing, stating that, 'An additional hour of light activity [which the study describes as exercise such as 'walking at a casual pace'] per day between age 12 years and 16 years was associated with an 8–11% decrease in depression scores.'[4]

Whilst the news that minor engagement in exercise can improve mental wellbeing is promising, the study also, sadly – and, perhaps, unsurprisingly – found that as children got older, they were less likely to exercise. This should be of some concern:

> An additional hour of sedentary behaviour per day was associated with an 8–11% increase in depression score at 18 years, and participants with persistently high or average sedentary behaviour levels between ages 12 years and 16 years had significantly higher depression scores at 18 years compared with those with persistently low sedentary behaviour.

Put simply, if we want to decrease the likelihood that children experience anxiety and depression now and also when they're adults, we must get them moving more whilst they're kids. Easy, right?

Apparently not.

Barriers to physical exercise

According to research[5] from Sport England, in the academic year 2019/2020, only 45% of young people were meeting the Chief Medical Officer's[6] guidelines of taking part in sport and physical activity for an average of 60 minutes or more every day, whilst 31% were doing less than an average of 30 minutes a day. The COVID-19 pandemic inevitably would have had some impact on these findings, yet to blame children's lack of physical activity on this alone would be to ignore the fact that students are getting much less physical education in schools than they used to. A survey[7] of nearly 600 Physical Education teachers, conducted by the Youth Sport Trust – whose aim it is to improve students' physical and mental wellbeing through sport and play – showed that in 2018, the minutes given to Physical Education lessons or activities in Key Stage 3 had declined by 20% over the previous five years, whilst the decline in minutes timetabled for Physical Education at Key Stage 4 was a staggering 38%. In other words, at an age where students become more sedentary, and more susceptible to developing a mental health disorder such as anxiety or depression, they are, quite perversely, getting *less* opportunity to exercise during the school day. Interestingly, in the same survey, 38% of Physical Education teachers attributed the decline in provision to the fact that core subjects have been given additional curriculum time.

PE or Physical Education?

Traditionally, the subject 'Physical Education' is referred to as 'PE' in schools: students take part in PE lessons in which they're taught the PE curriculum by PE teachers who belong to the PE department.

In this chapter, despite 'PE' being the language I am accustomed to, and despite 'PE' being 15 letters fewer to type than 'Physical Education,' I will be using the terms 'Physical Education' and 'physical education' throughout.

There are several reasons for this:

Firstly, for many people, the phrase 'PE' conjures up dreadful memories of the days when Physical Education lessons were synonymous with humiliation, abuse, and feelings of inferiority, often facilitated and perpetuated by cruel and sadistic Mr Sugdens[8] in short shorts.

Secondly, the phrase 'Physical Education' is preferable because the word 'physical' reminds us that Physical Education isn't just, as you'll soon read, about competitive sports. It's about *movement*, for all students, regardless of so-called 'ability.'

Finally, too many people fail to remember that Physical Education teachers are just that: educators whose job is no less important than that of any other teacher in a school.

The male Physical Education teacher: a surprising obstacle

The Youth Sport Trust's report into exercise and the mental wellbeing of boys, *What about the boys?*[9] found a surprising barrier to boys' willingness to engage in physical activity at school. Chris Wright, Head of Health and Wellbeing at the Youth Sport Trust, told me more about this:

> Interestingly, the male Physical Education teacher is a real barrier for boys at school. Previous Youth Sport Trust research showed that roughly 85% of male Physical Education teachers are competitive team sport-oriented, so when you look at the curriculum and what Physical Education departments are delivering, their provision is largely competitive team sports. And for the vast majority of boys, regardless of what the press or received wisdom tells you, competitive team sports are not what many boys want.

Barriers to a broad provision

So, if many boys do not want competitive team sports, why are Physical Education departments still allocating large amounts of curriculum time to teaching them? Wright explains further:

> I think it's easy to denigrate Physical Education teachers and say that they're the problem when, as with any other subject, accountability measures impact

what they can offer. They're under the same curriculum pressures as teachers in other subjects, but often, Physical Education teachers don't have the time, because of extra-curricular commitments, to work on developing their expertise. And let's not forget that we've lost 50,000 hours of Physical Education teaching in secondary schools since 2012 because of the overhaul to the education system. Why would any Physical Education teacher take a risk – and put time and effort into – teaching parkour, boccia, or skateboarding when they don't have the time or freedom to ensure they can teach those things well? Naturally, they'll revert to type and teach what they know: that is, competitive team sports.

Wright's frustration is palpable, and compelling. So, what's the solution?

Training is the solution. We're [the Youth Sport Trust] going to schools now and visiting Physical Education departments and we're asking them to completely review their pedagogy. The first thing we always ask Physical Education teachers is, 'Why? Why did you become a Physical Education teacher?' It might have been because they were good at sport, but I'd like to think that for most Physical Education teachers it's because they want to develop other kids in their physical, mental, and social prowess. When you start to unpick their 'why,' it's obvious that most Physical Education teachers want to do something different. We – and by 'we,' I mean school leaders and policy makers – just need to give them permission. We need to release them from the shackles of outdated curricula and expectations and allow them to explore what that looks like.

Poor training is something David Rowlatt,[10] Head of Physical Education in a secondary school in Cambridgeshire, also cites as a major barrier in preventing the introduction of broad curricula that could engage more pupils:

Physical Education teacher training is inadequate for encouraging broad activities. Too many trainees come through with minimal experience of anything outside the traditional and, worse, are often encouraged to get coaching badges in traditional sports. Courses which encourage a broad range of sports in Physical Education are few and far between and too many trainees are dependent on their training placement school. It's just easier to conform to traditional curriculum models.

The othering of non-sporty boys

The opportunity for physical activity does not only present itself in Physical Education lessons. That most cherished of school spaces – the playground – provides ample opportunity for students to engage in physical exercise. Dr Jon Swain, senior research officer at University College London's Institute of Education, spent many years looking at masculinity in schools, playing particular attention to the way boys use sport to construct their masculinity on the playground. Swain notes that boys draw upon many resources to construct their masculinity in the school space: intellectual resources, such as academic capability; economic resources, such as shows of material wealth, and cultural resources, such as being most in tune with the latest fashion, music, and social media trends. However, as Swain states, 'the most esteemed and cherished resource…[is] connected with an embodied form of physicality and athleticism.'[11] For many boys, the playground game of football provides an opportunity to practise the masculinity expected of them.

Unfortunately, when the dominant masculinity relies on athletic bodies and displays of sporting prowess, boys who do not conform to these expectations become othered, often in quite toxic ways. Swain refers to these boys as members of the 'subordinate group.' In one study, he notes:

> The subordinate group of boys were barely granted a look-in during the games of playground football and were also conceptualised as 'other' by the dominant group. Although they were sometimes allowed to occupy the same space on the pitch, they were not really part of the game: they were largely ignored, hardly got a kick of the ball, and were frequently publicly derided and ridiculed for their lack of skill and prowess.[12]

It gets worse:

> …This group of boys became feminised and subjected to various types of homophobic commentary in the form of name-calling such as 'Gaylord' and 'Poofter,' and remarks like, 'Why don't you go and play with the Brownies?'[13]

In Swain's observations, the dominant group of boys used accusations of homosexuality and/or femaleness as an insult for the non-sporty boys. People would be forgiven for thinking that Swain's observations, recorded over 20 years ago, are no longer relevant. These people would also be wrong. I interviewed Head of Physical Education, Darryn Knight,[14] who told me:

> 'Toxic masculinity' has been embedded in Physical Education lessons and school sport for years. My first-hand experience would have been when I was a child at school. Showing emotion was a weakness, a dent in our armour. We were told by the Physical Education teachers to maintain 'hardness' and to never show any kind of feelings. I often witnessed boys crying after making mistakes and being told to 'grow up' and to 'man up' by teachers and those around them. The changing rooms were ruled by hierarchy and violence and that was just the teachers; staff would sit in their office as we changed and then come and give a series of beatings for those students who didn't 'fit' the system. You were either a 'tough guy' or 'weak' and you would be punished for not fitting in.
>
> During my teenage and early adult years, I continued to play sport and the 'boys will be boys' attitude would continue to dominate changing

rooms. Extremely offensive and sexist language was the norm, and the most dominant boys in the team would be the architects of these themes. The toxic culture of the changing room was excused as 'banter.' The term 'banter' is a poisonous, dangerous, and shamefully easy way out for the perpetrators of such abuse.

Now, as an experienced Physical Education Teacher who has worked in a range of state and independent schools, many changing rooms are the same. Many changing rooms are still a breeding ground for 'banter.' I've witnessed staff ignore the noise or even get involved in order to 'build relationships' with the hard-to-reach students. This will be uncomfortable reading, but it's real hand experience. Boys will try to imitate the toxic masculine behaviours exhibited by their role models on TV and on social media and for some reason the school changing rooms have become a safe and acceptable space for them to do this. I've had to interrupt many conversations, for example, where I've caught boys talking disrespectfully about the women they've seen on programmes like *Love Island*.[15]

The 'toxic culture of the changing room,' as Knight terms it, extends beyond the changing room and into the lesson space, as attested by the frankly astonishing, highly troubling accounts, from recent school leavers, which opened this chapter.

Whether it's on the playground, in changing rooms, or in Physical Education lessons, sport in schools can still lead to some boys being ostracised and bullied for their lack of sporting or physical ability, whilst those that excel in sport can find themselves as part of a culture where toxic expectations of masculinity are expected, perpetuated, and encouraged.

The solutions

A. Reframe the role of the Physical Education teacher

Bullying, competitive Physical Education teachers such as the infamous Mr Sugden from Barry Hines' *A Kestrel for a Knave* are a thing of the past. The following case study illustrates how one school has reflected on the role and perception of the Physical Education teacher and made positive changes in the Physical Education department to improve physical and mental outcomes for students.

> **Case study: it starts at the door**
>
> Thomas Green, Head of Athletic Development, St Peter's RC High School
>
> Within a school, Physical Education departments operate in the grey expanse of a teacher's remit, sitting somewhere between traditional academic delivery and creating a hardworking, model citizen. Whilst this role isn't exclusive to the Physical Education

teacher, something about the shorts, a strong whistle and inconsistent tan lines seems to command an additional element of respect from many students – in particular, the boys.

It starts at the door.

Sport, for many students, can act as the anchor of the school journey, encouraging students to navigate the daily challenges that they may face. Every sport has its own rhythm that connects with students in their own unique manner and allows them to express themselves and transcend their own preconceptions of social stereotypes. The physical nature of the subject allows staff to highlight the importance of individuality whilst reinforcing behaviours that are expected of us as adults. This makes us incredibly mindful of our language and the way we conduct ourselves. From an academic standpoint, the contributory role of exercise on retention and learning is well documented but is often forgotten within a school environment (Ferrer-Uris et al., 2022).

Our contribution to the development of young men is not just through their physical education, but in demonstrating that varied personalities, abilities, and approaches are vital to a functioning society. Psychology will tell us that motivation, resilience, emotional cognition, self-control, and emotional regulation are all developed through sport (Cronin et al., 2022), so we pay close attention to how our students interact with one another and engage with challenge as they grow with us. Irrespective of ability, we have shared views of the type of young men we want leaving our gates after their tenure. Reverse engineering this process is a challenge, but the expectation that older students act as role models for the younger ones helps to make this more transparent. We also get this wrong, in small ways, on a daily basis, but we are a department that reflects, explores feelings – both mentally and physically – and will apologise.

We work hard to provide objectives and personal feedback that are achievable, whilst stretching students in our attempt to develop their own appreciation of 'intensity.' We praise the behaviours we wish to see and identify solutions to barriers, either real or perceived. As a team, we deliver these messages from different heights, tones, and timbres of voice, but the *message* is the same.

To ensure that our expectations are transparent, we have made a substantial investment into our Physical Education provision. Regular meetings have allowed the department to get on the same page regarding session structure. Every term, a new warmup specific to the sport is designed and carried out by the entire school. This process enables students to safely engage with a host of movement skills whilst working under time pressure. Over the first two weeks, teachers lead these so that the movements and terminology are modelled expertly. This allows demonstrations to be clear and to prevent any misinterpretations or misconceptions developing for the students. After this, specific students are allocated as leaders then assigned to certain portions of the warmup to model and peer-coach. Here, we are not only developing leadership, but an individual's ability to show vulnerability and receive help from another male. This process develops accountability and empowers our young men to know that, as a group, we are going to work diligently together as a team. A strong routine ensures that high standards are maintained and that these do not drift throughout the year.

> The first ten minutes of our lessons are dedicated to moving well and developing a student's appreciation of what hard work feels like. Does this fuel the narrative that young men should be strong, robust, and resilient? Yes. We believe they should be. We do this to combat the poor postural habits that students typically develop through a day spent sitting and ensure that students do not fear breathlessness, a dry throat, or discomfort within the context of an exercise routine. These are normal experiences that should accompany a successful Physical Education lesson. Students understand, acutely, the benefits of a well-structured warmup. Students will be self-regulating, aware of their movement deficiencies, and empowered to know that progression doesn't happen just because you wish for it. Anything worth earning takes time. A valuable lesson in all aspects of life, and a useful analogy for reluctant learners to carry into their academic lessons.
>
> Although we must provide an outcome-based assessment, we focus more on rewarding their own individual improvement. We vigorously challenge any negative attitudes or perceptions they have towards Physical Education. A shift in motivation and health usually accompanies this mindset. We encourage them to become their own expert in the assessment process whilst learning to avoid the debilitating impact of peer comparison amongst males.
>
> When working with young men, managing young male ego is an important part of the Physical Education teacher's role. The strongest guarantee of disengagement in our subject is a hostile and unsupportive culture. Success in our subject can therefore look very different, depending on the student context. Ensuring that individuals are given personal targets shifts their focus of attention inwards, allowing them to develop confidence in their ability to impact their physical health and, most importantly, their emotional and mental wellbeing.
>
> **Case study commentary**
>
> *The philosophy underpinning the approach here – which focuses on long-term progress for all students, regardless of their ability – could yield positive results in all school subjects. Curricula that focus on creativity, confidence, and resilience, rather than assigning a student exclusively with only a grade boundary could see long-term shifts in engagement, which could have really positive outcomes, particularly with boys who are disengaged in more traditionally academic subjects.*

B. Emphasise the mental health benefits of sport

In a study I mentioned at the start of this chapter, researchers recognised that, 'physical activity guidelines and strategies should more directly focus on the mental health benefits of activity.'[16] Strategies to promote physical activity are too focused on the physical benefits: better coordination, improved bone strength, cardiovascular benefits, and improved skill at a particular sport or exercise. However, the study's researchers believe:

> Given the early onset and increasing prevalence of depression in adolescents, promoting activity for its mental health benefits could be a more relatable message for young people to increase their activity.[17]

Excellent work around mental health is being done in schools all over the country which means that now, many students recognise the importance of good mental health. Not only this, but many schools are ensuring that students are well-equipped with the language of mental health. With this in mind, speaking about sport and exercise, but framing this with the additional benefits for sustaining good mental health, could be a great way of getting otherwise disinterested children engaged in sport and physical activity.

The following case study details how Lee Sullivan, author of *Is Physical Education in Crisis? Leading a Much-Needed Change in Physical Education*, completely overhauled his Physical Education curriculum to ensure that it became inextricably linked with mental wellbeing. It's quite remarkable:

Case study: a Physical Education concept curriculum

Lee Sullivan, Head of Physical Education, Upton Court Grammar School

It is well-documented that Physical Education's predominant form of delivery is a sport technique- and performance-focused perspective, which can often be criticised for being exclusionary and elitist in nature. After many years of teaching Physical Education, I found myself questioning my own future within education. I had lessons taken away and given to more 'academic' subjects, I was seeing the same sporty students at every extra-curricular club, and our own student voice surveys told us that a significant proportion of students were either not enjoying Physical Education or did not see the value in it. We were failing to nurture **physical literacy** – a term that describes the motivation, confidence, physical competence, knowledge, and understanding that develops in order to maintain physical activity at an appropriate level throughout life.[18]

Sadly, my thoughts were being echoed nationally, with only 51% of students strongly agreeing that they enjoyed sport,[19] with less than half of young people doing the recommended 60 minutes of physical activity per day.

Like in many Physical Education departments across the UK, my sports-driven curriculum was failing to meet the needs of my students and nurture their physical literacy. When a curriculum is obsessed with performance and proficiency, inevitably those not in the elite group will fail, which can have disastrous long-term ramifications. When referring to individuals who show little to no motivation in later life to engage in physical activity, Margaret Whitehead stated that 'establishing and maintaining physical literacy is highly dependent on experiences which individuals have encountered in respect of their involvement with physical activity.'[20]

It can be argued that the sports-driven curricula employed by the majority of Physical Education departments across the country are doing more harm than good. Whilst complex issues like childhood obesity and poor mental health are not the fault of Physical Education departments, Physical Education departments could design curricula and provide positive experiences that could reduce these issues long-term. For too long, we have not harnessed the full learning potential of sport.

Sport is so much more than techniques, skills, rules, and competition, but this was all we were delivering. Following extensive research, conversations with many other physical educators, and numerous hours spent reflecting, I realised that the future of Physical Education could in fact be very different. I was inspired by Julie Stern's work on conceptual learning; Margaret Whitehead and Elizabeth Durden-Myers' work on physical literacy, and practitioners including Alan Dunn and Lewis Keens, Phil Mathe and Will Swaithes. I now understood that Physical Education teachers had an opportunity like never before to re-examine what our subject has to offer.

A concept-driven approach to curriculum design is one that moves away from subject-specific content and instead emphasises 'big ideas' that span multiple subject areas. The purpose of the Concept Curriculum was to provide an inclusive hook for those students that had not previously been engaged through the sport-driven focus of a Physical Education lesson. It was to provide a positive experience within Physical Education so that students can build a strong positive relationship with physical activity, develop confidence and competence, and continue to reap the benefits of long-term engagement with physical activity for the rest of their lives.

Here are our five concepts, as they're taught across the school:

- **Year 7**: physical literacy
- **Year 8**: personal development
- **Year 9**: character development
- **Year 10**: leadership skills
- **Year 11**: active for life

The evidence is clear that if students experience negative experiences within Physical Education, they are more likely to be sedentary later in life. Our bread and butter as Physical Education teachers is to get the children active for sustained periods of time and develop movement competence. We should not replace physical activity or developing competence with character building, but we should offer learning that students deem to be more relevant to their lives and therefore more meaningful.

I believe that through a concept curriculum we can enhance the opportunity of meeting these two objectives by looking to develop character. Imagine a Physical Education lesson in which the focus is not only on the sport-specific skill, but that of a concept too, something every student will need in their lives. Take the concept of 'remaining positive' from our unit of work on resilience, for example. We continue to teach our sport-specific lesson, but the sport is no longer the destination; instead, it is the vehicle to relevant and meaningful learning. Here's how it works, in the context of a lesson on 'remaining positive.'

Our Physical Education lessons follow the LEAD structure:

1. **L**esson introduction

Here, students acquire an understanding of the term 'positivity' and what it means to remain positive despite encountering obstacles or failure.

2. **E**xplore, energise, and connect

Students now perform an activity that allows them to explore obstacles, and even failure. Perhaps they'll try a difficult skill such as a lay-up or jump shot in basketball. We want students to see, hear, and feel the concept of 'remaining positive.' We then ask linking questions to embed the learning and highlight the connection between 'remaining positive' and the physical activity. Questions might include: *How did remaining positive impact your progress in the previous task? How are resilience and remaining positive connected? Who demonstrated positivity in the task? How did they demonstrate it?*

3. **A**ctivity

In the main body of the lesson is physical activity. Students learn and practise movements to build competence and confidence within the activity.

4. **D**iscovery

Finally, students are encouraged to engage in self-reflection. Questions are posed, such as: *Give an example of a situation in your past where you have remained positive when faced with a challenge. How can remaining positive support you in another class? How can your understanding of remaining positive enable you to succeed in the future?* Sport-specific skills and physical activity are still vital to the lesson, but they are no longer the evaluative measure as to a student's progress or their ability in Physical Education.

Here is an example of the same process, applied to a lesson on body image:

Lesson concept: body image	
Lesson introduction	**Body image** is the perception that a person has of their physical self and the thoughts and feelings that result from that perception. Ask students to provide their own definition of body image or elaborate on the one given.
Explore, energise, and link	A student-led warmup whereby students conduct their own pulse raiser, static and dynamic stretches. During the warmup, students should discuss the questions raised in the acquire phase. **Link questions** Class discussion: • How are body image and self-worth connected? • What is the connection between body image and mental health? • How might your body image have impacted your ability to be successful in the previous task?
Activity	1. Students engage with a teacher-led mini HIIT workout that models how to motivate others, correct technique, and various movements. 2. Students should create their own HIIT training workout. In their groups, they should have one leader that is able to explain the exercises and discuss correct technique, whilst the remaining members demonstrate the movements, behind the leader.
Discovery	Students self-reflect, using the following question as prompts: • How have you felt about your body in the past? • How did you feel about your body in the lesson today? • How did it support or impact your motivation or confidence? • How can Physical Education support you further in maintaining a positive view of yourself in the future?

After teaching the Concept Curriculum for half a year, we sent out an optional Student Voice survey to every student. We knew the results of this survey would tell us if the curriculum had had the desired impact or not.

The results speak for themselves:

- 99% agree or strongly agree that they understand why physical activity is good for them
- 91% agree or strongly agree that they feel included in their Physical Education lessons
- 93% agree or strongly agree that they highly value Physical Education as part of their curriculum
- 87.5% value the learning they get from the Concept Curriculum
- 90% agree or strongly agree that the learning from the Concept Curriculum is relevant and meaningful
- 80% believe that the Concept Curriculum has improved their experience within Physical Education

We should strive to create a positive Physical Education experience for all, not just those that consider themselves 'sporty.' We should reward attitude and progress over performance and ability. We should aim to genuinely nurture physical literacy and build a lifelong relationship with physical activity, so that when students are older, they have the tools to manage and maintain their physical, social, and mental wellbeing. If students receive a bad experience in Physical Education now, it may impact their health and wellbeing forever.

C. Make engagement and participation your focus

Such is the quality of the work being done by the Physical Education Department at Herne Bay High School (see 'Boys Move' case study above), they have been identified by The Youth Sport Trust as a partner school. In this second case study from the school, Head of Physical Education Paul Beeson describes how, after recognising the essential role that regular physical activity has for adolescent wellbeing, he and his team increased measures of engagement for all pupils.

Case study: raising engagement

Paul Beeson, Deputy Head of Lower School and Physical Education Support Leader, Herne Bay High School

Performance. Assessment. Data. Progress. These are the words that fly around a school repeatedly. They are the clarion call of every senior and middle leader. They create demands of all teachers that, over the years, Physical Education departments have felt more inclined to appease. In the fight for Physical Education to be recognised as a core and valuable subject, Physical Education departments have, in part, become guilty of valuing grades and data over physical activity and enjoyment.

The power of Physical Education has never been more important. Beyond the obvious health benefits during a time when obesity and physical inactivity are quickly becoming one of the leading mortality contributors, Physical Education offers lessons around respecting rules and officials, socialising and interacting with others, confidence-building during difficult situations, teamwork and working with others, and the wellbeing benefits the come with just being outside in the fresh air.

Following a departmental review, and off the back of projects with Sport England and the Youth Sport Trust, we decided it was time to do things differently. We scrapped levels, performance targets, grades, and data tracking and we began to focus solely on engagement with physical activity and Physical Education. No data is tracked, no conversations are held around students 'meeting target grades' or 'making expected or below expected progress.'

The only thing we record is a student's engagement. We rate student engagement as follows:

- GREEN for **excellent engagement**: i.e., students do every task to the best of their ability, without questions
- AMBER for **good engagement**: i.e., students do all tasks, mostly to the best of their ability but at times could try harder
- RED for **less than expected engagement**: i.e., students put little effort into tasks

This is where we usually get the screams of, 'No assessment! How do you know students are making progress?' We understand people's perturbation.

We do still have an achievement grid:

	PERFORMANCE **Dedication**	**CHARACTER** **Respect**	**WELLBEING** **Kindness**
EXPERT	**Confidently**: • perform all simple and advanced skills consistently in pressurised situations • select and execute creative tactics successfully • assess whether improvements applied to my weaknesses have been effective	**Champion**: • high levels of engagement throughout the lesson • excellence through performance • the use of ambitious goals/targets to strive for further improvement when I leave school	**Promote**: • health and wellbeing to others • team/group cohesion • self-confidence within others
ADVANCED	**Accurately and fluently**: • combine simple and advanced skills/techniques with creativity • apply creative tactics/strategies to strengthen performance • show comprehensive understanding of how I can measure improvement within skills, techniques, and tactics	**Encourage**: • my peers to have a good level of confidence and self-belief in themselves • my peers to persevere with achieving their own goals/targets	**Continue**: • to develop my health and wellbeing • to have a positive influence on my team/group dynamics • to reflect on my self-confidence

	PERFORMANCE Dedication	**CHARACTER** Respect	**WELLBEING** Kindness
CONFIDENT	Effectively: • perform most advanced skills accurately and fluently • outwit opponents using their weaknesses • consider levels of performance through self- and peer-analysis	Sustain: • a high level of energy throughout the lesson • a level of confidence and self-belief to benefit my performance • my determination to achieve my goals/targets	Reflect: • on improving my own health and wellbeing • on my involvement within my team/group discussion • to improve my self-confidence
DEVELOPING	Clearly: • combine basic skills with evolving advanced skills under pressure • begin to identify strategies to outwit opponents • begin to think of methods to improve weaknesses	Explore: • the value of being physically active • why I need confidence and self-belief in my performances • how I can use goals/targets to improve my physical health	Understand: • how my level of exercise impacts my health and wellbeing • people's differences • the relationship between health and wellbeing

Sport and physical activity **155**

	PERFORMANCE Dedication	**CHARACTER** Respect	**WELLBEING** Kindness
FOUNDATION	Positively: • develop coordination and timing with simple skills • understand when to use skills and tactics • identify my strengths and weaknesses	Positively: • show respect throughout a lesson • understand the link between confidence and self-belief in sport • discuss the importance of being engaged in Physical Education and recognising the benefits of physical activity.	Positively: • apply myself in all aspects of a lesson • contribute to discussions throughout a lesson • discuss the relationship between health and wellbeing
BASIC	Engage: • and perform basic skills • in, and state, the basic techniques used within a sport • and comment generally on my own and others' performances	Engage: • in all tasks throughout the lesson • in discussion throughout the lesson • in identifying why this is important	Engage: • in all aspects of the lesson • alongside my peers • in identifying what health and wellbeing are

156 Sport and physical activity

> However, this grid isn't an assessment tool. Instead, it's used within lessons to identify aims and to get students thinking about their own performance levels. It also allows the students to see what they will be covering or learning about whilst in Physical Education.
>
> Note that the grid does not focus solely on athletic performance. Character and kindness are essential components too. We promote active and healthy lifestyles to young people, whilst teaching them about the role *these positive character traits, along with their wellbeing, have within their lives*. This enables us to lead a curriculum that is broad, inspiring, and engaging for all our students.
>
> Even without our achievement grid, we would argue that Physical Education ran for decades without assessment and still our local, regional, and national sports clubs and teams thrived. But Physical Education isn't just for students who show excellent progress in football. If we want to create excellent footballers, we invite them to our sports clubs or direct them to a coach outside of school. What we really want to see in our Physical Education lessons is students who are improving their physical literacy, who are confident in being active, and who are aware of the innumerable benefits this will bring to their wellbeing. This is something we feel we have achieved.

D. Deal with toxic 'changing room' cultures

Physical Education teacher Darryn Knight's earlier account of toxic changing room cultures makes for depressing reading. But there is some hope, as he explains:

> The toxic culture of the changing room can and should be challenged with supervision and role-modelling, which I am pleased to say are now increasingly common across all schools. There are no excuses anymore, and we must act quickly to see a change in our boys' behaviour. The biggest challenge we face is the dinosaurs left in the system – those who perceive the move towards inclusivity and sensitivity as 'wokeness;' those who continue to push their outdated and elitist views. Thankfully, Physical Education departments are more aware of the rise and success of women in sport and more Physical Education teachers are being inclusive, welcoming, and student-centred when planning and preparing lessons. We, as professionals, have a duty to challenge sexist language and violence and I believe many Physical Education teachers are now leading this wave through kindness, warmth, and an understanding that every student matters and expressing and acknowledging feelings is an important part of developing and becoming a young adult.

Knight's story has significant focus on the importance of inclusivity. One way of making changing rooms more inclusive is to explicitly teach students what is and what is not acceptable in terms of how students talk. Telling students what is and what is not acceptable in terms of how they speak to each other could have a significant impact on ensuring that stigmatisation becomes a recognised abhorrence,

HOW WE TALK IN PE

This changing room along with all sports environments in this school, is a safe and inclusive space. Successful students, successful sportspeople and successful teams lift others up, they don't just put people down. How we talk is an important part of making people feel good about themselves. In this changing room, and in our lessons, this is how we talk:

WE DO	WE DO NOT
Give encouragement to people who falter	Display homophobic, biphobic or transphobic behaviour. Invalidate the lived experience of no cisgendered folk
Talk about our problems with people with trust	Talk negatively about the way people look
Listen to people when they tell us how they are feeling	Talk in an inappropriate manner about topics of a sexually explicit nature. Sexualise other people
Remember that admitting weakness is a sign of strength	Mock people who we think are less good at sport, physical exercise or skills than we are
Voice our disapproval and challenge inappropriate or discriminatory comments	Shout, swear or use aggression towards people who make mistakes

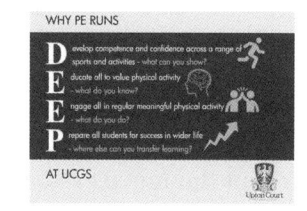

PE IS FOR EVERYONE

Figure 7.1

rather than the norm in schools where there are toxic changing room cultures. Students need to be told, from the outset, what sort of talk is not acceptable on the sports field, in the sports hall, or in the changing room. Teach students – through assemblies or dedicated lessons/parts of lessons – clear guidelines of what are acceptable topics and appropriate vocabularies for conversation. Ideally, Physical Education teachers should deliver these instructions, due to the fact that many boys look up to them as role models. Upton Court Grammar School have created a poster which very clearly outlines the rules of talk in PE at their school (See figure, 7.1 above).

E. Consider setting in Physical Education

In *BDT?* I called the practice of 'setting' students something that 'doesn't work,' 'problematic,' 'determined by unfair factors,' and 'morally wrong.' However, when it comes to Physical Education, setting could have some real benefits, particularly for those boys for whom Physical Education brings the risk of bullying, humiliation, or ostracism.

When I asked about the idea of setting for Physical Education on Twitter, I was surprised at how many schools did set in Physical Education. Naturally, I asked schools about why they did so. David Fawcett, author *Relearning to Teach*, tells me that when he got to his school, setting in Physical Education was already in place:

> But it was done badly. Pupils had been placed into sets based on ability, which is so subjective. Many had been put into lower sets simply because they were naughty, whilst some of the students in the top set had poor fitness levels. It was a mess. We switched to standardised fitness tests with the outcomes based on normative data and this allowed us to set based on fitness, which was determined by five different methods of testing.
>
> Now our sets are a lot more balanced, and students seem happier for it. Previously, children were being physically dominated by other children. Many said they felt intimidated in Physical Education because they couldn't run as fast, or as far, and so gave up. However, now pupils are more closely matched, they feel more confident in competing or working with others in their group.
>
> Our engagement is so much better. Very few students forget kit, ever. Those that do still participate more than they have ever done. Pupils feel safe and supported and I feel that sets may have been a part of this.

Although Fawcett's experience of setting is impressive, I still have reservations about the impact it would have on students' feelings of self-worth, knowing they were being systematically put into sets because they are of lower physical ability than others. And yet, given the research and anecdotes we've read here about the way boys with lesser physical prowess are routinely humiliated and marginalised in Physical Education, perhaps setting *is* something we should consider in Physical Education. I asked Bob Arnold, a Head of Physical Education,[21] about this conflict:

> Honestly, it can go one of two ways. Either less sporty or less active boys tend to be happy because they are away from the 'sporty lads' and can therefore feel more confident in their environment, or they feel that they have been lumped into 'bottom set' and feel demotivated because of it. Personally, I don't feel it is the setting itself that is the main driver of these negative feelings, but the style of teaching and language of the teachers themselves.
>
> I think there is definitely a case that in activities where students have shared ownership over success – such as team games like football, rugby, or netball – students should be set by ability or experience. Can you imagine what it must be like to be partaking in a rugby passing exercise where every time the ball is passed to you by a higher ability or more experienced player of rugby, you drop the ball? That is humiliating and really public. In fact, I don't think there's any subject so public as Physical Education and that can be a real challenge for less confident students. But, I think it's a challenge that setting can mitigate against.

> Setting can create supportive environments for students with those of similar experiences of team sport or physical activity. A disaffected student of Physical Education may be more likely to engage in activity knowing that they're away from the prying eyes of the 'sporty lads.' I think this is probably truer in Physical Education, because of the public nature of all success. In Maths, for example, success or failure isn't public – it's in the exercise book. Whereas in Physical Education, it's very difficult to hide your inability to hit or kick a ball.

Arnold acknowledges the potential pitfalls of setting, but like Fawcett, his argument for setting is compelling.

Unlike Fawcett, Arnold's department doesn't set students according to fitness levels. Instead, because of the role of 'shared success sports' in the setting rationale, students are set on games ability alone:

> We may have very talented gymnasts or swimmers in so-called 'lower' groups, but the team game aspect – and the frustration, anger, resentment, and embarrassment that comes with having students of differing abilities playing team sports together – dictates the set that students end up in.

Whereas in most other subjects I still think setting is morally wrong, I think there's a strong case for setting in Physical Education. Of course, this is only on the basis that all students, regardless of their set, receive excellent teaching based on high expectations, and where the quality of provision isn't determined by the set in which a student is placed.

F. Take a whole-school approach to physical activity

Case study: creating a community leader

I was recently surprised to learn of a school who have gone above and beyond in their attempts to improve activity levels in schools. Camersham Village High School[22] have recently created the post of 'Community Leader' whose job it is to raise awareness of, and engagement with, physical activity within the school community. Some key responsibilities in the role include:

- Work closely with the Physical Education Department and on-site sports centre to raise awareness of the importance of healthy body and mind
- Increase engagement levels with the school's activity spaces
- Identify students to receive free personal training sessions to build confidence with physical activity
- Seek opportunities for outdoor learning

- Build close relationships with feeder primary schools. Duties may include: support with curriculum development; support for delivering primary school PE lessons for primary feeders; leading CPD courses for primary school Physical Education leads
- Work with the catering staff to produce information about the nutritional value of foods served in school
- Produce a newsletter highlighting all physical activity matters in the school community
- Promote increased physical activity engagement with all members of the extended school community

I spoke to James Andrews, head of Physical Education at the school, about the role:

We're lucky enough to have an on-site sports centre. We had a situation where our sports centre closed post-COVID due to several managers leaving all at once, meaning we had to close it for three months. Then, when it reopened, we recognised a huge dip in activity levels, where our incoming Year 7 students and our links with our primary feeder schools had diminished due to COVID. So, increasing the physical activity lessons of incoming students became a big part of our whole-school recovery strategy.

I had already been approached, as Head of Physical Education, to come up with some ways of raising the profile of physical activity across the school community. I suggested various trips and a physical activity magazine that gets shared with students, staff, and parents. These ideas were added to the role of Community Lead that began in September of 2022. The role is in its infancy, but we absolutely intend to involve all school staff in raising physical activity levels somehow. We're going beyond simply putting on 'staff wellbeing sessions' that involve exercise. That's a shallow approach. We will do that, for sure, but in conjunction with other, more impactful ways of increasing activity sessions whole-school, such as engagement with the magazine and fundraising projects.

The role of Community Leader is exciting, and I don't know of any other school employing someone for something like this. To show our commitment to the role, the Community Leader is on a timetable of only about 25% teaching time. This way they can put all their efforts into the project.

Case study commentary

Camersham Village High School has made a staggering investment and commitment to improving physical health outcomes not only for the students, but for all people in the Camersham Village High School community. Yet why should we be surprised? All over the country, schools employ literacy coordinators because they recognise the importance of literacy in future life opportunities. We should not be surprised when a school employs someone whose job is dedicated to improving physical activity levels of students and staff, given the links between physical activity and future happiness and health.

The Creating Active Schools[23] (CAS) programme has been co-developed by researchers and practitioners to support schools in improving physical activity behaviours for their children and young people across the school day and beyond. CAS has provided a high-level overview of five aspects to consider, in order to create an active school. Here, Ian Holmes, CAS Manager at the University of Bradford, provides advice as to how schools can improve their physical activity provision:

1. **Get your policy right**. This is policy in practice, not on paper. Without a clear evidence-based physical activity policy, interventions will not embed. For example, decide your priorities and related benefits – e.g., *decide and agree your priorities and related benefits. Are you promoting physical activity for physical health, mental health, improved social skills, improved cognitive function, or all of the above? Make these clear to the stakeholders (e.g., senior leaders, school staff, children, parents) that need persuading.*

2. **Get your environments right**. Make sure your physical environments (indoors and out) support the physical activity policies you want to put in place. If you want to offer inclusive and varied opportunities to move (rather than traditional sport), do your indoor and outdoor spaces and related equipment/resources reflect this offer?

3. **Consider the capability, opportunity, and motivation of all stakeholders to promote and inspire physical activity**. Regularly consult and involve all stakeholders (senior leaders, staff, children, parents, wider community) in determining and developing your offer, making it everyone's responsibility over time. This will be an evolutionary process, as stakeholders can only provide feedback on what they know and have experienced. For example, boys will often ask for more football because that is their main exposure and what they know; when given the opportunity to build dens and climb trees in a forest area, many will choose this over the playground football match.

4. **Invest in, and improve, physical activity opportunities that have the best outcomes for ALL pupils**. CAS has identified seven opportunities that schools can take advantage of. Four of these are things that schools can control directly:

    i. Physical Education provision

    ii. Physical activity in other curriculum lessons

    iii. Physical activity at breaktimes

    iv. Events/visits related to physical activity

The other three are things that schools can influence:

   i. How students travel to and from school

ii. Community events

iii. Before-school/after-school clubs

Schools should focus on enhancing or adapting those opportunities that will make the most difference to all children in their school. For example, if your most inactive children don't relate to traditional sports, then you could start with addressing your Physical Education curriculum to make it more holistic, inclusive, and diverse. Secondary schools are also beginning to recognise the importance of active breaks/play for older children's ability to focus and perform at their best during lessons.

5. **Take small steps**. Be mindful of wide-ranging school priorities and existing workloads of staff. Look at how physical activity can be integrated into existing routines or parts of the school day, rather than adding further interventions. Think about 'nudge behaviours'[24] and getting as many stakeholders as possible to engage in a small way in the agenda. For example, even in a school with a behaviour policy that potentially conflicts with movement (e.g., silent corridors, students stay at their desk for the whole lesson), can students stand up to answer a question rather than putting their hand up? It isn't just about promoting moderate to vigorous physical activity. If we can reduce children and young people's sedentary time and promote movement that is both engaging and social, we are more likely to encourage wider participation through childhood and into adulthood. In this way, the next generation leads healthier, happier, and ultimately more fulfilling lives.

The final word

It was reassuring, as I conducted research for this chapter, to speak to so many Physical Education teachers who recognise the importance of inclusion in Physical Education. As a profession we need to recognise the important role that Physical Education teachers play in improving life outcomes for students. At the same time, we must not forget that all teachers – regardless of subject – have a role in espousing the benefits of increased physical activity, not only in terms of physical health, but mental wellbeing also.

Notes

1 All names have been changed.
2 Zhu, X., Haegele, J. A., & Healy, S. (2019). Movement and mental health: Behavioural correlates of anxiety and depression among children of 6–17 years old in the U.S. *Mental Health and Physical Activity*.
3 Ibid.

4 Kandola, A., Lewis, G., Osborn, D., Stubbs, B., & Hayes, J. F. (2020). Depressive symptoms and objectively measured physical activity and sedentary behaviour throughout adolescence: A prospective cohort study. *The Lancet Psychiatry*, *7*(3), 262–271.
5 Sport England. (2021). Active Lives Children and Young People Survey: Academic year 2019/20. Available at: https://sportengland-production-files.s3.eu-west-2.amazonaws.com/s3fs-public/2021-01/Active%20Lives%20Children%20Survey%20Academic%20Year%202019-20%20report.pdf?VersionId=4Ti_0V0m9sYy5HwQjSiJN7Xj.VInpjV6 (Accessed: 11th December 2021).
6 The Chief Medical Officer advises the government about all matters relating to health.
7 Youth Sports Trust. (2018). PE provision in secondary schools 2018. Available at: https://www.sportsthinktank.com/uploads/pe-provision-in-secondary-schools-2018---survey-research-report.pdf (Accessed: 11th December 2021).
8 If you don't get this reference, watch *Kes*. But only after you've read the book which inspired the film – it's called *A Kestrel for a Knave* and it's by Barry Hines.
9 Youth Sports Trust. (2021). *What about the boys?* Available at: https://ystcms.youthsporttrust.org/media/2hzn2fnt/boys-metal-health-final-report-2021.pdf (Accessed: 16th July 2022).
10 David Rowlatt is a pseudonym.
11 Swain, J. (2004). The resources and strategies that 10–11-year-old boys use to construct masculinities in the school setting. *British Educational Research Journal*, *30*(1), 167–185.
12 Swain, J. (2000). 'The Money's Good, The Fame's Good, The Girls are Good': The role of playground football in the construction of young boys' masculinity in a junior school. *British Journal of Sociology of Education*, *21*(1), 95–109.
13 Ibid.
14 Darryn Knight is a pseudonym.
15 *Love Island* is a reality TV show where scantily clad young men and women are encouraged to engage in romantic relationships and everything that romantic relationships between scantily clad young men and women might entail, on screen.
16 Kandola, A., Lewis, G., Osborn, D., Stubbs, B., & Hayes, J. F. (2020).
17 Ibid.
18 Whitehead, M. (2010). The Concept of Physical Literacy. In M. Whitehead (Ed.), *Physical Literacy throughout the Life Course* (pp. 10–20). Abingdon, Oxford: Routledge.
19 Sport England (2021).
20 Whitehead, M. (2010).
21 This is a pseudonym.
22 Because the role is in its infancy, the school have asked that their name and the names of teachers be changed.
23 See www.creatingactiveschools.org for further information.
24 Nudges are generally viewed as low-cost, behaviourally informed, choice-preserving solutions to various personal and societal issues. This means that nudges are generally easy to implement, are relatively effective, and allow people to make their own choices (Source: https://effectiviology.com/nudge Accessed: 11th July 2022).

References

https://effectiviology.com/nudge (Accessed: 11th July 2022).
Kandola, A., Lewis, G., Osborn, D., Stubbs, B., & Hayes, J. F. (2020). Depressive symptoms and objectively measured physical activity and sedentary behaviour throughout adolescence: A prospective cohort study. *The Lancet Psychiatry*, *7*(3), 262–271.

Sport England. (2021). Active Lives Children and Young People Survey: Academic year 2019/20. Available at: https://sportengland-production-files.s3.eu-west-2.amazonaws.com/s3fs-public/2021-01/Active%20Lives%20Children%20Survey%20Academic%20Year%202019-20%20report.pdf?VersionId=4Ti_0V0m9sYy5HwQjSiJN7Xj.VInpjV6 (Accessed: 11th December 2021).

Swain, J. (2000) 'The Money's Good, The Fame's Good, The Girls are Good': The role of playground football in the construction of young boys' masculinity in a junior school. *British Journal of Sociology of Education*, *21*(1), 95–109.

Swain, J. (2004). The resources and strategies that 10–11-year-old boys use to construct masculinities in the school setting. *British Educational Research Journal*, *30*(1), 167–185.

Whitehead, M. (2010). The Concept of Physical Literacy. In M. Whitehead (Ed.), *Physical Literacy throughout the Life Course* (pp. 10–20). Abingdon, Oxford: Routledge.

Youth Sports Trust. (2018). PE provision in secondary schools 2018. Available at: https://www.sportsthinktank.com/uploads/pe-provision-in-secondary-schools-2018---survey-research-report.pdf (Accessed: 11th December 2021).

Youth Sports Trust. (2021). *What about the boys?* Available at: https://ystcms.youthsporttrust.org/media/2hzn2fnt/boys-metal-health-final-report-2021.pdf (Accessed: 16th July 2022).

Zhu, X., Haegele, J. A., & Healy, S. (2019). Movement and mental health: Behavioural correlates of anxiety and depression among children of 6–17 years old in the U.S. *Mental Health and Physical Activity*.

8 Body image and eating disorders

The story

Written by James Downs

There was a long time before I was diagnosed with an eating disorder when I struggled with my body image. I was diagnosed with Obsessive-Compulsive Disorder[1] (OCD) when I was a teenager, but most of my preoccupations and behaviours were around the way I looked. I was convinced that others thought I was not just ugly, but offensively hideous – to the point I believed that someone driving on the road would crash their car if they saw me on the side of the road. I did everything I could to minimise how unacceptable I believed my body was to look at, including washing for hours before leaving the house and cutting my own hair every day.

I had been bullied when I was younger for being lanky, skinny, and feminine-looking. I'd also had puberty early, so I stood out because of my body. These experiences drummed into me that the way to fit in as a teenage boy was to look masculine, and that the way you look in general really matters. For me, my OCD was a way of social survival, and this only got worse as I got older and found school even harder to cope with. Slowly the focus of my worries extended to my weight and shape, and because I couldn't fulfil the masculine ideal of being muscly and not skinny, I rejected my body completely and started to lose weight. This is when I was diagnosed with Anorexia, and I have struggled with Anorexia and Bulimia ever since.

I became increasingly unwell, to the point that I had to leave school after my GCSEs. School wasn't supportive. I was extremely high-achieving, and the school was always firefighting behaviour problems and didn't have time to pay much attention to kids they knew would do well anyway. I was left to my own devices quite a lot, and I managed to miss most of a year of school before my parents were asked at parents' evening about where I had been. This is when I went to the doctors and managed to get some help, but the school struggled to understand. They thought that I was arrogant, and that I saw myself as above going to school because I had such good grades. Instead of understanding that I had a mental health problem, they treated me as though I was badly behaved; I didn't have the energy or support to try and get them to understand me and what I needed to take part in school. It was easier to leave and so I did, and just entered my exams without going to classes.

The research

Despite the unhappy stories of men like James, many people regard body image as predominantly a female issue. This is understandable. After all, idealised media portrayals of how women 'should' look have been in existence as long as the media itself. Recent attempts by certain elements of the mainstream media to include women of different shapes and sizes in their adverts, shows, and glossy photo shoots have gained attention, but only because, still, they defy the norm. Cellulite, stretch marks, and bingo wings remain niche in a world that values tiny waists, feline features, and impossible curves.

However, there is plenty of evidence to suggest that concerns about body image are not limited to girls and women. Sun-kissed and statuesque exemplars of male bodily perfection on television programmes such as *Love Island*; social media influencers whose abdominal muscles have abdominal muscles, and quite frankly startling blueprints of the masculine form found in online pornography means that, sadly, body image is a very real problem for many boys and men. One such sufferer was model and actor Tommy Hatto. Tommy now spends time working with the *Global Equality Collective* and goes round schools talking about his own struggles with eating disorders and body image. I spoke to Tommy about his experience of having an eating disorder at school and he provides real insight into the issue, particularly in terms of gender and masculinity:

Tommy Hatto's story

I was a very shy kid. Very introverted. At secondary school, when my friends started to date girls, nobody really put any interest into me. I was into girls, and I'd ask girls out and I'd get rejected. It made me incredibly sad. *Why is nobody paying any attention to me?* was the question I constantly asked myself. I attributed it to the way that I looked, and I started comparing myself to the boys who were always dating – the popular kids, the sporty kids. Also, that was what was being projected in the movies I was watching. In films, it's always the sports guys or the in-shape guys who would date the cheerleaders, whilst the geeky introverted people like me were literally the outcasts.

I wasn't very good at Physical Education. I played lots of computer games and stayed in. Because of this, I guess you could say I had a bit of puppy fat. The summer before my

> last year in school, I went to Thailand to visit family. I remember my family pulling at my body fat and making little comments about it. That was when I first seriously started to think I was fat. So, I decided I'd get in shape.
>
> All I knew about getting healthy was that you had to eat less. I cut out everything. I would have half a grapefruit for breakfast, a single chicken breast for lunch, and then whatever my Dad cooked me for dinner. I started running. I was too insecure to go to the gym, so I'd do muscle work in the garden or in my bedroom. The weight would just fall off. That's where I got into the trap, because losing weight did feel good. Whenever I would hit a plateau I would think, 'I need to get compliments off people. I need to do something more.' So then, I'd eat less and less until I got to the point where I was eating the minimum I could, without eating nothing at all. Then, when I did eat, I would make myself sick.
>
> When people showed concern regarding my weight loss, I became very defensive. I felt as though they were trying to sabotage me, trying to ruin my life. I believed they wanted to prevent me from losing weight and looking good.
>
> I was in and out the doctors'. My hair was falling out, my skin was awfully bad. I had anaemia. And still, I was in denial about having an eating disorder. As a boy, how could *I* have an eating disorder? I couldn't. Eating disorders were a girl issue. And if anybody found out that I was at the doctors' for this, God knows what they would've said. The stigma attached to boys having eating disorders would mean that I'd be perceived as girly, and I'd be bullied even more than I already had been.

Thankfully, Tommy has now recovered and uses his experiences to educate and enlighten others. Hopefully, his work will help to reduce the stigma that prevented him from discussing his own eating disorder and body image issues with someone who could've supported him.

You could say that Tommy's work has never been so important. Research from the Royal College of Psychiatrists shows that between 2015/2016 and 2020/2021, there was a 128% increase in hospital admissions for boys and young men with eating disorders.[2] In 2010 the number of boys in England, Scotland, and Wales going into hospital for an eating disorder was 235. In 2018 the figure was 466.[3] In fact, 2018 was the first time that the number of boys being admitted to hospital for an eating disorder increased at a faster rate than that for girls.

Of the 310 children admitted into hospital for Bulimia treatment in 2018–19, 7% were male. 5% of the 2,043 children treated for Anorexia in the same year were boys.[4] These statistics point to the devastating impact of body consciousness and body anxiety on the mental wellbeing of girls, but for male sufferers of Bulimia and Anorexia, the experience of these disorders is no less traumatic. However, the prevalence of these two disorders on any discussion about body image could detract from our awareness of another, lesser-known body image disorder that is more likely to affect men and boys than women and girls: Bigorexia. Before we discuss Bigorexia, it's important that we understand its foundations.

Anorexia

Anorexia (or Anorexia Nervosa) is a serious mental illness where people are of low weight due to limiting how much they eat and drink. They may develop 'rules' around what they feel they can and cannot eat, as well as things like when and where they'll eat. Anorexia can affect anyone of any age, gender, ethnicity, or background.[5]

Bulimia

Bulimia (or Bulimia Nervosa) is a serious mental illness. It can affect anyone of any age, gender, ethnicity, or background. People with Bulimia are caught in a cycle of eating copious quantities of food (called bingeing), and then trying to compensate for that overeating by vomiting, taking laxatives or diuretics, fasting, or exercising excessively (called purging). Treatment at the earliest possible opportunity gives the best chance for a fast and sustained recovery from bulimia.[6]

Fitspiration

In 2020, 87% of children aged between 12 and 15 had a social media account.[7] The most popular social media site in the UK was Instagram, an app which many young people turn to for health and fitness advice and inspiration. The commonly used term for this social media-based fitness inspiration is 'fitspiration,' often abbreviated to 'fitspo.' A quick search of the hash tag #fitspo in Instagram's search engine returns 74.8 million[8] photos (selfies, before and after images, etc.), videos and memes featuring young, musclebound men offering their advice as to how others can achieve similar levels of perceived physical perfection. 'Fitspo' is distinct from 'Thinspo' – which glorifies weight loss and *encourages* eating disorders – in that it appears to promote a lifestyle where healthy eating, fitness, and strength are valued. There is also – particularly with male 'fitspo' exponents – a significant emphasis on aesthetics: low body fat and high muscle mass are a must.

An Australian study into the 'fitspo' phenomenon noted that men were just as likely to be objectified as women, albeit in different ways. The study found that:

- Depicted men were highly muscular
- Images of men focused on stomachs, nearly all of which had visible abdominal muscles
- Images of men rarely focused on weight loss or thinness
- There was a trend of increased muscle mass images in men over time[9]

Bigorexia

The brawn-swathed men slathered all over Fitspo posts and television programmes like *Love Island* have led to a rise in what many people call 'Bigorexia.' Bigorexia, also known as muscle dysmorphia, is an anxiety disorder that leads someone to believe that they are too small or skinny, or that they are never muscly enough. Sufferers of Bigorexia become fixated on gaining muscle, which can often lead to excessive and dangerous weight training, restrictive eating practices, and a reliance on anabolic steroids as a means of achieving muscle growth.

Bigorexia is more commonly observed in men than in women. A 2019 study of nearly 15,000 participants found that 22% of men, compared to 5% of women, reported having eating disorders linked to working out and attempts to gain muscle.[10] It is believed that one in ten young male gymgoers in the UK suffers from Bigorexia,[11] whilst figures from the US suggest that almost 6% of US students have the disorder.[12] Bigorexia mainly affects men in their 20s and 30s, but the average age of onset is 19 years old.[13] This early onset could be explained by statistics from the UK which show that, 'almost half of secondary boys would consider exercising with the specific intention of building muscle and bulking up (48%).'[14] A fifth of secondary-age boys claim to already having done this previously, 'suggesting that a staggering 69% of boys aspire to a muscular physique.'[15] Alarmingly, of these boys, '10% would consider taking steroids to achieve their goals.'

School and boys' body image

According to the *Picture of Health?* report by Credos, based on a survey of 1,005 boys in UK primary and secondary schools, school is an uncomfortable place for boys with low body confidence:

> School…is where boys feel the most pressure about the way their body looks, with just over one-third (35%) of boys feeling this way; secondary boys (38%) are more likely than primary boys (29%) to feel the most pressure at school.
>
> For boys who have been bullied (35%), this pressure is even more intense. Nearly half (45%) of boys who have been bullied feel the most pressure at school, compared with 30% of those who have never been bullied.[16]

Sadly, given that this is such an issue, over half (56%) of boys would find it difficult talking to a teacher about their body confidence.

The fact is that body image and eating disorders are increasing in prevalence amongst male students. It's important that we work appropriately to help victims or those at risk, fast.

The solutions

A. Spot the signs of eating disorders

Charlotte Markey is a psychology professor at Rutgers University-Camden in the US and author of *Being You: The Body Image Book for Boys*. I interviewed Markey and she explained one of the key differences between boys' and girls' experiences of eating disorders:

> Unlike girls, boys are very behaviourally focused. Boys have been gendered to *do* things. Sometimes, when girls have concerns about how they look, they don't do things – they restrict. They restrict their exercise. They restrict their food intake. When boys are concerned about their image, however, they go to the gym. They control what they eat. They take supplements. Because of this, many boys with a body or eating disorder appear to look very healthy, which can make it difficult to notice the problem.

This could explain why many teachers (and parents) are much slower to notice the signs of eating disorders in boys.[17]

BEAT is the biggest eating disorder charity in the UK. Their website contains lots of advice for teachers, parents, and carers on how to spot the signs of eating disorders. What follows is a list of signs for teachers to look out for, for four specific eating disorders. It is important that for Anorexia and Bulimia, which are traditionally regarded as exclusively female disorders, teachers remind themselves that boys who display any of the signs listed could also potentially be at risk of, or suffering from, one of the two disorders.

Anorexia

Aside from the physical signs of weight loss, teachers should also look out for other, behavioural signs of developing anorexia. Children who are developing Anorexia, or already suffering with it, may:

- Say that they have eaten earlier or will eat later, or that they have eaten more than they have
- Be untruthful about how much weight they have lost
- Undergo a process of strict dieting and avoid food they think is fattening
- Count the calories in food excessively
- Eat only low-calorie food, or limit the type of food they will eat
- Miss lunch
- Avoid eating with other people

- Hide food
- Cut food into tiny pieces to make it less obvious they have eaten little or to make food easier to swallow
- Eat very slowly
- Take appetite suppressants, such as slimming or diet pills
- Be obsessive or exhibit rigid behaviour, particularly around food
- Be irritable
- Exercise excessively – this might involve exercising when not physically well enough to do so, or feeling guilty or anxious about not exercising
- Vomit or misuse laxatives
- Withdraw and isolate themselves socially
- Wear baggy clothing to hide their body, due to self-consciousness or to make weight loss less noticeable
- Fall behind academically

Adapted from advice found at: https://www.beateatingdisorders.org.uk/get-information-and-support/about-eating-disorders/types/anorexia

Bulimia

Children who are developing Bulimia, or already suffering with it, may:

- Frequently check body shape or weight or avoid looking at their body or checking their weight
- Compare their body with those of others
- Eat large amounts of food
- Purge after bingeing by vomiting, over-exercising, using laxatives, diuretics or fasting
- Disappear during or soon after eating in order to vomit
- Organise life around shopping, eating, and purging behaviour
- Be secretive, especially about eating
- Hoard food
- Have mood swings
- Be irritable

- Engage in social withdrawal
- Self-harm
- Exercise excessively

Adapted from advice found at: https://www.beateatingdisorders.org.uk/get-information-and-support/about-eating-disorders/types/bulimia

Bigorexia

Children who are developing Bigorexia, or are already suffering with it, may:

- Exercise excessively
- Display rapid muscle or weight gain
- Miss out on social activities in favour of exercise
- Eat lots of food, regularly
- Be observed regularly using protein shakes or dietary supplements
- Train, despite injury
- Display acne, increased facial hair growth, and enlarged breasts (in men) due to steroid abuse
- Display aggression or mood swings[18]

Binge Eating Disorder

Binge Eating Disorder is a mental illness where people eat very large amounts of food without feeling like they're able to control the amount they're consuming. Children who are developing Binge Eating Disorder, or are already suffering with it, may:

- Buy lots of food
- Organise their life around bingeing episodes
- Hoard food
- Eat very rapidly
- Eat when not hungry
- Eat until uncomfortably full
- Avoid eating around others
- Engage in social withdrawal

- Display signs of irritability

- Experience mood swings

Adapted from advice found at: https://www.beateatingdisorders.org.uk/get-information-and-support/about-eating-disorders/types/binge-eating-disorder

B. Watch how you speak about bodies

> 'Wow. You've shot up over the summer!'
> 'I need a few strong boys to help me take these books next door.'
> 'I eat far too many cakes in the staffroom. Can't you tell?'

It's not uncommon for teachers to make references to the physical bodies of either students or themselves. Whilst innocent enough in intention, the reality is that at best, such comments, when heard repeatedly over a whole school career, and from the mouths of many different teachers, suggest that bodies are an acceptable object of praise or negativity. This could make students who don't fit the judgement criteria – kids who haven't 'shot up' over summer, for example, feel uncomfortable. I asked Charlotte Markey about the importance of language when it comes to talking to students about bodies:

> Language is really important, especially for teachers and parents. We're an appearance-obsessed culture and we don't want to reinforce that. We want to show students that people are valued for things other than how they look, and we really need to put energy into commenting on when students are kind, clever, or funny. Teachers play such a pivotal role in kids' sense of self and so they should try not to comment on external attributes – such as how tall or strong someone is – because people actually have very limited control over these things.

C. Talk about the mental-health benefits, rather than the aesthetic benefits, of exercise

In Chapter Seven, I mentioned that emphasising the mental health benefits of sport could be a great way to get more students involved in Physical Education at school. However, focusing on the mental health benefits of sport also has the additional benefit of detracting from – and therefore giving less importance to – the effect of exercise on how the body looks. Teachers who tell boys that they need to exercise in order to 'get more hench' or to get muscles or a six-pack for summer, means that an aesthetically pleasing body becomes more desirable than a physically healthy body. This puts unfair pressure on boys who do not match this ideal, regardless of the frequency and intensity of the exercise they engage in.

D. Teach boys about the dangers of steroid abuse

I've spoken at many schools to teenage boys about body image, and Bigorexia is always the thing that really captures their interest. When I tell boys about the negative consequences of steroid abuse, I'm always met with audible sounds of shock and surprise from the audience. Which tells me that I'm telling them something they need to hear. I get my information from the NHS website. Here's what could happen to boys who choose to abuse steroids:

- Hair loss
- Breast development
- Severe acne
- Stomach pain
- Increased risk of prostate cancer
- Infertility
- Shrunken testicles
- Erectile dysfunction
- Reduced sperm count[19]

It's important that boys are told this for two reasons: firstly, it could deter boys who are thinking about abusing anabolic steroids from doing so. Also, it could make boys who are currently abusing steroids seek help.

E. Teach about body confidence and the manipulation of the male body in advertising and social media

It's not just female bodies that are mutilated by Photoshop wizards of the advertising and media industries. Male bodies are also stretched, twisted, and pinched to create a more masculine ideal. If we can teach boys this, it may better help them to scrutinise the unrealistic male bodies plastered all over social media, reality TV shows, and yoghurt adverts. Media Smart is the education body of the Advertising Association. On their website, they have free resources, built around Credos' *A Picture of Health?* report, to help teachers educate students about the way images of the male body are manipulated for public consumption.

 The PowerPoint presentation mentioned in the lesson plan below can be accessed here: https://mediasmart.uk.com/body-image-advertising-11-14yrs

Lesson: male body image and advertising

Stage one (5 minutes)

Show students slide two of the PowerPoint presentation (figure 8.1), with a quote from a boy of their age interviewed for the Credos report, but do not inform them of the identity of the speaker. Ask students to create a personal mind map in their books by responding to the thinking prompts on the slide. Ask students who are willing to share one or two ideas to create a class mind map on the board or on paper.

Body Image and Advertising

"Some people might think that they have to have a specific body shape. They should have … a fit body type."

Boy, aged 10, from Cardiff

Think about…?
- Who you think might be speaking
- What they might be talking about
- Why they might be saying this

Media Smart – Body Image and Advertising | © Media Smart 2017. All Rights Reserved.   OPENING EYES

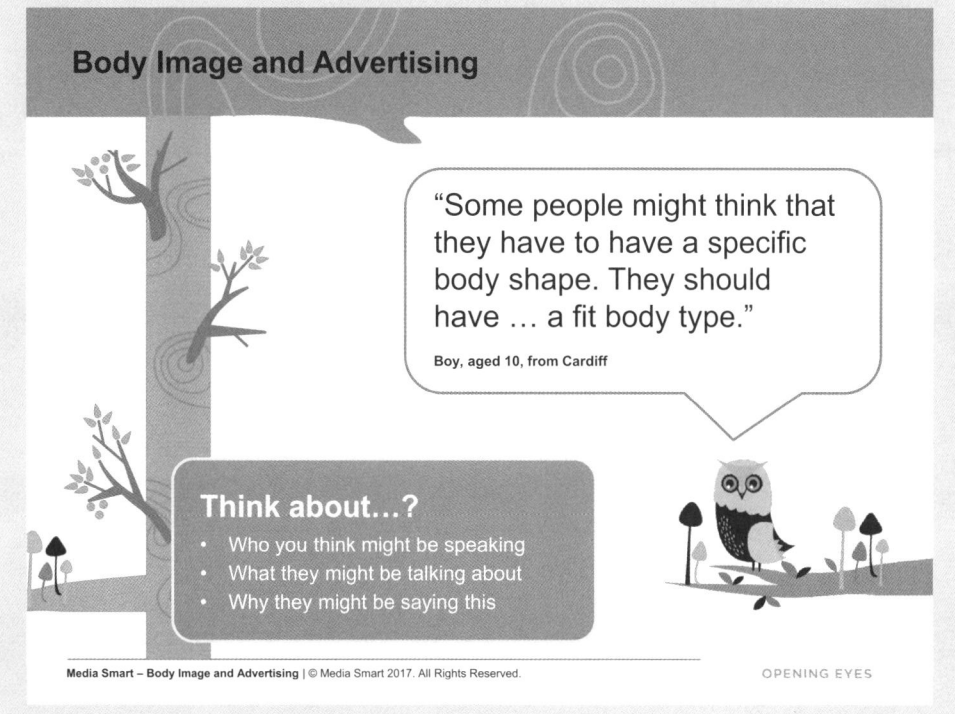

Figure 8.1

Stage two (5 minutes)

Now reveal to the class that the quote was taken from a boy, roughly their age. Ask them how this compares to their original thoughts about who said the quote to gauge their understanding. Are they surprised by the quote's origin? Why/why not? Question whether they made any assumptions about the gender of the speaker when first reading the quote, or seeing the subject of the lesson. Why do they think that girls' body image is more often discussed than boys'?

Develop the discussion by finding out what they understand by the term 'body image,' asking students to add suggestions to their starter activity mind maps before introducing the definition on slide three for further clarity. As a class, compare how the definition on the slide is similar or different to their initial ideas of what body image means and invite a few students to put it into their own words. Ask the class to note down the final definition in books or write it on the board for reference. Explore the question of what it might mean to have positive body image – emphasise that this is not tied to how people look, but how they feel about themselves.

Stage three (15 minutes)

In pairs, students are given the following scenario:

> Imagine you work for an advertising agency that is designing an advert to sell a pair of jeans to young men. You have access to photo technology, and as much money as you need to make the best, most persuasive, advert possible to encourage people to buy your jeans.

Teachers can choose whether students draw their proposed advert, summarise it in a short paragraph or discuss it in pairs, dependent on time. Afterwards, ask students to explain their choices; why did they design their advert this way?

Stage four (10 minutes)

In pairs, students are given an A5 printout with a doctored image of a boy of their age on one side and the natural image of the same boy on the other. Sheets should be handed out folded in half, so they first see only the altered image. Some pairs will have a picture of the boy with a thinner body shape visible, and other pairs will have a picture with a more muscular body shape visible.

Aim to spread the different versions of the worksheet evenly around the room. Ask students to think about how they would describe the body and add a few annotations to the image of the body's features that are the most noticeable or that stand out to them the most. Then ask them to unfold the worksheet to find the natural (or the altered) body shape and circle any differences they can see. How would they describe the second body and how is it different to the first? After looking at the images, students feed back their thoughts to another pair with a different version of the worksheet. Encourage students to use these thinking prompts (from slide seven of the PowerPoint) to get the discussion going:

- What has been changed? Get students to look at specific parts of the body to see if they have been altered in any way. Guide them to make functional descriptions rather than judgements on looks: for example – what is different about the arms? How would you describe the legs?

Use the PowerPoint slide (figure 8.2) to explain that these images have been altered to reflect how pictures are sometimes changed in the media:

Body image and eating disorders **177**

Body Image and Advertising

Activity: Spot the Difference

What impact do you think these images might have on young people, especially if they didn't realise the images had been altered?

MediaSmart
OPENING EYES

Media Smart – Body Image and Advertising | © Media Smart 2017. All Rights Reserved.

Figure 8.2

- **Has anything surprised you about these images?** They may think it is creating an unrealistic body ideal for boys or be surprised that the media changes images in this way. They may not have realised the extent to which images can be changed – or they may believe that images get altered even more than these ones.
- **Do girls have a different insight?** The girls in the class may expect images of boys to be altered in this way – or are they surprised to see that these images are altered in a similar way to images of girls?
- **Why do you think these changes are made?** What do they think is the media's motivation for altering images?

As a class, discuss what impact they think these images might have on a young person their age, especially if they did not realise changes had been made. Likely answers may include: *It may make someone feel less positive about their own body, or they might not want to talk about the way it makes them feel.*

Stage five (15 minutes)

Show students slides 9–11 (figures 8.3, 8.4, and 8.5) and introduce them to the three boys' personas on the screen. Explain that they will be taking on the persona of one of these boys. Give additional prompts as needed for students who may struggle to imagine another person's life and routine, or who may worry that they might get this 'wrong.'

Their first task is to map out five moments during a typical day when he might encounter the media and advertising. After a few minutes, students share feedback on these moments, and what types of media or advertising they might see – e.g., a billboard on the bus to school or sponsored content on social media. Use your own examples to develop discussion further, or to stimulate conversation with students who are having trouble thinking of different ideas.

Ahead of the class, source a few examples of adverts or media that might be aimed at young men, or feature young men in the images. It is important to choose a representative and diverse selection of adverts which include people from a range of ages, ethnicities, and cultural backgrounds. Avoid selecting extreme examples for shock value as this can have unintended negative consequences. For instance, while most students might recognise a highly exaggerated image of muscular men as unrealistic, someone with a distorted sense of body ideals may see this as inspiring and a true representation of body norms. If you have access to the internet during the lesson you may also wish to include TV or video ads and watch these together as a class.

Arrange the class into pairs or small groups. Each group picks one of the personas and a moment in his day. Ask them to discuss how the boy may engage and respond to the images shown in the advert he saw during this moment. Look over an example

Body Image and Advertising

Activity: A Day in the Life

Boy one: Joe, 12

Joe catches the bus to school, enjoys gaming and hanging out with friends at home. Has an older brother who is 15.

Media Smart – Body Image and Advertising | © Media Smart 2017. All Rights Reserved.

MediaSmart
OPENING EYES

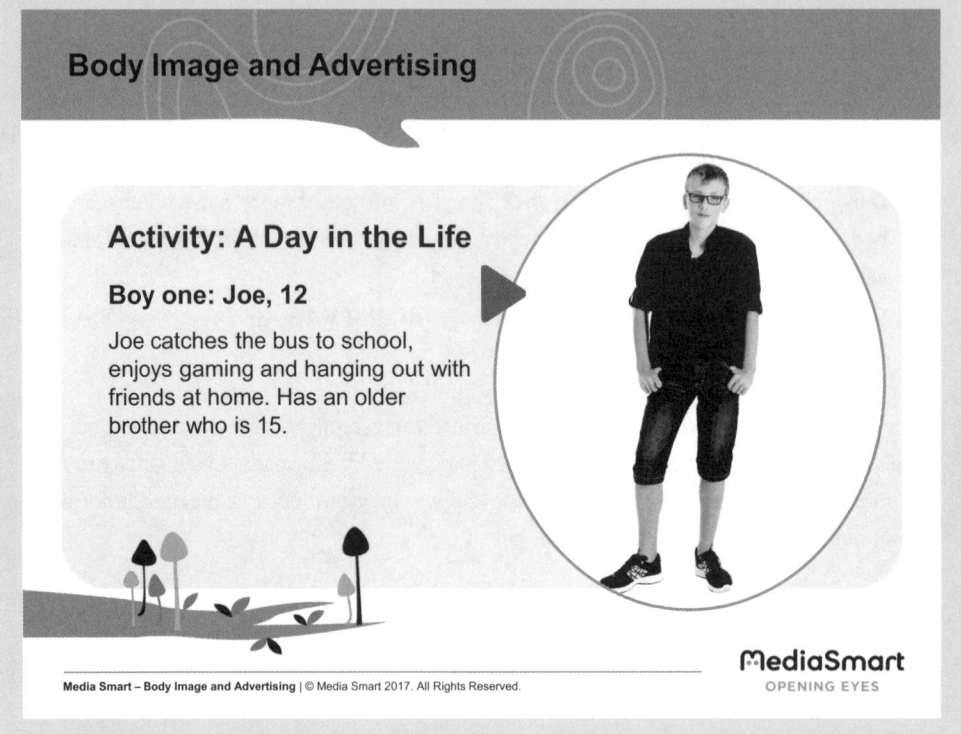

Figure 8.3

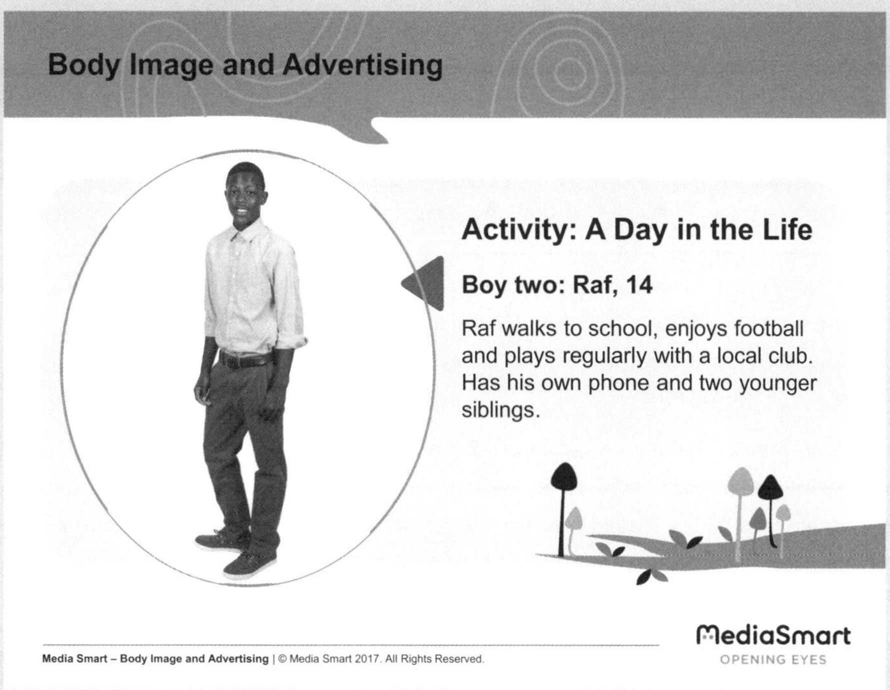

Body image and eating disorders 179

Body Image and Advertising

Activity: A Day in the Life

Boy two: Raf, 14

Raf walks to school, enjoys football and plays regularly with a local club. Has his own phone and two younger siblings.

Media Smart – Body Image and Advertising | © Media Smart 2017. All Rights Reserved.

MediaSmart
OPENING EYES

Figure 8.4

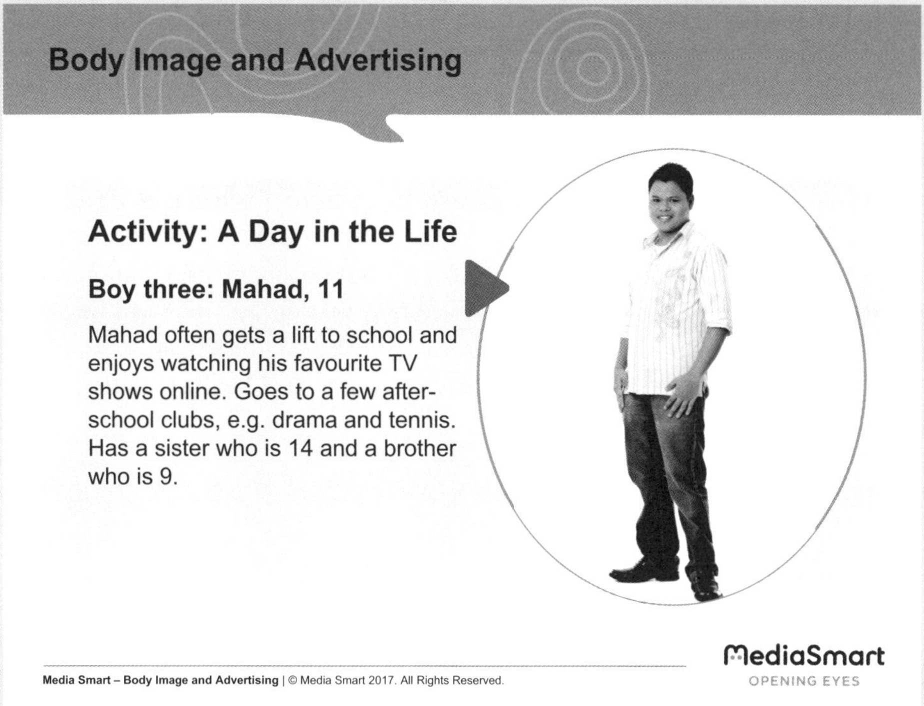

Body Image and Advertising

Activity: A Day in the Life

Boy three: Mahad, 11

Mahad often gets a lift to school and enjoys watching his favourite TV shows online. Goes to a few after-school clubs, e.g. drama and tennis. Has a sister who is 14 and a brother who is 9.

Media Smart – Body Image and Advertising | © Media Smart 2017. All Rights Reserved.

MediaSmart
OPENING EYES

Figure 8.5

as a class first to check for understanding. Encourage them to role play the different scenarios, first scripting out what the character might say, before rehearsing ways of talking about, responding to, and giving advice on the body image issues raised in their character's day. Focus on turning conversations away from talking about or comparing appearance and instead focus on building emotional resilience. You may wish to note, on the white board, suggestions that the class find particularly effective. Students who feel confident can also share their role plays with the class, with others providing kind, specific, and helpful feedback on their suggested responses, focusing on conversations that encourage characters to celebrate their individuality.

Stage six (5 minutes)

Return to the original annotated quote from the lesson starter. Spend a few moments summarising what was discussed at the start of the class. Ask students to build on their initial mind maps. They should use the information they have learnt throughout the lesson about positive body image to add more ideas about the advice they might give to the boy to think more positively about his body. If possible, they should use a different-coloured pen to help them visualise what they have learnt and to easily see which notes refer to their improved understanding of body image and the impact of the media and advertising.

The final word

When Charlotte Markey wrote her book on boys' body image, she was surprised about the degree of self-consciousness that boys experience. Boys told Markey that they hated taking their shirts off where social situations required it, such as a trip to the beach or swimming pool, but also in more formal settings such as school changing rooms.

Hopefully, having read this chapter, you will not be surprised when you hear a boy express insecurity about his body. No doubt, you will also be saddened. But, by viewing body insecurity, or body disorders, through a mixed-gender lens rather than a purely female one, we can help boys to realise that healthy bodies come in all shapes and sizes.

Notes

1 Obsessive-Compulsive Disorder is a mental health condition where you have recurring thoughts and repetitive behaviours you cannot control.
2 Royal College of Psychiatrists. (2022, May 18). Hospital admissions for eating disorders increased by 84% in the last five years. Available at: https://www.rcpsych.ac.uk/news-and-features/latest-news/detail/2022/05/18/hospital-admissions-for-eating-disorders-increased-by-84-in-the-last-five-years (Accessed 8th December 2022).

3 BBC Radio 4 *Woman's Hour: Boys and eating disorders: 14 tips for parents*. Available at: https://www.bbc.co.uk/programmes/articles/W3KsZDLWDp0jXXp0d9M0P/boys-and-eating-disorders-14-tips-for-parents (Accessed 8th April 2022).
4 NHS Digital. (2019). *Hospital Admissions for Eating Disorders*. Available at: https://digital.nhs.uk/data-and-information/find-data-and-publications/supplementary-information/2019-supplementary-information-files/hospital-admissions-for-eating-disorders (Accessed 8th April 2022).
5 BEAT. (n.d). Anorexia Nervosa. Available at: https://www.beateatingdisorders.org.uk/get-information-and-support/about-eating-disorders/types/anorexia (Accessed: 8th April 2022).
6 BEAT. (n.d). Bulimia Nervosa. Available at: https://www.beateatingdisorders.org.uk/get-information-and-support/about-eating-disorders/types/bulimia (Accessed: 8th April 2022).
7 Statista Research Department. (July 2021). Does your child have a social media account? *Statista*. Available at: https://www.statista.com/statistics/272509/children-active-on-social-media-in-the-uk-by-age (Accessed: 8th April 2022).
8 Search conducted on 8th April 2022.
9 Carrotte, E. R., Prichard, I., & Lim, M. S. (2017). 'Fitspiration' on social media: A content analysis of gendered images. *Journal of Medical Internet Research*, *19*(3).
10 Nagata, J. M., Murray, S. B., Bibbins-Domingo, K., Garber, A. K., Mitchison, D., Griffiths, S. (2019). Predictors of muscularity-oriented disordered eating behaviors in U.S. young adults: A prospective cohort study. *International Journal of Eating Disorders*, 52, 1380–1388.
11 Athar, A., Rotherham, N., Talwar, D. (2015). Muscle dysmorphia: One in 10 men in gyms believed to have 'bigorexia'. *BBC Newsbeat*. Available at: https://www.bbc.co.uk/news/newsbeat-34307044 (Accessed: 8th April 2022).
12 Bo, S., Zoccali, R., Ponzo, V. et al. (2014). University courses, eating problems and muscle dysmorphia: Are there any associations? *Journal of Translational Medicine*, 12, 221.
13 Olivardia R. (2001) Mirror, mirror on the wall, who's the largest of them all? The features and phenomenology of muscle dysmorphia. *Harvard Review of Psychiatry*, *9*(5), 254–259.
14 Credos. (2016). *Picture of Health?* Available with subscription at: https://adassoc.org.uk/credos/picture-of-health (Accessed: 13th April 2022).
15 Ibid.
16 Ibid.
17 Credos (2016).
18 Roden, C. (2019). Promoting positive body image in boys. *The Optimus Blog*. Available at: https://blog.optimus-education.com/promoting-positive-body-image-boys (Accessed: 8th April 2022).
19 NHS. (2022). Anabolic steroid misuse. Available at: https://www.nhs.uk/conditions/anabolic-steroid-misuse/#:~:text=The%20penalty%20is%20an%20unlimited,be%20banned%20from%20competing%20professionally (Accessed: 16th July 2022).

References

Athar, A., Rotherham, N., Talwar, D. (2015). Muscle dysmorphia: One in 10 men in gyms believed to have 'bigorexia' *BBC Newsbeat*. Available at: https://www.bbc.co.uk/news/newsbeat-34307044 (Accessed: 8th April 2022).

BBC Radio 4 *Woman's Hour – Boys and eating disorders: 14 tips for parents*. Available at: https://www.bbc.co.uk/programmes/articles/W3KsZDLWDp0jXXp0d9M0P/boys-and-eating-disorders-14-tips-for-parents (Accessed: 8th April 2022).

BEAT. (n.d.-a). Anorexia Nervosa. Available at: https://www.beateatingdisorders.org.uk/get-information-and-support/about-eating-disorders/types/anorexia (Accessed: 8th April 2022).

BEAT. (n.d.-b). Bulimia Nervosa. Available at: https://www.beateatingdisorders.org.uk/get-information-and-support/about-eating-disorders/types/bulimia (Accessed: 8th April 2022).

Bo, S., Zoccali, R., Ponzo, V. et al. (2014). University courses, eating problems and muscle dysmorphia: Are there any associations? *Journal of Translational Medicine*, 12, 221.

Carrotte, E. R., Prichard, I., & Lim, M. S. (2017). 'Fitspiration' on social media: A content analysis of gendered images. *Journal of Medical Internet Research*, *19*(3).

Credos. (2016). *Picture of Health?* Available with subscription at: https://adassoc.org.uk/credos/picture-of-health (Accessed: 13th April 2022).

Marsh, S. (2017). *Eating disorders in men rise by 70% in NHS figures. The Gwuardian.* Available at: https://www.theguardian.com/society/2017/jul/31/eating-disorders-in-men-rise-by-70-in-nhs-figures (Accessed: 8th April 2022).

Nagata, J. M., Murray, S. B., Bibbins-Domingo, K., Garber, A. K., Mitchison, D., Griffiths, S. (2019). Predictors of muscularity-oriented disordered eating behaviors in U.S. young adults: A prospective cohort study. *International Journal of Eating Disorders*, 52, 1380–1388.

NHS Digital. (2019). *Hospital Admissions for Eating Disorders*. Available at: https://digital.nhs.uk/data-and-information/find-data-and-publications/supplementary-information/2019-supplementary-information-files/hospital-admissions-for-eating-disorders (Accessed 8th April 2022).

NHS. (2022). Anabolic steroid misuse. Available at: https://www.nhs.uk/conditions/anabolic-steroid-misuse/#:~:text=The%20penalty%20is%20an%20unlimited,be%20banned%20from%20competing%20professionally (Accessed: 16th July 2022).

Olivardia, R., (2001). Mirror, mirror on the wall, who's the largest of them all? The features and phenomenology of muscle dysmorphia. *Harvard Review of Psychiatry*, *9*(5), 254–259.

Roden, C. (2019). Promoting positive body image in boys. *The Optimus Blog*. Available at: https://blog.optimus-education.com/promoting-positive-body-image-boys (Accessed: 8th April 2022).

Royal College of Psychiatrists. (2022, May 18). Hospital admissions for eating disorders increased by 84% in the last five years. Available at: https://www.rcpsych.ac.uk/news-and-features/latest-news/detail/2022/05/18/hospital-admissions-for-eating-disorders-increased-by-84-in-the-last-five-years (Accessed 8th December 2022).

Statista Research Department. (July 2021). Does your child have a social media account? *Statista*. Available at: https://www.statista.com/statistics/272509/children-active-on-social-media-in-the-uk-by-age (Accessed: 8th April 2022).

9 Pornography

The story

An aspect of my research for this chapter involved asking friends, the public at large and even trusted work colleagues if they would be prepared to be interviewed about this subject in the strictest confidence. One brave person agreed to an interview:

Matt Pinkett: For how long have you been addicted to pornography?
Porn Addict: Well, to be fair, I started watching the free stuff online when all my mates at school were on about it and doing the same, so probably in Year 8 or 9 or something. So, we would have been around 13 or 14 years old. That was a long time ago now. But you know what? I still don't see myself as addicted. My doctor says I'm an addict, and my therapist too, but I don't feel pornography has really f*cked my life up. Like, I really, really enjoy watching it. It turns me on. It's fun…I'm not harming anybody.
MP: Okay, but might it be the case that you're harming yourself?
PA: Not really. Watching porn hasn't impacted me in a way that hurts me physically.
MP: Some porn addicts report having trouble maintaining or even getting an erection.
PA: Actually, there is that, I suppose. I usually struggle to maintain an erection with just 'normal' sex. I can only get really turned on – and stay that way – when I'm doing something a bit more filthy, like you see in most porn videos.
MP: Can you define 'filthy' for me?
PA: You know, messy oral and stuff like that. To be honest, for me, I think I would even have trouble getting an erection with regular sex now. It typically has to be something more than that. Legal stuff, but not your normal vanilla[1] stuff. I just can't get into it that much if I'm just having sex with one person and doing normal, routine sex stuff.

DOI: 10.4324/9781003250722-10

MP: That's interesting. Does that make forming romantic relationships difficult?

PA: Now you say it, yeah. When I meet women, I'm always, right from the off, trying to find out if they're into oral, anal, or other stuff. If they're not, I just don't really find them sexy for very long. And even when I do like them, they usually think I'm a weirdo for being into it. So it's quite tough. Quite lonely, I guess. Not many women want to fall in love with a man who wants to have sex in the way that I want to have sex.

MP: Do you feel that watching pornography has made you violent during sex?

PA: No. No way. I have watched so much pornography for so many years and I still don't like the violent sh*t. I immediately scroll past any videos that look violent or brutal. I've certainly never been aggressive or violent in sex, apart from one time, but I definitely didn't initiate that.

MP: How do you mean?

PA: Well, I was once with a woman, and after a couple of weeks of us having sex, she asked me to put my hands around her throat during sex. I told her I wasn't into that, but she looked genuinely disappointed, so I went along with what she wanted even though I didn't particularly enjoy it. Then I remember she texted me a few days later saying she wanted someone more dominant. Maybe more…masculine, I guess.

Then a few weeks later I was texting a new woman and we eventually started talking about sex. I texted her something about spanking her and then it got to the point where I mentioned putting my hands around her neck…

MP: How did she react?

PA: She was disgusted. She told me I was out of order and that she didn't want to know me any more.

MP: How did you feel?

PA: This was four years ago, and I still regret saying that. It's just not me. I hate myself for that. I don't know what I was thinking. When I think about it now, even though I was uncomfortable with it, I still mentioned the choking thing because I've seen it so often in porn. I thought that everyone was doing it.

The research

Pornography

It's difficult to know exactly how much pornography boys watch. Estimations about the proportion of adolescent males accessing pornography vary from study to study. Some studies, for example, have shown that 83–100% of male adolescents have accessed pornography (compared to 45–80% for girls), whilst in other studies, figures have been as low as 19–30% for all adolescents.[2] Even then, the frequency with which pornography is accessed ranges from once, to every so often, and to every day. What all studies tend to agree on is that more boys watch pornography than girls.

Boys and pornography viewing habits in the UK

A UK study[3] from 2020, looking at pornography viewing habits in 1,100 UK adolescents aged between 11 and 16, found that 48% of teenagers had watched pornography. The older a teenager is, the more likely they are to have accessed pornography. The study found that 56% of boys had viewed pornography compared to 40% of girls. Of the boys who had seen pornography, 59% had done so as a consequence of actively seeking it out, whilst for girls this figure was 25%.

Pornography and mental health

There is plenty of research to suggest that viewing pornography can have a damaging effect on a person's mental health. A huge study of over 45,000 adolescents, looking into the link between pornography viewing habits and mental health, concluded that adolescents who view pornography frequently reported 'lower levels of happiness and higher levels of stress, sadness and hopelessness.'[4] This hopelessness, the study suggested, could also be linked to the higher rates of suicidal ideation and suicidal attempts also reported by high-frequency pornography users.

Another study found that people who were exposed to pornography in childhood, 'had significantly more depression and less life satisfaction in adulthood than those exposed at a later age or who had never used pornography.'[5] This same study cites shame as an important factor in this process:

> The shame that may result from interest in pornography or behaviours relating to pornography (seeking it out in private, masturbation, acting out sexual behaviours learned in pornography) may become internalised over time and lead to decreased mental health and general life satisfaction.[6]

Pornography and body image

Research into adult viewers of pornography has found that men who watch pornography frequently are more likely to view mesomorphic bodies – large muscle mass, low body fat bodies, like those of most male porn actors – as a masculine ideal. Not surprisingly, these men are also less likely to be satisfied with their own bodies.[7]

There isn't much research into the way pornography affects the way young people perceive their own bodies. However, a 2018 Internet Matters survey[8] of over 2,000 parents of teenagers concluded that 27% of young people who watched pornography experienced 'poor self-esteem as they judge themselves against the actors.' This would suggest that our boys are negatively judging the size of their own penis against that of the male actors in the video, not to mention the sexual desirability of a large, muscular, waxed chest. They may also be making potentially damaging judgements about the desirable physical appearance of future sexual partners. This same survey also indicated that '34% of parents say it [watching pornography] harms their child's body image.' From the scant research which is available on this topic – and there needs to be more – there does not appear to be any difference between how girls and boys worry about what other people will think of their bodies because of pornography.

In her 2021 book, *Pornography and Public Health*, Emily Rothman makes an interesting point about the recent dramatic rise in the popularity of so-called amateur pornography.[9] Unlike the muscle-honed bodies observed in studio-produced pornography, amateur pornography contains a far higher proportion of what we might refer to as 'real bodies' – bodies of different shapes and sizes. Rothman tells us that research suggests that 'in comparison to older pornography consumers, younger audiences disproportionately prefer amateur pornography.'[10] Because of this:

> It's possible that young people are choosing to watch pornography that features average-looking bodies more than their elders did or do, and that whatever we think we know about how watching pornography affects body image should not be applied to the younger generation.[11]

In other words, we've a few more years to go before we can start to investigate the impact of amateur pornography on the way boys will later go on to view their bodies.

Penis size

It's fair to assume that boys who regularly watch pornography may experience hang-ups about the size of their penis. After all, if the prevalence of Instagram fitness gurus with bulging muscles means that our boys also want bulging muscles, then surely the well-endowed men of pornography will inspire a longing for a large appendage in the boys who regularly watch porn. Pornography expert Emily Rothman admits in her book that whilst, 'to [her] knowledge, there have been no studies of the average penis size of pornography performers,' it is 'reasonable to conclude that pornography likely tends to feature larger-than-average penises in length and girth.'[12] However, according to Rothman, research is mixed. Some studies show that pornography consumption does lead to greater dissatisfaction with the size of one's penis; other studies show otherwise and that in fact men feel more pleased with the size of their penis if they frequently watch pornography.

Where students express concern with the size of their penis, I'd suggest that directing their emphasis towards making future sexual partners feel comfortable and cared for is a far greater use of their time and…ahem…energy.

Pornography and relationships

Healthy, loving, romantic relationships are hugely beneficial for a person's mental wellbeing.[13] But sadly, for people who watch pornography frequently, the capacity to seek out and form healthy, committed relationships could be more elusive. In her summary of the research, Bonnie Young discusses several ways that access to pornography at a young age can impact a person's ability to form healthy, loving sexual relationships:

> ...because children lack maturity and real-life sexual experiences, they are especially susceptible to internalisation of inaccurate portrayals of human sexuality. If left uncontested, these beliefs about sexual relationships may create dissonance, disappointment, or unmet expectations as these individuals seek to form sexual relationships in adolescence and adulthood.

Young goes on to explain that children who have accessed pornography at a young age grow up making comparisons between themselves and the pornography they have seen. What's more, they believe that what they see in pornography presents a realistic representation of sex and sexuality. Such comparisons can be really damaging. As Young states, such comparisons:

> ...may lead to dissatisfaction and distress, especially when their partner's or own behaviour cannot or does not mirror pornographic material.[14]

Pornography and sexual aggression

In the chapter *Sex and Sexism* in *BDT?* I stated that:

> ...despite the prevalence of violence in pornography, there is no reliable evidence to suggest that exposure to violent pornography alone turns those that watch it into people who will commit acts of sexual aggression, including rape.[15]

Since the publication of *BDT?*, researchers Christopher Ferguson and Richard Hartley have conducted a meta-analysis of over 70 research studies into the impact of pornography on sexual aggression, stretching as far back as the 1970s, and concluded that 'evidence did not suggest that nonviolent pornography was associated with sexual aggression.' The link between watching violent pornography and later sexual aggression was described as 'weakly correlated.'[16]

As I wrote in *BDT?* when the watchers of violent pornography go on to commit sexually violent acts, this is usually because of 'other risk factors' such as narcissism and a violent upbringing at play.'

Pornography and the objectification of women

Perhaps male regular watchers of pornography find it difficult to form romantic relationships because they see women as, primarily, sexual objects rather than people who need love, care, and support. Many longitudinal studies have showed that adolescents who view pornography more frequently are also more likely to perceive females – and this will necessarily include their classmates, their friends, and even some female school staff – as, primarily, sex objects. One study showed that even after six months, Dutch adolescents who were exposed to pornography still regarded women as sex objects above anything else.[17] Other studies in America[18] and Japan[19] have yielded similar results.

Men who display misogynistic attitudes are more likely to suffer with their mental wellbeing,[20] but far greater damage is done to the female victims of sexual objectification. As Barbara Fredrickson and Tomi-Ann Roberts explained in their summary of the research picture, *Objectification Theory: Toward Understanding Women's Lived Experiences and Mental Health Risks*, the victim accumulation of objectifying experiences 'may help account for an array of mental health risks that disproportionately affect women: unipolar depression, sexual dysfunction, and eating disorders.'[21] Combatting such attitudes at a young age could improve the mental health of both males and females.

Sexual objectification and boys

Boys are more likely than girls to see sexual messages in the media as desirable. They're also more likely to perceive the messages as accurate representations of 'real life.' One study found that boys are more susceptible than girls are to objectifying women, notably after watching sexually explicit material in video games.[22] Despite this bleak picture, recent research has found that boys (and girls) are less likely to view women as sex objects as the intensity of 'Porn Literacy' education increases.[23]

The solutions

Porn Literacy is essential, not only to boys' mental health, but crucially to the girls who suffer because of the sexist attitudes that can arise out of frequent pornography viewing. The solutions that follow, whilst initially centred around making boys more pornography-literate, also include advice on wider issues such as consent, and how boys can hold each other accountable when sexist attitudes are apparent.

A. Create the right conditions for discussion

Discussing pornography frankly and openly is important. However, it's fair to say that the school environment isn't necessarily where students are going to feel that they can discuss pornography and sex freely. Therefore, it's important that teachers and facilitators of pornography education sessions do all they can to ensure that conditions are adapted and suited to ensure students feel able to talk about what can be a potentially uncomfortable, doubtlessly embarrassing, possibly hilarious, and increasingly necessary topic in a way that leaves them feeling safe and comfortable. *Beyond Equality* is a national organisation that works with schools and universities on helping boys to rethink their masculinity. Since their inception they've spoken to over 65,000 young people on topics ranging from mental health, consent, and toxic masculinity to pornography. In their report, *The Imagine Toolkit*, they clearly outline how to create prime conditions for discussing pornography effectively, appropriately, and safely:

1. **Adapt to the group**. Make sure that any pornography or sex education is tailored to the specific needs of the group. Needs will vary depending on things such as age and gender composition. Carrying out a baseline survey before the session can help to understand the needs of a particular group.

2. **Mind the age gap**. You should use more concrete and less abstract concepts with younger students. Be aware that the presence of the adult will have different impacts depending on the age of session participants.

3. **Set a timetable**. Plan the workshop from start to finish. Ensure that there is adequate time left for exercise, breaks, and feedback.

4. **Expect the unexpected**. In discussions about sex and pornography, things rarely go to play. Be prepared to cut out elements of your planned session if the discussion goes in an unexpected, but important, direction.

5. **Adapt your style**. At times you will need to lecture and at others you'll need to facilitate and encourage discussion. Sometimes you'll need to be authoritative whilst at others, it may help to be more jovial or light-hearted. Be aware of this and adapt depending on the focus of the session. Make sure that you stay connected with the group. Ask questions, be participative and interactive. Notice the energy and adjust.

6. **Acknowledge your flaws as well as those of others**. Acknowledge your own flaws as a tool for connection with the group and encouraging discussion. There is no need to punish students for having sexist or prejudiced *thoughts*. Instead, you should show students that they are responsible for how they *act*.

7. **Get somebody else involved**. Two heads are better than one. Many situations are easier to handle if there are two facilitators instead of one. It is less demanding than doing it alone and provides a feedback mechanism. It also provides reassurance and a self-regulating mechanism for school-based facilitators who may be working within previously unexplored territory with their students. The fear of overstepping professional boundaries, or the discussion getting out of control, would be lessened with another adult present.

8. **Come well-rested**. Facilitating workshops is demanding. Make sure that facilitators work together to create time for preparation and rest before a session, and reflection and rest after the session.

B. Be clear on what's acceptable and what's not

If pornography exposure in childhood and adolescence is a problem, it's important that we manage the problem optimally. To do this, it's important that both teachers and students are fully aware of the facts around what's legal, what's acceptable, and what isn't when it comes to discussing pornography with young people.

Here are some important facts.

The law

- **Adolescents who have watched, or are in possession of, pornography are *not* breaking the law.**

Any potentially beneficial educational discussions around pornography could be hindered if students feel stigmatised for having watched it. For most adolescents, a burgeoning interest in sex is quite natural. Students should not be made to feel vilified for watching pornography as such stigmatisation not only invokes feelings of shame but prevents meaningful and engaging discussions about pornography and the impact of watching it. Jo Morgan, founder of Engendering Change,[24] a consultancy which specialises in gender, sexuality, sex education, and wellbeing, spoke to me about the importance of destigmatising pornography in school:

> We need to discuss porn with children in a way that's not sensationalist, and not judgemental as well. If you can talk about porn in a way that doesn't engender shame then you're much more likely to get engagement from the person that you're talking to. So, any discussion about pornography needs to start with making it absolutely clear that some people in the room will be disgusted by porn; some might watch it every now and then with no adverse negative impact; some people might have niche pornographic interests; some may have concerns about how much pornography they're watching. The fact is, everyone in that room is going to have a different filter through which they hear what you say. It's important to be open from the get-go to ensure nobody feels left out or feels unusual.

- **Extreme adult pornography is illegal.**

Anybody who watches extreme adult pornography – pornography in which a person's life is threatened; where a person's anus, breasts, or genitalia are likely to suffer serious or permanent injury; or where necrophilia or bestiality are present – is committing an illegal offence.

Despite the rise of pornographic (and even more mainstream reading) material featuring acts of bondage, domination, submission, and masochism (BDSM), it remains an offence under UK law to injure another person for the purposes of sexual gratification. Many students who view pornographic material will have been exposed to any number of videos featuring (usually, hopefully) consensual kink activities which may include the apparent or real hurting of one or more participants and may also include verbal and physical degradation of a participant. They may have become aroused by such scenes and may also believe that such activities are part of 'normalised' sexual behaviour. It is vitally important to explain to students that while kink has become more mainstream, and those engaging in consensual kink activities should not be judged as 'wrong' or 'deviant' for becoming aroused by these activities, firstly, the majority of performers are carefully trained before engaging in these types of sexual activity; secondly, great care is typically taken to 'hurt, but never harm,' participants. Furthermore, there are laws governing this type of sexual activity which students need to be very aware of. Students need to know that 'rough sex' injuries (or even death resulting from rough and possibly consensual sex) can be prosecuted since UK law was changed in 2020. 'Rough sex' can no longer be used as a defence for injuring or killing a partner, even accidentally.[25]

- **Sexual, eroticised, partially or fully naked photographs of people under the age of 18 are illegal to possess, send, or receive**.

To make, send, upload, possess, send, or view images that may be *considered* sexually explicit of somebody under the age of 18 is illegal. Therefore, teenagers can break the law if they take and send sexually explicit photographs of themselves or a partner, even if the photographs are taken within the parameters of a supposedly consensual loving relationship. The Crown Prosecution Service does not tend to prosecute for these offences. Instead, a warning tends to be offered. Nevertheless, prosecution is possible, and students need to be made aware of this.

A vital document

In 2021, the Department for Education produced an extremely useful report entitled *Sexual violence and sexual harassment between children in schools and colleges*. It's a document I strongly recommend people working in schools read. In the report the DfE outlined very clearly what constitutes sexual violence and what constitutes sexual harassment. The report tacitly acknowledged the role that gender – specifically, masculinity – plays in sexual violence and harassment in schools when it advised that sexually inappropriate behaviour 'should never be passed off as "banter," "just having a laugh," "part of growing up" or "*boys being boys*".'[26]

Sexual violence

The report defined sexual violence according to the Sexual Offences Act of 2003, as follows:

Rape: A person (A) commits an offence of rape if: he intentionally penetrates the vagina, anus, or mouth of another person (B) with his penis, B does not consent to the penetration, and A does not reasonably believe that B consents.

Assault by penetration: A person (A) commits an offence if: s/he intentionally penetrates the vagina or anus of another person (B) with a part of her/his body or anything else, the penetration is sexual, B does not consent to the penetration, and A does not reasonably believe that B consents.

Sexual assault: A person (A) commits an offence of sexual assault if: s/he intentionally touches another person (B), the touching is sexual, B does not consent to the touching, and A does not reasonably believe that B consents. (Schools should be aware that sexual assault covers a very wide range of behaviour so a single act of kissing someone without consent or touching someone's bottom/breasts/genitalia without consent can still constitute sexual assault.)

Causing someone to engage in sexual activity without consent: A person (A) commits an offence if: s/he intentionally causes another person (B) to engage in an activity, the activity is sexual, B does not consent to engaging in the activity, and A does not reasonably believe that B consents. (This could include forcing someone to strip, touch themselves sexually, or to engage in sexual activity with a third party.)

Knowing the definitions of these offences can be incredibly useful in the fight against boys' casual use of words like 'rape'. In *BDT?* I discussed how I have used these definitions educationally when faced with boys using phrases like 'rape' in a casual or joking manner. I used the example of how I responded to an incident where a boy told me that he had got 'absolutely raped' – he meant beaten – whilst playing a computer game the night previously:

> Ben, rape is when a man puts his penis into a person's vagina, anus, or mouth without consent. Rape can ruin lives and can have serious lifelong effects on the victim. Using the word casually, as you are doing, is insensitive and inappropriate. Do you understand that? Want me to explain further?[27]

Obviously, such frank explanations rely on strong relationships between teacher and pupil and sensitivity to any potential triggers. However, when used judiciously with age-appropriate pupils, the frank and anatomical language, free from any salacious or deliberately crass or offensive flourishes, can make children realise the seriousness of the problem of using such language inappropriately.

The definition (given above) of sexual assault is also something I think many boys and girls need to be made aware of. As the report explains, sexual assault may not always involve 'violence' or injury. It can be kissing someone without consent or touching someone's genitalia. The key for students to understand is that it is carried out without consent being given.

Sexual harassment

In *BDT?* I published details of everything the government classes as sexual harassment. I do it again here in the hope that schools, if they haven't already, use the information to structure behaviour policy and educate both staff and students on what exactly constitutes unacceptable sexist or sexualised behaviour:

Sexist or sexualised language

- Telling sexual stories
- Making lewd comments
- Making sexual remarks about clothes and appearance
- Calling someone sexualised names
- Sexual 'jokes' or taunting

Physical behaviour

- Deliberately brushing against someone
- Interfering with someone's clothes
- Displaying pictures, photos, or drawings[28] of a sexual nature
- Upskirting[29]

Online sexual harassment

- Non-consensual sharing of sexual images and videos and sharing sexual videos
- Inappropriate sexual comments on social media
- Exploitation, coercion, and threats

The information above can and should be used to educate students about those sexist or sexualised behaviours that are not acceptable. Here's a lesson plan you can use or adapt.

Lesson: understanding sexual harassment, sexual assault, and rape

Preamble

This lesson starts by making students aware of shocking statistics with regard to sexual harassment faced by female pupils in schools. It then teaches students what the government defines as sexual harassment or violence.

Stage one

Teacher to tell students that gender is a 'hot topic' that can often invoke lots of strong emotions in people. Therefore, people must be honest and open today, but also respect each other. Males should remember that females in the session have had experiences that they couldn't possibly relate to. Equally, females in the session must appreciate that many males will feel 'targeted' during this session. This session isn't about blame. It's about moving forward together.

It's very important that you warn students that rape, sexual abuse, and sexual harassment will be discussed during the session. If they wish to leave, they can. Of course, if you know of students who will be triggered by these topics, speak to them in advance of the session. Remind students that if they are affected by any of the things discussed in the session, there are people in school they can talk to.

Stage two

Quiz students on the following questions. A whole-class show of hands will suffice.

1. What percentage of girls at mixed-sex secondary schools have experienced some form of sexual harassment?
    a) 12%
    b) 21%
    c) **37%**
    d) 52%
2. How many teachers in mixed-sex secondary witness sexual harassment at least on a weekly basis in schools?
    a) 7%
    b) 14%
    c) 27%
    d) **32%**
3. How many girls have been subjected to unwanted physical touching of a sexual nature whilst at school?
    a) 5%
    b) 11%
    c) **24%**
    d) 32%
4. Of girls who have been subjected to sexual harassment at school, how many reported it to a teacher?
    a) 4%
    b) 14%
    c) 34%
    d) **54%**

(*All data from UK Feminista report,* It's Just Everywhere. *Available at: https://ukfeminista. org.uk/wp-content/uploads/2017/12/Report-Its-just-everywhere.pdf*)

Take time to discuss the statistics that have featured in the quiz. It could be useful to mention that the statistics may not present an accurate picture due to under-reporting, or because some victims of sexual harassment or abuse will not realise that they've been harassed or abused.

Stage three

Display the following statements on the board:
- People talk about sexual assault or inappropriate sexual behaviours as if they're not big problems
- People tell sexually explicit jokes
- Sexual harassment is tolerated, rather than punished
- Boys are made to believe that men should be dominant and sexually aggressive
- Girls are made to believe that they should be submissive and sexually passive
- Boys are made to believe that they should be sexually experienced
- Girls are made to believe that they should not be 'frigid'
- Girls and women are taught how to avoid being abused or raped, rather than boys being taught that they shouldn't abuse or rape

Ask students to have a discussion in pairs or groups about whether they think any of the statements are true in wider society. Then, ask if these things are true within the school's community. Discuss.

Reveal that in fact, the statements above are what defines a 'rape culture.' A rape culture is a society or environment that trivialises the sexual assault and abuse of women. Explain that it's very important that in school, we do everything we can to challenge and stop these sorts of beliefs and behaviours.

Stage four

Students are to complete the card-sort activity in which they are given 12 cards, featuring 12 behaviours:

Telling sexual stories	Making sexual comments	Sharing sexual images and videos	Rape
Deliberately brushing against someone	Interfering with someone's clothes	Telling sexual jokes	Drawing inappropriate images
Calling someone sexualised names	Assault by penetration	Making sexual remarks about clothes and appearance	Sexual assault

In groups, students should spend around ten minutes putting these behaviours into either one of these three categories:

- Sexual violence
- Sexual harassment
- Neither

After ten minutes, get feedback from students to see what they put in each category.

Stage five

Then, go through each of the individual behaviours, providing explanatory answers as to which category each behaviour fits. Teachers should go through the answers carefully and sensitively, giving students the chance to voice their opinions or questions, should they have any. Answers are as follows:

Sexual harassment

Calling someone sexualised names

Calling somebody derogatory names, such as 'slut' or 'slag,' which make negative judgement about someone based on their sexual activity, real, imagined, or otherwise, is not acceptable.

Telling sexual stories

Talking about your own sexual activity, or even talking about sex in films, computer games, or pornography in the presence of someone who hasn't consented, could make someone feel extremely uncomfortable. This person could be a fellow student or teacher. Either way, it's harassment.

Making sexual comments

Even seemingly harmless innuendoes or inappropriate references to sex in the presence of someone who does not consent could cause considerable discomfort, upset, and even trauma.

Sharing sexual images and videos

It is also against the law for anybody under the age of 18 to send images of a sexual nature to anybody, regardless of whether the person you're sending them to is a boyfriend or girlfriend.

Deliberately brushing against someone

If there is reasonable evidence that a child has deliberately brushed against another child for the purposes of making physical contact of a sexual nature (such as to make contact with sexual or sexualised body parts) then this can be considered harassment.

Interfering with someone's clothes

This doesn't mean grabbing someone's tie! However, trying to pull down someone's trousers, lifting a skirt, or pinging a bra strap is sexual harassment.

Telling sexual jokes

Joking about your own sexual activity, or even telling jokes of a sexual nature, could make someone else feel incredibly uncomfortable and, as such, this is considered harassment.

Drawing inappropriate images

This includes drawings of body parts or of human beings that are overtly sexualised. If images are sexual to the point where they make someone else feel discomfort, it might be considered harassment.

Making sexual remarks about a person's clothes or appearance

Comments about people's bodies, or the way they dress, and making sexualised assumptions based on these comments (for example, 'She's wearing a short skirt so must be up for it...') is sexual harassment.

Sexual violence

Rape

A person commits an offence of rape if: he intentionally penetrates the vagina, anus, or mouth of another person with his penis, without consent. If somebody feels they have been raped, they should report it to the police immediately. The fact that the legal definition rape defines it as penetration by a penis means that only men can legally commit rape under UK law. Of course, women can force another person to have sex with them. Although that's not *legally* rape, it is just as wrong and just as distressing for the victim as legally defined rape.

A woman may be charged with rape only if she procures another person who is then raped by a man.

Assault by penetration

Assault by penetration occurs when a person intentionally penetrates the vagina or anus of another person with a part of her/his body or anything else, the penetration is sexual, and the person does not consent. If a person believes they have suffered from assault by penetration, they must report it immediately.

Sexual assault

A person commits an offence of sexual assault if s/he intentionally touches another person, the touching is sexual, and the person does not consent to the touching. If a person believes they have been subjected to a sexual assault, they must be report it immediately.

Neither

Reveal that, surprisingly, none of the behaviours fits into the 'Neither' category.

Stage six

Give students the opportunity to voice any surprise they may have about where certain behaviours fit. Perhaps they feel surprised that drawing inappropriate images is classed

> as harassment, for example. Maybe they feel that some sexualised behaviours, such as wolf-whistling or staring that makes the object of the staring feel uncomfortable, have been missed. Explain that these behaviours would come under the heading of 'sexual harassment.'
>
> ***Stage seven***
>
> Remind students that if they have been affected by anything in the session, they can speak to somebody in school. Reiterate the school's safeguarding policy and any in-school reporting procedures which are in place for students to report concerns. Also, direct them to external child support services such as Childline.

C. Redefine masculinity

Since the release of *BDT?* in 2019, I've visited many schools and talked to students of all genders about what 'masculinity' means for them. What I've found is that, sadly, sexist behaviours or sexual inappropriateness are inextricably linked with student perceptions of masculinity or maleness in schools.

As teachers, parents, and other adults working closely with young people we must be alert to – and prepared for recognising and challenging – toxic masculine behaviour in our various contexts. We have a responsibility to support students in redefining masculinity and enabling frank and open discussion of what it means to be a man today.

Inspired by activist Tony Porter's excellent TED[30] talk, *A Call to Men*, the workshop below helps students to reflect on masculinity, reflect and recognise its toxic sexual elements, and redefine masculinity in the context of their own school setting.

> **Lesson: redefining masculinity**
>
> **Preamble**
>
> This lesson asks students to reflect objectively on masculinity in wider society, and then on masculinity within their own school setting. The session ends with asking students to define a new, positive masculinity to aspire to within school and in the wider community.
>
> ***Resources***
>
> - Sticky notes
> - Board and board marker
> - Empty cardboard box with 'The Man Box' written on it

Stage one

Seat students in groups. It's up to you whether you want mixed-gender or same-gender groups.

Begin by telling students that gender is a 'hot topic' that can often evoke lots of strong emotions in people. Therefore, people must be honest and open today, but also respect each other. Males should remember that females in the session have had experiences that they couldn't possibly relate to. Equally, females in the session must appreciate that many males will feel 'targeted' during this session. This session isn't about blame. It's about moving forward together.

Tell students that the session will contain references to rape, and they are free to leave the room if it's a subject that makes them too uncomfortable or distressed. As with the previous lesson plan, be alert to any students for whom this session may be overwhelming because of personal experience and ensure they can discuss concerns, or opt out, before you deliver the session.

Stage two

Explain to students that they are going to watch a TED talk called, *A Call to Men* by a male feminist ally called Tony Porter. Tell students that Porter does reference and describe (not in any graphic detail) a gang rape. Students (and staff) are welcome to leave the room during this section if it makes them feel uncomfortable.

Emphasise that during the video, the presenter talks about a concept known as 'The Man Box.' Explain that students should pay extra attention here, as there will be an activity on 'The Man Box' after the video.

Watch the video. It is available here:

https://www.ted.com/talks/tony_porter_a_call_to_men?language=en

Discuss with students any immediate responses to what they have seen.

Note: Session leaders are advised to watch Tony Porter's talk in advance of the session. This can help them to prepare discussion questions for students.

Stage three

Bring to the centre/front of the room a cardboard box with the phrase **MAN BOX** written very clearly on the front of it.

Organise students into groups of three or four students. Hand out sticky notes to groups and ask them to remember as many 'behaviours' as they can from the Man Box described in Porter's *A Call to Men* TED talk. Following their discussion, groups should write down each individual item from the Man Box on a separate sticky note.

After five minutes, asks groups to feed back on the items. Once a correct item is identified, fetch that note from the group and physically put it inside the Man Box in the centre/front of the room. As you collect each item, discuss it with the class.

For reference, when taking feedback from students, the Man Box items identified in the video are:

- Do not show weakness or fear
- Demonstrate power and control (especially over women)
- Be aggressive
- Protect people
- Do not be 'like a woman'
- Be heterosexual
- Be tough
- Do not be 'like a gay man'
- Be brave
- Make decisions – do not ask for help
- Be athletic
- View women as property/objects

Once you have collated as many correct items as possible from students, you can then go onto the next step.

Stage four

Students must now add extra items to the Man Box. These must be items that they feel were missed out of Porter's TED talk. Their additions must be *school-specific* and describe those negative masculine behaviours observed in their own school. Some possible contributions might be:

- Boys must never be seen to be working hard in lessons
- Boys must not be good at 'creative' subjects like Drama or Dance
- Boys must tell sexist jokes
- Boys must joke about sex
- Boys must be cheeky to their teachers

Get students to volunteer their answers and discuss them with the class. Add the answers to the Man Box.

Stage five

It's now time to create a 'new masculinity' for your school. Before this happens, however, we need to get rid of the current items in the Man Box.

> Make a song and dance of finding a bin. It can be one in the classroom already, but could be more entertaining, more purposeful if a student or member of staff is charged with leaving the room to find a bin. When the bin is 'found,' bring it to the centre/front of the room. Students must take it in turns to come up, pull an item out of the Man Box, read it aloud, then put it in the bin. If the binning of the items is accompanied by scathing comments, all the better.
>
> **Stage six**
>
> With a board pen, the teacher inserts the word 'New' on the Man Box. It now reads **NEW MAN BOX**.
>
> Students must then come up with positive features of a 'new masculinity' to be upheld by boys – and men – in the school. Students must write them down on separate sticky notes and put them in the New Man Box as and when they are created.
>
> Possible contributions might include:
>
> - Boys work hard
> - Boys call each other out on sexism
> - Boys accept that it's okay to be homosexual
> - Boys talk about their feelings
> - Boys realise that there are more important things than physical strength
> - Boys are kind
> - Boys ask for consent before hugging
>
> After this, the teacher spends some time picking out sticky notes, discusses the items and records the best contributions on the board under the heading: The New Man Box at [School Name].
>
> This 'manifesto for new masculinity' can be typed up and printed out for students. Alternatively, it can be used as a focus for a whole-school effort to address and focus on the items contained within.

D. Teach boys to call each other out

The idea that men need to call out sexism when they see it has gained traction of late,[31] and rightly so. After all, the sad truth is that misogynists are more likely to listen to men than the women who are their victims. However, what is often ignored in the frustrated exhortations about some men's lack of action when witnessing another man being sexist or sexually inappropriate is that for many men, calling other men out can be extremely dangerous: after all, we already know that men are far more likely to be victims, as well as the perpetrators of violent crime.[32]

The dangers of men calling men out

Quite recently, I found myself in a pub. Sitting next to me were two men discussing a female colleague who had recently gained a promotion. The men were very drunk and, as a result, very loud. One of the men – let's call him 'Barry' – exclaimed to the other, 'She only got promoted 'cos she's f*@ked everyone, you know?' Upon hearing this information, Barry's friend – let's call *him* 'Nigel' – nodded in enthusiastic and knowing agreement. In fact, Nigel revealed, he knew it was true because he himself had engaged in sexual relations with the woman in question whilst at work.

Barry, clearly impressed, then remembered that he'd *also* had sex with the same female colleague and so the pair felt it necessary to outline the exact details of their innumerable sexual couplings with the woman.

As I sat there, trying to think quickly about how I could challenge Barry and Nigel effectively, but without getting my head kicked in, my eyes fell upon the three young women working behind the bar. It became very apparent, very quickly that these bartenders also felt very uneasy about the tone and nature of Barry and Nigel's drunken reminiscing.

So I said something.

'Fellas, is it okay if you stop talking the way you are? It's pretty disgusting language you're using and you're making everybody feel uncomfortable.'

'Shut the f*ck up, Big Ears. It's a pub. We can say what we want.'

'Erm…well, actually…I disagree. You see —'

'Do you want to take this outside?' Barry spat at me.

It was playing out just as I feared. I was being asked to go outside for a punch-up. I can't remember whether I stood up to escape, or if I stood up to accept their challenge of a scrap outside, but stand I did. And it's lucky I did because, as I stood up, my eyes fell upon a badge glinting on the table next to Barry's mobile phone. And, poking out of a Nigel's wallet was yet another, identical badge: a Metropolitan Police badge.

'You're coppers and you're asking me out for a fight?' I said.

The moment they realised that I knew they were police officers, it became a little more difficult for Barry and Nigel to a) continue to degrade and embarrass women the way they were and b) smash my face in. They left.

Thankfully, that night, a fortuitous turn of events means that I was able to call two idiots out, without putting myself in harm's way, and when she woke up the next morning, my five-year-old daughter still had a father in relatively good nick. But it could have ended very differently.

Social danger

Calling men out doesn't just put men at risk of physical harm. It turns out that calling out men on their sexism can impact your social relations too. When I was much younger, I used to play five-a-side football with a group of friends. After one game, as we were having post-match drinks on the front patio of a local drinking establishment, one of my teammates saw fit to shout at a young woman who was walking, on her own, past the pub. He thought that telling this woman that she had nice breasts (the language he used was slightly less formal) was a perfectly acceptable, even complimentary thing to do. I told him otherwise, wrongly assuming that the rest of the guys I was with wouldn't take issue with the tactfully gentle, but educational and assertive, reproach that I had offered.

How wrong I was.

Instead, somebody told me to 'calm down' whilst another pal told me to 'stop being so woke.' One so-called friend enquired as to when it was that I 'got so boring.' I felt that I was being unfairly treated, which put me in a foul mood, and they weren't too happy either. Suddenly, these people I'd called friends for years were now the enemy; they had become people whose views and values didn't align with my own. And to them, I was a party pooper, an outsider who didn't know how to have fun. I left the pub early and never played football with them again.

Of course, I realise now that I don't need friends whose idea of fun is shouting at and objectifying women. But, by the same token, the truth is that I lost friends. Friends I had cared about, and that was difficult.

No excuse

I haven't told these stories to dissuade men from intervening when they witness other men degrading, objectifying, being sexist or sexually abusive about or to women. I believe that men *should* intervene when they witness other men being sexist or sexually abusive to women. It's with regret that I think back to my own sexist behaviours as an adolescent. It's with greater regret that I reflect on the times that I have mistreated women as an adult – an adult who should've known better. Now, as I look back, I rue the times I wasn't held to account for my behaviour and I'm grateful for the times I was.

So, it's important that we teach our boys to call out sexism and inappropriate behaviour when they see it. However, we do have to face the reality that if we want our boys to be good people who do the right thing in these situations, we must also accept that these boys are potentially at significant risk of physical harm or social ostracism. As a result, it's important that we try and teach boys to call each other out safely.

What follows is a system that empowers boys to call out sexism or sexually inappropriate behaviour whilst minimising the risk of physical harm and social exclusion. I call it the 'Come off it, mate' method.[33]

'Come off it, mate' method

Calling out non-friends

Step one: frown

It may be that boys see somebody they don't know being sexist or sexually inappropriate. It may be another boy in school outside of their year or friendship group. It may be a man in a public place or on public transport. If this is the case, it's important that the boy/s show their disapproval of such behaviour, whilst minimising the risk of antagonising the perpetrator of it. The safest way to do this is to frown.

Of course, there are caveats. If frowning could put the boy/s at risk, this step should be ignored. For example, I wouldn't advise a lone 12-year-old boy to frown at a gang of football fans being sexually inappropriate to a woman on a train late at night.

Step two: report

If a boy witnesses somebody being out of order, they must report it immediately to somebody in a position of authority. In school, this would be a teacher or other adult. Outside of school it may be a member of rail or bus staff, the police, or a manager of a nearby shop or restaurant.

In situations where no authority figure is present, but a woman is at significant risk of danger, the police should be called and then boys should alert other members of the public, until there are enough people to jointly call out the behaviour without risk of physical harm.

Calling out friends

Step one: frown/ignore

If a boy hears a friend say something sexist, or is present when a friend engages in sexually inappropriate talk or behaviour, the very least he should do is make his disapproval clear. This can be in the form of frowning, but in cases where this isn't an option – it may be that the offending behaviour has taken place over text message or social media, or it may be that the caller-outer does not feel comfortable frowning at someone he considers a close friend – the offending comment should be completely ignored. After all, if a boy sends a sexist joke over WhatsApp and nobody responds or reacts to it, he should learn pretty quickly that that sort of behaviour isn't welcome.

Step two: say, 'Come off it, mate'

More powerful than simply frowning/ignoring is direct verbal disapproval of the offending behaviour. A simple, 'Come off it, mate' is a clear and unambiguous statement of disapproval that is less easily ignored than a frown or silence. The use of the word 'mate' is helpful as it tells the offender, 'It's not you I do not like, but your behaviour.' Of course, 'mate' can be dropped if the caller-outer feels it appropriate to do so. It may be the case that realising a friend is sexist means that perhaps they're not the sort of person you want as a friend.

Step three: educate and interrogate

For boys who feel confident enough to do so, the next stage of calling somebody out is education. Saying, 'Come off it, mate' gives the caller-outer time to think of questions or statements that can make the offender rethink their behaviour. Some example questions or statements might be:

- How would you feel if somebody said that about you?
- How do you think that makes her feel?
- Do you honestly think that's a good way to be?
- How would you like it if someone just grabbed you without asking?
- It's not 1978. We don't talk like that now.
- That's not a cool way to talk about women.
- You do know that's a criminal offence, right?

Of course, it may be that the person making the offensive comments doesn't care about what they've done and responds to the caller-outer's questions or attempts to educate with rudeness and contempt. This is where the next step comes in handy...

Step four: report

The caller-outer should report the behaviour if they deem it necessary to do so.
  A note:
  I have spoken about this system at many schools, and it's most powerfully used when boys and girls are told about the 'Come off it, mate' method in situations where everybody is together, such as in a year group assembly. Once everybody has heard about what 'Come off it, mate' signifies, it becomes a powerful tool which nobody can feign ignorance of. *Regularly reinforcing the message and method in future assemblies, with posters and discussion in subject lessons and tutor times is vital. For the method to work, all school staff need to be aware of it and regularly remind students how to use it.*

E. Teach consent effectively

Recent research tells us that boys are far less likely than girls to believe that consent is necessary prior to sexual activity. Given the gender power imbalance observed in lots of pornography – where men are aggressively and often violently dominant over subservient, passive females – this is perhaps unsurprising. Consent, then, is something we must teach well. Really well. Justin Hancock has over 20 years of experience in sex and relationships education. As well as being the creator of unsurpassable sex education resources through his website *BISH training*, Hancock is also the author of *Let's talk about consent*. Hancock has given me permission to include the following from his blog post, *Top tips for teaching about consent*[34]:

> **Top tips for teaching about consent**
>
> Justin Hancock
>
> 1. **Don't oversimplify consent**
>   Oversimplifying consent to, 'Just say no' or, 'Wait for an enthusiastic yes' messages is not likely to be helpful. Consent is an extremely complicated topic because it relates to how we feel about ourselves, how we relate to others, and what our cultures tell us we should and shouldn't do. The best Relationships and Sex Education (RSE) is when young people are asked to think about things *themselves*. Simply being told, lecture-style, what to think isn't real or relevant for them and won't give them the tools to help them in real life.
> 2. **Don't just tell people what consent is. Let them practise it**
>   Just giving a legal definition of consent, or showing a brief video, is one way of teaching about consent. However, much more useful would be for people to *practise* discussing and giving consent. If you can bring in experiential learning activities then students can learn about what makes negotiation difficult; how asking for our needs to be met can be tricky; how to handle power differences; what it feels like to meet your own and other people's needs; and explore the messages they get from society about this.
>
>   You could try the handshakes activity (see lesson on consent and handshakes, below), which has comprehensive instructions and tips for negotiating consent.
>
>   Additional resources for this activity can be located on the website listed in Footnote 34.
> 3. **Open up conversations exploring the difficulties**
>   Young people love talking about consent in detail. It can bring up so much around social norms, ethics, politics, gender, power, and structural inequality. Good RSE needs to allow students to reflect on, to consider, and to change or build upon their values or ethics.
> 4. **Don't just make it about the person saying no**
>   It's vitally important that we don't reinforce some of the problematic messages about consent when we teach about consent. We certainly should not be putting the emphasis on people to be saying, 'No,' which puts the responsibility on victims of assault and not on perpetrators. Whilst we can say that it should be okay to say, 'No,' and to give people some tools to help them do this, we should be spending more time teaching everyone about how to recognise and respect a 'No' and how to increase the opportunities for others to say 'No' to us.

5. **Bring in media and messages**

    Ask students to critically review famous film clips and ask them to explore how the characters are relating to each other around consent. You could also ask students to think about the messages that mainstream media, and sexually explicit media, send out about consent, choices, and agency.

    It's important not to do this as a way of exonerating perpetrators of sexual violence (i.e., 'it was looking at porn that made me do it'). However, we can look at the sources of consent education we have and consider how useful they all are. Media reflects, but also reinforces, the dominant narratives we have around power, gender, sexuality, relationships, and ourselves. Critiquing this is important because we can't escape culture and much of our culture does not encourage consensual practices with each other or with ourselves.

6. **Talk about power**

    As we have seen in the recent iteration of #MeToo activism, consent and power differences are intertwined. In context, some people were more vulnerable to sexual assaults and rapes because there was so much at stake for them – their careers, livelihoods, and reputations – if they didn't yield to their attackers' wants. Their attackers knew this. Sadly, this is not something which we can safely say is a thing of the past. This is still something that affects all of us, in Hollywood and beyond.

    We all have different levels of power and privilege because society awards some people more status than others because of their identity (race, disability, gender, sexuality, class, age, etc). We can also experience differences, and sometimes imbalances, in power in a relationship if, for example, one of us is more confident or experienced than another. Because of this, it's harder for some people to ask for what they want (or what they don't want) from sex and relationships. This must be part of what we teach about consent.

7. **Be clear on what sex is**

    Make sure students know that 'sex' is not just intercourse[35] and that actually, sex can include a wide range of intimate practices and activities. Even if you teach some really great stuff about consent, it will be undermined if you don't teach inclusively and holistically about what sex actually is. Sex is about diverse sexual practices that people may or may not enjoy; it's not just about intercourse or penis-in-vagina sex. If you teach that that's what sex is, then as well as excluding everyone in society who doesn't have that kind of sex, you are also sending a non-consensual message about what kind of sex is acceptable and expected.

8. **Model consent**

    We can bring good consensual practice into the classroom even when we aren't teaching about consent. When putting people into small groups we could ask students if they want to be put into groups, or whether they'd prefer to choose their own groups. Small groups means that some students can feel more comfortable participating than in larger groups. When asking people for contributions you could ask open questions and not put people on the spot. Sex Education lessons are not the place for 'cold-call' questioning! You can also subtly give people the option not to participate in a lesson, or in an aspect of a lesson, if you sense that they might find it uncomfortable. For example, in the handshakes lesson, young people could be observers of other people shaking hands rather than taking part in handshakes themselves.

Of course, if you want to venture a step further, you could talk about how consensual it is that students have to be in your classroom, or at school at all. What would consensual schooling look like?

Lesson: consent and handshakes

Preamble

This lesson helps students to explore what consent may feel like and what makes getting and giving consent easier or harder.

Stage one

Handshake one

Explain to students that they will be shaking hands with someone else in the classroom. There will be three rounds of handshakes so some hand sanitiser will be useful! Clearly explain to students that although they may feel pressure to take part in the handshakes, there's absolutely no need to do so if they feel uncomfortable. They can simply greet each other with a non-contact gesture instead.

Explain to the group, 'This is a lesson about consent and what that means. First of all, I'd like everyone to greet each other, and shake hands if you want to.' Give enough time for as many people to shake hands (or alternative) with as many people as they like. Once everyone has settled back down, ask the group the following questions and make sure different views are heard. At this point the participants will still be a bit wary of what's going on, so you might want to keep this part of the discussion a bit shorter.

- How was that?
- How was it compared to other handshakes you've had?
- What's the secret to a great handshake? (People might talk about firmness, or the context – e.g., who's doing the handshake and when)
- On a scale of one to ten how was it? (Usually this gets between four and seven)

Then explain that you would like them to shake hands again.

Stage two

Handshake two

Explain the following: 'This time I'd like you to shake hands again, but I'd like you negotiate it, through discussion with the person you're shaking hands with, considering the following:'

- Do you want to shake hands with left or right hand?
- Do you want to go up and down or side to side?
- How firm do you want it to be? (Allow time for the inevitable giggles to subside) Negotiate this on a scale of one to ten
- How long would you like it to go on for, or how many shakes would you like?
- Do you want to dry your hands first?
- Do you want to do something else altogether? A fist bump? A shoulder bump? A hug?

Then allow everyone to exchange their negotiated greeting. Notice what happens in the room – there's often more laughter and smiling. It also takes longer. Then ask the following questions:

- How was that?
- How was it compared to other handshakes you've had?
- On a scale of one to ten how was it? (Usually this gets between six and nine)
- How did it compare to the first handshake?" (People often say, 'it was more mutual,' 'we knew what was going to happen,' 'it was more fun,' 'there was more eye contact…')
- Did anyone prefer the first handshake? (Try to convince people that this isn't a trick question – it's important that people feel they can say they did. They might say 'it was less awkward,' 'it was over more quickly,' 'it was more fun,' 'it was more exciting not knowing how it was going to be…')

Now tell students that neither 'first handshake' nor 'second handshake' was ideal. Instead, we could try being more 'third handshake.'

Stage three

Handshake three

Now students will explore how people can incorporate the best of both handshakes. Explain, 'I'd like you to shake hands for one last time, but this time I'd like you to try and get a balance between first handshake and second handshake. Try to keep it fun and spontaneous but also try to find ways of communicating with the other person to make sure that you and they are both into it (and can stop if you want). Really pay attention to them. Look for body language, eye contact, facial expressions, that kind of thing.'

Notice what happens in the room and then ask some of these questions:

- How was that handshake?
- How did it compare with the first two?
- On a scale of one to ten how was it?
- Think about how you communicated to each other about the handshake. What did you do or say? Play it back in your head in super-slow motion. What happened?

People might think about:

- How they stood
- How they looked at each other
- How 'in tune' they were with the other person
- Whether they copied or mirrored what the other person was doing
- How the moments of connection and disconnection felt
- What kind of words they might have used
- The noises they made
- How the facial expressions were. *Did they make faces themselves? Did their partner change expression? What did they think this expression meant? Did they adjust their handshake once they reacted to that expression?*

Often the 'third handshake' is the preferred handshake of the group. Ask the group to think of why this is. Usually, they say that they really felt a connection this time.

I sometimes then ask people to do another 'third handshake' but this time with someone they haven't shaken hands with yet. This is to test whether we can have a good mutually enjoyable handshake with someone that we have never shaken hands with before.

Stage four

Explain to students that the activity was all about consent. A useful script is as follows:

'You might know that consent means agreeing to do something.' Tell students that sex *without* consent is quite categorically rape or sexual assault. Also, someone must be able to give their consent. This means that if someone is drunk or nearly unconscious or felt they weren't able to say 'No' (because of a power imbalance or even peer pressure) then it's not consensual. Also, just because someone hasn't said 'No' doesn't mean 'Yes.' So, if someone says 'No,' or their body language or face indicate they are uncomfortable, you should stop.'

Then:

'Let's talk about what consent feels like and how do we have the sex we might want to have? Today, you've all been able to practise how good consent feels.

'When people first shook hands today, they were shaking hands in the way that they are expected to, or they just took part more passively in someone else's handshake.

'Often when people have sex, they take a "first handshake" approach. They often don't (or can't) negotiate or say what they want but rely on an internal "script" for what counts as sex. Sex in this case might mean, "One thing leads to another," "Foreplay," and then "Intercourse" (penis or toys in vagina or anus).

'This approach works for some people and some people like that kind of sex because it can be spontaneous and exciting. However, sometimes it can lead to rubbish sex because people aren't able to talk about what they actually like, or they don't have bodies that can enjoy that kind of sex. Sometimes it can result in sex that isn't consensual: either like feeling forced to take part in someone else's handshake, or doing it because it's expected, or one thing leading to another without anyone checking in that this is what you wanted.'

This is a lot of information, so at this point make sure students have understood everything. Accept questions. Then explain:

'If people were more "second handshake" about sex then it would be really difficult (to have sex) because everything would have to be negotiated. There might be so much negotiation about every single thing (kissing, touching, words, taking clothes off, etc.) that it would take away a lot of the fun and spontaneity. Sometimes being a bit "second handshake" is important and some people are able to talk about sex like this. There are ways to be "second handshake" when we're planning sex with someone. This might be our texting what we enjoy, or talking together about different kinds of sex we might want to try. However, a lot of people find this really difficult.

'The key is to be more "third handshake." This means *really* paying attention to what each other wants and trying to make it mutually pleasurable. So, focus on the tiny micro-communications of the other person: eye contact, nodding or shaking heads, facial expressions, noises, short words or phrases like, "oh yeah" or, "a bit gentler," how bodies move towards or against each other, moving hands etc.'

Stage five

At the end of the session, have a discussion, using these prompts.

- Are there times when you feel like you can't say 'No' to a handshake? Did that happen in this lesson? Why?
- How might our self-perception/how we feel about ourselves affect how much we feel we can have the sex (or handshakes) that we actually want to have?
- Think about the words used to describe different people who have sex – what difference would that make? For instance, what are sexually active men called compared with what sexually active women are called?
- What makes asking for the sex (or handshake) you want – or don't want – more difficult? What makes it easier?
- Are there times when it's better to talk more than others?

F. Consider the gender make-up of sessions you deliver for Porn Literacy education

It's important, when teaching students about the impact of pornography (as well as the related topics discussed in this chapter such as body image and expectations, redefining masculinity in your school, calling out sexist behaviour, and consent) that you think carefully about whether you're going to teach in same-gender or mixed-gender groups. Here are some pros and cons of each:

	Pros	**Cons**
Same-gender groups	• Boys may feel less self-conscious about discussing issues relating to sex and relationships with no girls present • Might enable boys to focus more tightly on the problems associated with masculinity, and masculinity more generally • Could leave girls feeling that they are being marginalised and not getting the same level of input as the boys. Therefore, efforts should be made to ensure that positive interventions are put in place for girls, particularly with regard to consent and expectations within a sexual relationship	• Dividing groups into 'boys' and 'girls' could reinforce the gender binary • Dividing groups into 'boys' and 'girls' neglects the needs of trans or non-binary students
Mixed-gender groups	• Gives the opportunity for boys to hear and better understand girls' experiences and perspectives • Helps to create and develop mutual understanding between boys and girls • Provides the opportunity for boys and girls to work together to promote gender equality and change gender violence	• Girls may be exposed to sexist or sexually inappropriate abuse • Boys will not feel comfortable discussing sex, or issues relating to it, openly in front of girls • Boys may feel pressure to lie about their experiences and thoughts around the issues being discussed, in order to save face

Adapted from the *Imagine Toolkit* by Beyond Equality.[36]

The final word

I could have written a whole book about this topic. There are people that have. Pornography and sex are difficult issues full of nuance, complicated by the fact that they can be embarrassing for students and teachers to talk about frankly and openly. And yet, this is a topic that needs attention. At time of writing 50,046 submissions have been made to the *Everyone's Invited* website,[37] a website that invites students in UK schools and universities to recount their experiences of being victims of sexual abuse, assault, and harassment. That number will be far bigger now. It may be that your school features on the list of schools, published on the organisation's website, where sexual abuse has taken place.

It is only through education that the scourge of sexual abuse, assault, and harassment can be eradicated. I urge schools to seek out the teachers and other education professionals who are willing to have those difficult and awkward conversations. Seek out those adults in schools who feel passionately that something must change.

Notes

1 'Vanilla' is a term which refers to sexual activity which is regarded as conventional or unadventurous with no notable features.
2 Horvath, M. A., Alys, L., Massey, K., Pina, A., Scally, M., & Adler, J. R. (2013). *'Basically… porn is everywhere': A rapid evidence assessment on the effects that access and exposure to pornography has on children and young people*. Available at: https://kar.kent.ac.uk/44763 (Accessed: 27th April 2022).
3 Martellozzo, E., Monaghan, A., Davidson, J., & Adler, J. (2020). Researching the affects that online pornography has on U.K. adolescents aged 11 to 16. *SAGE Open*, *10*(1), 215824401989946. https://doi.org/10.1177/2158244019899462
4 Cho, E. (2016). Frequent internet pornography use: Korean adolescents' internet use time, mental health, sexual behavior, and delinquency. *International Journal Of Human Ecology*, *17*(1), 27–37. https://doi.org/10.6115/ijhe.2016.17.1.27
5 Young, B. (2017). *The Impact of Timing of Pornography Exposure on Mental Health, Life Satisfaction, and Sexual Behavior*. Brigham Young University. Available at: https://scholarsarchive.byu.edu/etd/6727 (Accessed: 27th April 2022).
6 Ibid.
7 Tylka, T. (2014). No harm in looking, right? Men's pornography consumption, body image, and well-being. *Psychology of Men & Masculinity*, 16, 10.
8 Internet Matters. (2019). Impact of seeing pornography on children: Parental concerns. Available at: https://www.internetmatters.org/wp-content/uploads/2019/04/Internet-Matters-Infographic-Impact-of-seeing-Online-pornography-on-children.pdf (Accessed: 13th July 2022).
9 Amateur pornography is a genre of pornography featuring actors who are not paid for filming. It generally features what we might term 'real' people (as opposed to actors) filming in real-life settings (a domestic house environment or hotel room rather than a porn studio).
10 Rothman, E., (2021). *Pornography and Public Health*. Oxford University Press.
11 Ibid.
12 Ibid.

13 Braithwaite, S., & Holt-Lunstad, J. (2017). Romantic relationships and mental health. *Current Opinion in Psychology*, *13*, 120–125.
14 Young, B. (2017).
15 Pinkett, M., & Roberts, M. (2019). *Boys Don't Try?* UK: Routledge.
16 Ferguson, C., & Hartley, D. (2020). Pornography and sexual aggression: Can meta-analysis find a link? *Trauma, Violence and Abuse. 10*(1).
17 Peter, J., & Valkenburg, P. (2009). Adolescents' exposure to sexually explicit internet material and notions of women as sex objects: Assessing causality and underlying processes. *Journal Of Communication*, *59*(3), 407–433.
18 Wright, P., & Tokunaga, R. (2015). Men's objectifying media consumption, objectification of women, and attitudes supportive of violence against women. *Archives Of Sexual Behavior*, *45*(4), 955–964.
19 Omori, K., Zhang, Y. B., Allen, M., Ota, H., & Imamura, M. (2011). Japanese college students' media exposure to sexually explicit materials. *Journal of Intercultural Communication Research*, *40*, 93–110.
20 Wong, Y. Joel, Ho, Moon-Ho, Wang, Shu-Yi, & Miller, I. S. (2016). Meta-analyses of the relationship between conformity to masculine norms and mental health-related outcomes. *Journal of Counseling Psychology*, *64*.
21 Fredrickson, B., & Roberts, T. (1997). Objectification theory: Toward understanding women's lived experiences and mental health risks. *Psychology of Women Quarterly*, *21*, 173–206.
22 Dill, K., Brown, B., & Collins, M. (2008). Effects of exposure to sex-stereotyped video game characters on tolerance of sexual harassment. *Journal of Experimental Social Psychology*, *44*, 1402–1408.
23 Ibid.
24 Jo Morgan is a multiple award-winning trainer and former PHSE teacher who has now turned her talents to consulting and training full-time. You can find out more about her incredibly important work here: engenderingchange.co.uk
25 You can find out more here: https://www.gov.uk/government/publications/domestic-abuse-bill-2020-factsheets/consent-to-serious-harm-for-sexual-gratification-not-a-defence
26 Department for Education. (2021). Sexual violence and sexual harassment between children in schools and colleges: Advice for governing bodies, proprietors, headteachers, principals, senior leadership teams and designated safeguarding leads. Available at: https://assets.publishing.service.gov.uk/government/uploads/system/uploads/attachment_data/file/1014224/Sexual_violence_and_sexual_harassment_between_children_in_schools_and_colleges.pdf (Accessed: 17th May 2022).
27 Pinkett and Roberts (2019).
28 That's right. The ubiquitous penis drawings scrawled in many schools are not acceptable and should be sanctioned as sexual harassment.
29 *Upskirting* is where someone takes a picture under a person's clothing without their permission, and it is illegal in the UK.
30 Technology, Entertainment, Design. TED talks are free, online talks and conferences whose themes are categorised under the slogan, 'ideas worth spreading.'
31 Thorp, N. (2021). Men, it's your responsibility to call out misogyny – not ours. *Metro*. Available at: https://metro.co.uk/2021/03/19/men-its-your-responsibility-to-call-out-misogyny-not-ours-14273170 (Accessed: 27th April 2022).
32 Office for National Statistics. (2021). The nature of violent crime in England and Wales: Year ending March 2020. A summary of violent crime from the Crime Survey for England and Wales and police recorded crime. Available at: https://www.ons.gov.

uk/peoplepopulationandcommunity/crimeandjustice/articles/thenatureofviolentcrimei nenglandandwales/yearendingmarch2020#groups-of-people-most-likely-to-be-victims-of-violent-crime (Accessed: 11th May 2022).

33 While the solutions and lesson plans in this section deal primarily with challenging sexist and misogynist behaviour from boys/men directed towards women, the methods are equally applicable to any form of sexualised abuse, which may also be homophobic or transphobic in nature. Call it out, *every* time.

34 Hancock, J. (2017). Top Tips for Teaching about Consent. Available at: https://bishtraining.com/top-tips-for-teaching-about-consent (Accessed: 12th July 2022).

35 i.e., sex with penetration.

36 Beyond Equality, MAN, Emancipator. (2018). *The Imagine Toolkit*. Available at: https://uploads-ssl.webflow.com/5fe38f96354a9a59b3a05cd1/6059e8cda501da4f5637adbd_IMAGINE-Toolkit-EN.pdf (Accessed: 15th June 2022).

37 Everyone's Invited. (2022). Available at: https://www.everyonesinvited.uk (Accessed: 21st June 2022).

References

Beyond Equality, MAN, Emancipator. (2018). *The Imagine Toolkit*. Available at: https://uploads-ssl.webflow.com/5fe38f96354a9a59b3a05cd1/6059e8cda501da4f5637adbd_IMAGINE-Toolkit-EN.pdf (Accessed: 15th June 2022).

Braithwaite, S., & Holt-Lunstad, J. (2017). Romantic relationships and mental health. *Current Opinion in Psychology*, *13*, 120–125.

Cho, E. (2016). Frequent internet pornography use: Korean adolescents' internet use time, mental health, sexual behavior, and delinquency. *International Journal Of Human Ecology*, *17*(1), 27–37. https://doi.org/10.6115/ijhe.2016.17.1.27

Department for Education. (2021). Sexual violence and sexual harassment between children in schools and colleges: Advice for governing bodies, proprietors, headteachers, principals, senior leadership teams and designated safeguarding leads. Available at: https://assets.publishing.service.gov.uk/government/uploads/system/uploads/attachment_data/file/1014224/Sexual_violence_and_sexual_harassment_between_children_in_schools_and_colleges.pdf (Accessed: 17th May 2022).

Dill, K., Brown, B., & Collins, M. (2008). Effects of exposure to sex-stereotyped video game characters on tolerance of sexual harassment. *Journal of Experimental Social Psychology*, *44*, 1402–1408. Available at: https://www.gov.uk/government/publications/domestic-abuse-bill-2020-factsheets/consent-to-serious-harm-for-sexual-gratification-not-a-defence

Everyone's Invited. (2022). Available at: https://www.everyonesinvited.uk (Accessed: 21st June 2022).

Ferguson, C., & Hartley, D. (2020). Pornography and sexual aggression: Can meta-analysis find a link? *Trauma, Violence and Abuse*, *10*(1).

Fredrickson, B., & Roberts, T. (1997). Objectification theory: Toward understanding women's lived experiences and mental health risks. *Psychology of Women Quarterly*, *21*, 173–206.

Hancock, J. (2017). Top tips for teaching about consent. Available at: https://bishtraining.com/top-tips-for-teaching-about-consent (Accessed: 12th July 2022).

Horvath, M. A., Alys, L., Massey, K., Pina, A., Scally, M., & Adler, J. R. (2013). *'Basically… porn is everywhere': A rapid evidence assessment on the effects that access and exposure to pornography has on children and young people*. Available at: https://kar.kent.ac.uk/44763 (Accessed: 27th April 2022).

Internet Matters. (2019). Impact of seeing pornography on children: Parental concerns. Available at: https://www.internetmatters.org/wp-content/uploads/2019/04/Internet-Matters-Infographic-Impact-of-seeing-Online-pornography-on-children.pdf (Accessed: 13th July 2022).

Martellozzo, E., Monaghan, A., Davidson, J., & Adler, J. (2020). Researching the affects that online pornography has on U.K. adolescents aged 11 to 16. *SAGE Open*, *10*(1), 2158244r01989946. https://doi.org/10.1177/2158244019899462

Office for National Statistics. (2021). The nature of violent crime in England and Wales: Year ending March 2020. A summary of violent crime from the Crime Survey for England and Wales and police recorded crime. Available at: https://www.ons.gov.uk/peoplepopulationandcommunity/crimeandjustice/articles/thenatureofviolentcrimeinenglandandwales/yearendingmarch2020#groups-of-people-most-likely-to-be-victims-of-violent-crime (Accessed: 11th May 2022).

Omori, K., Zhang, Y. B., Allen, M., Ota, H., & Imamura, M. (2011). Japanese college students' media exposure to sexually explicit materials. *Journal of Intercultural Communication Research*, *40*, 93–110.

Peter, J., & Valkenburg, P. (2009). Adolescents' exposure to sexually explicit internet material and notions of women as sex objects: Assessing causality and underlying processes. *Journal Of Communication*, *59*(3), 407–433.

Pinkett, M., & Roberts, M. (2019). *Boys Don't Try?* UK: Routledge.

Rothman, E. (2021). *Pornography and public health*. Oxford University Press.

Thorp, N. (2021). Men, it's your responsibility to call out misogyny – not ours. *Metro*. Available at: https://metro.co.uk/2021/03/19/men-its-your-responsibility-to-call-out-misogyny-not-ours-14273170 (Accessed: 27th April 2022).

Tylka, T. (2014). No harm in looking, right? Men's pornography consumption, body image, and well-being. *Psychology of Men & Masculinity*, *16*(10).

Wong, Y., Joel, Ho, Moon-Ho, Wang, Shu-Yi, & Miller, I. S. (2016). Meta-analyses of the relationship between conformity to masculine norms and mental health-related outcomes. *Journal of Counseling Psychology*, *64*.

Wright, P., & Tokunaga, R. (2015). Men's objectifying media consumption, objectification of women, and attitudes supportive of violence against women. *Archives Of Sexual Behavior*, *45*(4), 955–964.

Young, B. (2017). *The Impact of Timing of Pornography Exposure on Mental Health, Life Satisfaction, and Sexual Behavior*. Brigham Young University. Available at: https://scholarsarchive.byu.edu/etd/6727 (Accessed: 27th April 2022).

10 The final, final word

Since the publication of *Boys Don't Try?* hundreds of educators and parents have been in touch to tell me how reading it has caused them to make alterations – some big, some small – in their practice, to improve academic, emotional, and social outcomes for boys. I'm particularly proud of the work many schools are doing on sexism, and I hope that *Boys Don't Try?* makes things better for girls, too.

It is my sincerest hope that this book has a similar impact. Because boys *do* cry. They get scared, and they get lonely. They want to be good. They want to love and be loved. It is my hope that we, as a profession dedicated to improving the life chances of young people, use the advice within this book to ensure that our boys become men who aren't afraid to be vulnerable; men who seek help when they need it, before it's too late; men who lift other people up, rather than put other people down; men who treat other people with respect and dignity. Men who talk and men who listen.

Boys do cry.

So, let's make them smile.

Index

Pages followed by "n" refer to notes.

accountability: angry behaviour 20–21; individual 106
active ideation 70n3
adolescents: anger in 11, 12–13; early and late adolescence 97; emotional expression 12–13, 75; gender differences in expressing emotions 12–13; LGBTQ+ identity 116; listening skills 83; longitudinal study, long-term 140; mental health disorders 2; new struggles for boys in maintaining friendships 97–98; physical activity and mental health 139–140; pornography, access/viewing habits 184, 185, 188, 190; role models for 116; self-harm by 51; sexism of 203; *see also* children; suicide/self-harm prevention
advertising 174–180; manipulation of the male body in 175–180
affinity humour 88
aggression: and anger 13, 14; humour 88; outdated expectations of male aggression 28–29, 53; *see also* anger; violence
Akala (rapper, journalist and author) 42
amygdala 8
Anderson, Eric 99
Andrews, James 160
anger 6–25; adult male, problems with 11–12; and aggression 13, 14; antecedents 9–10; articulating 15; and attention 13; benefits of 7–8, 13–14; blaming for negative events 10; Calm Plans (case study) 15–17; classroom strategies 3; concept/description 8, 13–14; destigmatising 17; excessive focus on behaviours, and not causes 7; expression and experience of 11, 12–13; feeling of, contrasted with expression of 14; fictional case study (student thought experiment) 6–7; gender differences 11–13; helping pupils to manage 14–17; holding pupils and teachers accountable for behaviour 20–21; and later violent acts in boys 12; as a normal human emotion 8, 13; physical effects 9, 12, 14; plans for managing 15–17; proactive management 13; reasons for feeling angry 9–11; recommendations in relation to 13–21; research 7–13; and shame 7; taboo of 7; teaching pupils about 13–14; time out method of managing 17–20
anger management techniques 14, 15
Anna Freud Centre 59
Anorexia 165, 167, 168, 170–171
Anti-Bullying Alliance 133
anti-depressant use 1, 49
anxiety and depression 6
Arnold, Bob 158
assault by penetration 192, 197
Astley, Gemma 116–117

Atta, Dean, *The Black Flamingo* 127, 128
attention-seeking 60
autism, specialist education 15–17
Awoyelu, Emmanuel 27–28, 36, 40–42

BAME classroom 40, 44n24
banter, teacher: bad banter, by male teachers 86–88; defining 86; and mental health 88
Bartram, Brendan 118–120
Batchelor, Billy 136
Bates, Laura 1
BDSM (bondage, domination, submission and masochism) 190
BEAT (eating disorder charity) 170
Beeson, Paul 151
Beyond Equality, *The Imagine Toolkit* 189
Bhopal, Kalwant 39
Bigorexia 4, 169, 172, 174
Binge Eating Disorder 172–173
biographical essays 109
Bishop, Rudine Sims 35, 36
Black-African/Caribbean boys 3, 26–46; afro hair contravening social policy, claims of 33–34; 'blackness' and 'whiteness' 44n10; bullying, racist 41–42; defining characteristics of 27–28; disciplining 30–31; feeling marginalised 33; lack of understanding from White people in authority 32; ostracism 33; racial prejudice 28, 29–34; stereotyping 29; stigmatisation 33; teachers' reactions to misbehaviour of White and Black children 30–31; whether naturally more naughty, violent or aggressive 28–29; *see also* ethnic minority backgrounds; exclusions of groups from school; Gypsy, Roma and Irish Travellers (GRTs)
body confidence 169, 174–180
body image 165–182; and advertising 175–180; body confidence, teaching about 169, 174–180; 'fitspiration' 168; lesson plan example 175–180; manipulation of the male body in advertising/social media 174–180; and penis size 186; personal story 165–166; and pornography 185–186; recommendations in relation to 173–182; research 166–169; school and boys' body image 169; steroid abuse, teaching boys about dangers 4, 174; talking about mental health benefits, not aesthetic benefits of exercise 173; watching speech about bodies 173; *see also* body confidence; eating disorders; media; social media
Boman, Peter 12–13
books for children 35–36; diverse texts appraisal form 36–38; whitewashing of literature 36, 45n32
boys: aggressive behaviour 13, 28–29, 53; assertiveness 13; Black-African/Caribbean *see* Black-African/Caribbean boys; body image 169; close friendships, struggle to maintain 97; destructive/self-destructive behaviours 53; emotional expression 11, 12–13, 53, 75, 97–98; encouraging calling out for inappropriate sexual behaviour 201–205; expression of anger 12, 13, 53; fear of appearing 'gay' 96, 97, 98, 121; improving attitudes to school 12–13; male sexuality, unwanted and ignored problems 73; mental health of *see* mental health of boys; relationships with fathers 13; rethinking the way teachers engage with in school 72; setting up talking groups for 80–82; and sexual objectification 188; steroid abuse, teaching about 4, 174; talking about issues 75–76; talking to about friendships 103; teaching how to listen 82–85, 103; as victims 3; whether naturally more naughty, violent or aggressive 28–29, 53; *see also* anger; friendships; girls; masculinity; men; talking about problems
Boys Don't Try (*BDT?*) (Pinkett) 1, 93n21, 157; and exclusions from school 28, 34; and sexual harassment/violence 187, 192, 193, 198; and suicide/self-harm prevention 53, 54; and talking about problems 76, 79, 86

Boys Move initiative, case study 137–139; dodgeball 137; laser tag 138; tug of war 137–138; walking and talking 138–139
brain 8
'bromances' 98–100, 110; benefits of bromantic relationships 99–100; components of 'bromantic' attachment 99; lesson 101–103; literary, exposing pupils to 100–101; physical intimacy 99; recognition of 100–103
Bryson, Tina 18
Bulimia 165, 167, 168, 170, 171–172
bullying, racist 41–42
Byrom, Helen 82

calming techniques 14–15
Carter, Carol 36
Casablancas, Julian 21n1
Centre for Literacy in Primary Education (CLPE) 44n25; *Reflecting Realities* report 35–36
Chamberlain, Nira 39
'changing room' cultures, toxic 156–157
Chetty, Darren 36
children: asking directly if suicidal 54–55; books 35–36; engaging in connection projects 106; expression of emotions 75; gender differences in expression and experience of anger 12–13; physical activity and mental health 139–140; self-harm 51; social media accounts 168; *see also* adolescents; boys; girls; suicide/self-harm prevention
Chu, Judy 98, 99
code switching 35
coming out: as gay 120–123; as trans female 129–131
community leader, creating 159–160
Concept Curriculum, Physical Education 147–151
confidence: body 169, 174–176; lack of 8, 114–115, 128; and physical activity 146, 148, 149, 152–154, 159
consent to sexual activity: all sexual activity, teaching about 207; bringing in media and messages 207; causing someone to engage in without 192; considering the gender make-up of sessions delivered 212; and handshakes 208–211; letting others practice 206; model consent 207–208; not emphasising the person saying 'no' 206; not oversimplifying 206; opening up conversations 206; power, discussing 207; teaching about 206–208; *see also* pornography; pornography, discussing in school; rape; sexual assault; sexual harassment; sexual violence
contagion, suicide 62–63
Co-operative learning (Slavin) 105
Cope, Thomas 120–123
COVID-19 pandemic 77, 106
Cox, D. L. 12
Crane, James 105
Creative Active Schools (CAS) programme 161
Crick, N. R. 12
Crown Prosecution Service 191
crying 11, 12
curriculum: audit questions 38; embedding LGBTQ+ literature in 126–128; Physical Education (PE) 147–151
Cushing, Ian 34
cutting oneself 1, 53

Dalai Lama 21n1
Daniels, Steve 20–21
De Botton, Alain 21n1
Deffenbacher, Jerry 11
Denton, Phil 80
Department for Education and Skills (DfES) 29; *Sexual violence and sexual harassment between children in schools and colleges* 191
destructive/self-destructive behaviours, in boys 53
Devlin, Hannah 11
dialect 34–35
Dickens, Charles, *Christmas Carol* 101
disciplining of Black boys 30–31
Durden-Myers, Elizabeth 148

eating disorders: Anorexia 165, 167, 168, 170–171; Bigorexia 4, 169, 172, 174; Binge Eating Disorder 172–173; Bulimia 165, 167, 168, 170, 171–172; under-eating, as self-harm 53; gender differences 1; spotting signs of 170–173; *see also* body image; eating disorders
Ekman, P. 9, 10
emotions: anger as a normal human emotion 8; comparing with the weather 79–80; helping pupils to recognise emotional nuance 80; normalising male emotional talk 79–80; openness, importance of 79; vocabulary for specific emotions 80; *see also* anger
Engendering Change (Morgan) 190
essay writing 109
essentialism 43n4
ethnic minority backgrounds: bullying, racist 41–42; employing more staff from 40; involving of parents in children's education 39; racial bias of teachers 28, 29–34; school trips, taking account of diverse cultures 41; terminology 44n10; *see also* Black-African/Caribbean boys
Evans, Laura 132–133
Everyone's Invited website 213
exclusions of groups from school, avoiding 3, 26–46; bias of teacher 28, 29–34; children's books 35–36; curriculum audit questions 38; diverse texts appraisal form 36–38; external providers, making use of 40–41; gender differences 3; injustices 26, 28, 43; involving parents from ethnic minority backgrounds 39; and mental health disorders 26–27; not feeling included 26–27; policing language, being mindful of 34–35; racist bullying, dealing with 41–42; recommendations in relation to 34–36; research 27–34; school trips, taking account of diverse cultures 41; *see also* Black-African/Caribbean boys; Gypsy, Roma and Irish Travellers (GRTs)

Fagot, Beverly 13
Fashanu, Justin 128
Fawcett, David 159; *Relearning to Teach* 158
femininity, rejection of 98
Ferguson, Christopher 187
fight, flight or freeze response 8
final presentations 109
'fitspo' 168
Ford, Joseph 58, 59
Foster, Alex 112
Fredrickson, Barbara 188
friendships 3, 95–111; boys' comments on 95–96; boys' problems with 97–98; boys' struggle to maintain close relationships 97; calling out friends for inappropriate sexual behaviour 204–205; complexity of male friendships 100; connection projects, engaging children in 106; female 97; gender differences 96–97; group work, effective use of 104–106; and importance of talking for boys 76, 103–104; importance to mental health 97; looking for opportunities to create connections 104–109; and mental health 97; nature of male friendships 96–97; normalising loving male relationships 100; recommendations in relation to 100–109; research 96–100; seating plans, changing 104; secrets, sharing 97; *see also* 'bromances'; talking about problems
Friesen, W. V. 9, 10
Fuggle, Peter 59–60
Furlong, M. 12

Garson, Mikael 136
Gately, Stephen 121
gay men 95, 96, 112–114, 118, 119, 121–126, 128, 132; being openly gay 113, 114, 124, 126; fear of appearing 'gay' 96, 97, 98, 121; *see also* homophobia; homosexuality; LGBTQ+ and masculinity in schools
Gelman, S. A. 43n4
gender differences: anger 11–13; assertiveness 13; crying 11, 12; disclosure of mental health issues 74;

eating disorders 1; exclusion rates 3; friendships 96–97; responses to disclosures about problems 83; suicide/self-harm 3, 50, 52–53; violence and aggression 12, 28–29, 53; *see also* boys; girls; men; stereotypes; women
gender socialisation 73
girls: anger, expressing 11, 12; crying in 11, 12; cutting themselves 1, 53; expression of emotions 11, 12, 75; mental health of 2; pressures on 1–2; self-harm, likelihood of 51, 52; *see also* boys; women
Global Equality Collective 166
Goethe, Johann Wolfgang von, *The Sorrows of Young Werther* 62–64
Green, Thomas 144–146
group work, effective use of 104–106
GRTs *see* Gypsy, Roma and Irish Travellers (GRTs)
Gypsy, Roma and Irish Travellers (GRTs) 3, 26–46; defining characteristics of 28; feeling marginalised 33; negative attitude of teachers to 29–30; stereotyping 29; stigmatisation 33; whether naturally more naughty, violent or aggressive 28–29; *see also* Black-African/Caribbean boys; exclusions of groups from school

Hancock, Justin, *Let's talk about consent* 206
handshakes 208–211
Hartley, Richard 187
Hatto, Tommy 166–167
Headstrong (youth mental health charity) 52
Hines, Barry 144
homophobia 98, 113, 114, 118–120, 123, 126, 128, 131, 136, 143, 215n33; abuse 123, 127, 131; fragility-induced 98; tackling 132–133; *see also* gay men; homosexuality; LGBTQ+ and masculinity in schools
homosexuality 113, 114, 118–120, 123, 124, 126, 134n1, 143; *see also* gay men; homophobia; LGBTQ+ and masculinity in schools

Hulgus, J. F. 12
humour: affinity 88; aggressive 88; creative language use 90; cynicism 89; examples 89; harnessing effectively 85–90; importance in building relationships with pupils 86; improving mental well-being, using for 86–88; jokes 89; props and media types, use of 89; role play 90; stereotypes 89; stories 89; teacher performance 90; and teasing 89–90

I Feel, I Need cards 90
initial calming 14
Inspector Calls, An (J. B. Priestley) 63, 64, 65, 101
Instagram 168
instruction, direct 83
Internet Matters survey 185
interviews: feeding forward 108; gold nugget stories 107; *The Listening Project* 107–109; modelled interviewing 107; pornography 183–184; practice, added benefits 107; preparing for 108–109; question selection 108; recording 108–109; selecting interviewee 108; skills practice 108

Jacklin, C. N. 12
James, Megan 15–17
jokes 89

Kara, Bennie 38–39
Khan, Faheem 132–133
King, Martin Luther 40
Knight, Darryn 143, 144, 156

language: creative use 90; policing, being mindful of 34–35; suicide/self-harm prevention 68
Lerner, Jennifer 10
lesson plan examples: body image 175–180; 'bromances' 101–103; listening 84–85; sexual harassment/violence 193–198; *see also* teachers
LGBTQ+ and masculinity in schools 112–135; coming out 120–123; education 118–120; embedding LGBTQ+ literature

in the curriculum 126–128; identity 4; impact of establishing an LGBTQ+ group at school 116–117; mental health statistics 4; tackling homophobia 132–133; teachers being true to themselves 124–126; trans female, coming out as 129–131; vulnerability, embracing 124–126; whole-school approach to raising inclusivity 132–133; *see also* gay men; homophobia; homosexuality

listening 3; eliciting a range of experiences 107; modelled interviewing 107; in pairs 83–85; positive responses 83; practice interviews 107; project 106–109; teaching boys how to listen 82–85, 103; *see also* talking

Listening Project, The (Nelson and Way) 106–109

loneliness, normalising 104

Luhrmann, Baz 67

Maccoby, E. E. 12

McDonagh, Chelsea 34–35, 39, 40, 42

macho culture 97, 98

McKellen, Sir Ian 113–115

Mackenzie-Chalmers, Tom 124–126

Markey, Charlotte 173, 180; *Being You* 170

masculinity 72, 73, 86, 143, 166; and anger in men 11–12, 53; and 'bromance' 99–100; cultural expectations 88, 98, 142; defined by rejection of femininity 98; exaggeration by boys 98; and LGBTQ+ in schools 112–135; and male friendships *see* friendships; and mental health of boys 2; 'new masculinity' 198, 200, 201; perceived associations with physical and emotional strength 74; and pornography/sexual violence 189, 191; redefining 198–201, 212; as stoicism in the face of adversity 49; 'toxic' 143, 144, 189; *see also* LGBTQ+ and masculinity in schools

media: and body image 4, 174–180; guidelines for reporting suicide 62–63, 65; idealised images of women 166; LGBTQ+ and masculinity 120; mainstream 166, 207; types for enhancement of learning 89; *see also* social media

Media Smart 174

men: expression and experience of anger 11; normalising male emotional talk 79–80; problems with anger 11–12; reasons for reluctance to talk 74; reluctance to ask for help 49, 74, 92n3; violent crimes committed by 12; *see also* boys; masculinity; women

mental health: of adolescents 2; anti-depressant use 1, 49; Australian research 2; and benefits of anger 8; of boys *see* mental health of boys; designated professionals 59; exclusions from school, effect on 26; of girls 1, 2; good, case study examples for promoting 80–82; humour, using to improve 88–90; importance for teachers of supporting 3, 51, 54; importance of friendships for 97; importance of talking for 3, 74, 75, 81; in LGBTQ+ community 4; limitations of teachers in relation to 51, 100; listening, importance of 82–83; maladaptive indicators of 88; and physical activity *see* mental health and physical activity; and pornography 185; and suicide contagion 62; undiagnosed problems and suicide 66; *see also* suicide/self-harm prevention

mental health and physical activity 4, 139–140; emphasising the mental health benefits of sports 146–151; talking about mental health benefits, not aesthetic benefits of exercise 173

mental health of boys: and banter 88; gender differences in self-harm 52; joined-up approach required 49; and masculinity 2; reasons for writing about 1–2; and school exclusions 26–27; talking, importance of 3, 74, 75, 81; Western narrative of 73–74; *see also* anxiety and depression; body confidence; body image; boys; eating disorders; suicide/self-harm prevention; talking about problems

Michael, George 121

Milford-Haven, Clare 47–49

misogyny 188, 201, 214n31, 215n33
Moran, Caitlin 1
Morgan, Jo 190
MSN Messenger (online instant messaging platform) 121, 134n8
muscle dysmorphia 169
Myers, Martin 32

Nelson, Joseph D., *The Listening Project* 106–109
newly qualified teacher (NQT) 32

objectification, sexual: and boys 188; of women 187–188
Objectification Theory (Fredrickson and Roberts) 188
Obsessive-Compulsive Disorder (OCD) 6, 165, 180n1
Ofili, Chris 39
Ong, Scott 136
open questions 103–104
Ougrin, Dennis 51, 63
over-exercising, as self-harm 53

Palmer, Donald 39
Papageno Effect 66
Papyrus (suicide prevention charity) 50, 63, 64
Pascoe, C. J. 98, 99
Patkar, Sachin 136
penetration, assault by 192, 197
physical activity and sports 4, 136–164; barriers to a broad provision 141–142; barriers to physical exercise 140; Boys Move initiative, case study 137–139; confidence-building 146, 148, 149, 152–154, 159; creating a community leader 159–160; dealing with toxic 'changing room' culture 156–157; making engagement and participation one's focus 151–156; and mental health in children and adolescents 139–140; othering of non-sporty boys 142–144; recommendations in relation to 144–162; taking a whole-school approach to 159–162; talking about mental health benefits, not aesthetic benefits of exercise 173; *see also* Physical Education (PE)
Physical Education (PE) 137; Concept Curriculum 147–151; Key Stage 4 140; male PE teachers as obstacles 141; reframing the role of the PE teacher (case study) 144–146; setting, considering 157–159; *see also* mental health and physical activity; physical activity and sports
physical intimacy 99
physical literacy 147
Picture of Health? report (Credos) 169, 174
Pillay, Priya 15–17
Pinkett, Matt 183–184; *see also Boys Don't Try (BDT?)* (Pinkett)
play groups 13
poetry 72–73
Porn Literacy 188, 212
pornography 4, 183–216; access to 184; amateur 213n9; and body image 185–186; boys and pornography viewing habits in the UK 185; 'come off it, mate' method 204–205; extreme adult pornography illegal 190–191; friends, calling out 204–205; gender power imbalance 205; interview with author 183–184; law 190–191; and mental health 185; no excuses permitted 203; non-friends, calling out 204; and objectification of women 187–188; and penis size 186; recommendations in relation to 188–213; redefining masculinity 198–201; and relationships 187; research 184–188; sexual, eroticised, partially naked photographs of people under 18 illegal 191; and sexual aggression 187; sexual violence 191–192; social danger 202–203; teaching and discussing *see* pornography, discussing in school; teaching boys to call each other out 201–205; understanding sexual harassment, sexual assault and rape 193–198; and 'vanilla' sexual activity 183, 213n1; violent 187; watching or in possession, not breaking the law 190; *see also* consent

pornography, discussing in school: acknowledging flaws 189; adapting one's style 189; adapting to the group 189; being clear about what is acceptable 190–198; creating the right conditions for discussion 188–189; expecting the unexpected 189; involving others 189; minding the age gap 189; rest for teachers, ensuring 189; timetable, setting 189

Porter, Tony, *A Call to Men* (TED talk) 198, 199, 200

postvention 53

prefrontal cortex 8

Priestley, J. B. 63, 64, 65, 101

PSHE (personal, social, health and economic) education 3, 13, 14, 84

racial prejudice 28, 29–34

rape 191, 192, 197

Reach Out Project, The 27

Relationships, Sexual Health, and Parenthood resource, Scotland 124

Relationships and Sex Education (RSE) 206

Roberts, Mark 1

Roberts, Tomi-Ann 188

Robinson, Stefan 99, 100

Rogers, Bill 14

role play 90

Romeo and Juliet 63, 64, 66, 67; Luhrmann's version 67

Rose, Amanda 83, 85; *Girls' and Boys' Problem Talk* 75–76

Rothman, Emily, *Pornography and Public Health* 186

Rowlatt, David 142

Rowling, J. K. 36

Rye, Stacey 32, 41

Sakyi, Kwame S. 104

Samaritans 47, 63, 64, 65; 'Step by Step' programme 53

school trips, taking account of diverse cultures 41

schools: exclusion of Black-African/Caribbean boys and GRTs from 26, 27; as high-pressure environments 11; improving boys' attitudes to 12–13; LGBTQ+ and masculinity in 112–135; rethinking the way teachers engage with boys in 72; sport and PE *see* mental health and physical activity, physical activity and sports, Physical Education (PE); *see also* Black-African/Caribbean boys; exclusions; Gypsy, Roma and Irish Travellers (GRTs); lesson plan examples; teachers

self-harm *see* suicide/self-harm prevention

SEND (Special Educational Needs and Disabilities) 15–17

Senior Leadership Team (SLT) 20, 132

sexism 201–203, 215n33, 217

sexual assault 192, 197

sexual harassment: calling someone sexualised names 196; deliberately brushing against someone 196; drawing inappropriate images 197; interfering with someone's clothes 196; lesson 193–198; making remarks about clothes/appearance 197; making sexual comments 196; online 193; physical behaviour 193; sexist or sexualised language 193; sharing sexual images and videos 196; telling sexual jokes 197; telling sexual stories 196

Sexual Offences Act (2003) 191–192

sexual violence 191–192; assault by penetration 192, 197; rape 191, 192, 197; sexual aggression and pornography 187; sexual assault 192, 197

Siegel, Daniel 18

Slavin, Robert 105

Smith, D. C. 12

social media 121, 130; accounts, of children 168; and body image 174–180; and communication 76, 77; images 138; influencers 166; Instagram 168; LGBTQ+ identity and masculinity 124, 130; offensive behaviour on 204; platforms 124, 127; role models on 144; status updates 76; suicidal ideation 64; *see also* media

Sport England 140
sport/physical activity *see* physical activity and sports
Stabb, S. D. 12
Standard English 35
stereotypes 29, 30, 89, 97; *see also* gender differences
Stern, Julie 148
steroid abuse, teaching boys about dangers 4, 174
stigmatisation, avoiding 17, 33, 50, 59, 190
Stone, Matt 116–117
Stonewall (organisation on rights for LGBTQ+) 4, 113, 125, 134n4
Strengthening Minds 20
substance abuse 1
suicidal thoughts/suicidal ideation 70n3
suicide/self-harm prevention 47–71; aftermath-blame talk, avoiding 66; asking about self-harming behaviour 59–60; asking directly if suicidal 54–55; attention-seeking, reframing thinking on 60; avoiding 'no-framing' 58–59; avoiding positive portrayal of suicide 67; being honest about one's own reaction 57; concern, expressing 59; cutting oneself 1, 53; defining prevention 54; defining self-harm 52; excessive detail, avoiding 65; following standard disclosure protocol 57; gender differences 3, 50, 52–53; glorifying suicide, avoiding 67; guidelines for teachers 64–68; having a critical approach to suicide 67; intervention 54; language, correct 68; learning to recognise signs of self-harming behaviour 55–56; methods and context, exercising caution when referring to 65–66; not expecting immediate cessation of self-harming behaviour 57; not trying to be a therapist 57; over-identification and risk of imitative behaviour 65–66; over-simplification, avoiding 66; own natural negative responses, honouring 57–58; Papageno Effect 66; personal account of a parent 47–49; postvention 53; prevalence amongst boys and men 2, 49–50; reasons for self-harm 52; recommendations in relation to 54–69; reducing access to means 60–61; research 49–54; responding to disclosures appropriately 56–60; responsible teaching 62–64; safety plans 61, 69; self-harm a predictor of suicide 51; statistics on suicide 49–50; stigmatisation, avoiding 59; substance abuse 1; support services, signposting 61–62; teachers and child suicide 50–51; thinking of impact of topic on pupils 64–65; trying not to react strongly 57; ultimatum, avoiding 57; undiagnosed problems 66; unusual methods, taking care when discussing 65; *Werther* effect (suicide contagion) 62–64
Sullivan, Lee 147–151; *Is Physical Education in Crisis* 147
Swain, Jon 142, 143

talking about problems 72–94; case studies 77–78, 80–82; and dependence upon social media 76, 77; disclosure of mental health issues 74; gender differences in responses to 83; and gender of teachers 75; helping pupils to recognise emotional nuance 80; humour, harnessing effectively 85–90; *I Feel, I Need* cards 90; importance for mental health 3, 74, 75; and male friendships 103–104; male sexuality, unwanted and ignored problems 73; normalising male emotional talk 79–80; open questions 103–104; positive responses to disclosures 83; post-pandemic issues 77, 106; reasons for men's reluctance to talk 74; recommendations in relation to 76–91; reluctance of men to talk 49, 74, 92n3; reminding pupils of how to talk 76–78; research 74–76; *see also* boys; friendships; listening
teachers: accountability of 20–21; banter, by male teachers *see* banter, teacher; bias of 29–34; and child suicide 50–51;

on consent issues *see* consent to sexual activity; guidelines for discussing self-harm and suicide 64–68; male PE teachers as obstacles 141; performance 90; reactions to misbehaviour of White and Black children 30–31; supporting mental health 3, 51, 54; tackling of bias 34; teaching responsibility about suicide 62–64; *see also* lesson plan examples
teasing 89–90
Thatcher, Margaret 119, 124, 134n1
'thinspo' 168
time out method, *TIME* magazine article, controversy 17–20
toddler behaviour 13
transgender students 50; trans female, coming out as 129–131
Traveller Movement, The 28, 42, 43n2; *see also* Gypsy, Roma and Irish Travellers (GRTs)
Twitter 124

Vaughan, Andrea 64
violence: biological and environmental factors 28; gender differences in relation to 12; men as victims as well as perpetrators 201; nature of 22n11; pornography 187; verbal 86; whether boys are naturally more violent or aggressive 28–29, 53; *see also* aggression; anger; rape; sexual assault; sexual violence
vulnerabilities, responding to: LGBTQ+ and masculinity in schools 124–126; and male friendships 104

Way, Niobe 97, 99, 103–104; *The Listening Project* 106–109
Werther effect (suicide contagion) 62–64
White, Adam 99
Whitehead, Margaret 148
women: expression and experience of anger 11; female teachers, discussing personal issues with 75; friendships 96–97; objectification of 187–188
Woolley, Charlotte 1; *The Lost Girls* 38
Wright, Chris 141, 142

Young, Bonnie 187
Young, Will 121
Youth Sport Trust (YST) 137, 141